Classics & **Contemporaries**

BOOKS by JOHN W. ALDRIDGE

Literary Criticism

After the Lost Generation

In Search of Heresy

Time to Murder and Create

The Devil in the Fire

The American Novel and the Way We Live Now

Talents and Technicians:
Literary Chic and the New Assembly-Line Fiction

Classics and Contemporaries

Fiction

The Party at Cranton

Social Commentary

In the Country of the Young

Edited Works

Critiques and Essays on Modern Fiction

Discovery #1

Selected Stories by P. G. Wodehouse

Classics & Contemporaries

John W. Aldridge

UNIVERSITY OF MISSOURI PRESS • COLUMBIA AND LONDON

Copyright © 1992 by
The Curators of the University of Missouri
University of Missouri Press, Columbia, Missouri 65201
Printed and bound in the United States of America
All rights reserved
5 4 3 2 1   96 95 94 93 92

Library of Congress Cataloging-in-Publication Data

Aldridge, John W.
    Classics and contemporaries / John W. Aldridge.
    p. cm.
    Includes index.
    ISBN 0-8262-0822-3
    1. American literature—20th century—History and criticism.
2. English literature—20th century—History and criticism.
I. Title.
PS221.A617   1992
810.9'005—dc20   92-6694
                                                                                               CIP

∞™ This paper meets the requirements of the
American National Standard for Permanence of Paper
for Printed Library Materials, Z39.48, 1984.

Designer: Kristie Lee
Typesetter: Connell-Zeko Type & Graphics
Printer and Binder: Thomson-Shore, Inc.
Typeface: Century Schoolbook and Century Expanded

Once Again for Patsy

Contents

Preface	ix
Acknowledgments	xiii
The Erotic Passion of Henry James	1
Notes toward the Definition of T. S. Eliot	9
The Saddest Story of Ford Madox Ford	17
Edmund Wilson's Twenties	23
Hemingway's Last Big Novel	29
The Sun Also Rises: Sixty Years Later	39
Biographing Faulkner	49
Mailer on Miller	54
The Death of the Lions	59
Afterthoughts on the Twenties	69
Homage to Malcolm Cowley	79
Céline and the Hateful Horror of It All	87

J. P. Marquand, Esquire	95
Steinbeck's Knightly Little People	104
The Final Novels of Algren and Farrell	108
James Gould Cozzens: By Writing Possessed	112
Robert Penn Warren's Legend of the South	118
The Appalling Diaries of Evelyn Waugh	126
World War II and the American Novel	130
James Jones's Men at War	139
Catch-22: Twenty-five Years Later	144
Donald Barthelme and the Doggy Life	152
No One in Charge	157
William Gaddis and the "Ongoing Situation"	165
John Barth: Versions and Reversions	171
Robert Coover's Party Animals	180
Norman Mailer: Conquering the Bitch Goddess	186
A Mailer Masterpiece	194
William Styron's Holocaust Chic	198
Saul Bellow's Struggle with the Cosmos	209
Wright Morris Country	217
Little Magazines and the Great Gray Middle	225
Index	235

Preface

This book contains a selection of my literary essays produced between 1968 and 1991. Some of them have been expanded since their first periodical appearance and, in more than a few, portions deleted by editors because of limitations of space or taste have been restored. In all but two instances I have resisted the temptation to update essays by incorporating discussion of materials that have become available since the time of the original writing. That would have required the revision of just about everything presented here and surely proved to be an unending and pointless labor. I have, however, added postscripts to the essays on Hemingway's *Islands in the Stream* and the little magazines because subsequent posthumously published Hemingway works in the first case and recent literary developments in the second seemed to make further commentary imperative.

The arrangement of the essays in a collection of this kind must always be somewhat arbitrary. I might have presented them in the order in which they were written and first published, but that would not have provided any intelligible form or continuity. I decided, therefore, to arrange them according to the historical periods with which the writers discussed are most commonly identified or during which they were at the most visible or productive stages of their careers. Thus, James, Eliot, and Ford are grouped together as early classic modernists; Wilson, Hemingway, Faulkner, Henry Miller, and Cowley who were also classics but more specifically associated with the twenties; Céline, Marquand, Steinbeck, Algren, and Farrell who were most productive in the thirties; and Cozzens, Waugh, and Warren who were all active over this same period but who enjoyed their largest share of public attention in the forties—Cozzens with *Guard of Honor,* Waugh with *Brideshead Revisited,* and Warren with *All the King's Men.*

A younger generation of writers began to emerge after the second World War, so I have grouped together those I discuss, partly because some wrote specifically about the war, others because they are contemporaries, the essays about them following my assessment of the literary influences of the war. James Jones wrote almost exclusively about military life during the war, while Joseph Heller in *Catch-22* produced our most compelling satirical portrait of that life. The studies that follow all concern other writers of about their age, while the concluding essay is a generalizing discussion of the classic modernist movement and its relation to the literary situation as I envisioned it at the beginning of the seventies.

In reading over these essays I have realized, as I did not realize quite so clearly before, that while writing them I carried in my mind a certain image of the kind of audience I expected to address, and I am not at all sure that such an audience exists today or, for that matter, existed even at the time I thought I was writing for them. I am speaking of a readership of educated people who have some serious interest in literature and yet who are perhaps only slightly acquainted with formal literary criticism. I suspect that it was a readership of this sort, made up of what Henry Ladd Smith once called "the superior few," that older book critics such as Wilson and Cowley were able to address with such ease and assurance back in the twenties and thirties. They wrote their reviews and essays for *New Republic* and *The Nation.* They discussed books and ideas in a literate, intelligent fashion with apparently complete confidence that they would be understood, and the "few" responded, oftentimes vehemently, sometimes boorishly, but they responded because they too read and at their leisure discussed books and ideas in a cultural atmosphere, however thinning, in which books and ideas had some living relation to the daily conduct of life.

From the beginning of my career and from my first book of criticism, *After the Lost Generation* (1951), through the several that followed, I must have taken it for granted that these were the kinds of readers I expected to reach, for that is what Wilson and Cowley, the idols of my youth, had taught me to expect. Yet it is obvious that, for undoubtedly complex and arcane reasons, serious literary criticism in our time has mostly ceased to address and does not really wish to address such readers, for it has become, at its most academic, more and more parochially preoccupied with the theory of literature and progressively less preoccupied with literature. Today it is scarcely distinguishable in its approach from theoretical work in the fields of anthropology, philosophy, and linguistics.

Among the existing less academic periodicals that continue to publish critical discussion of literature, only *The New York Review of Books* regularly offers, in the form of long, often much too long essay-reviews, this kind of discussion in any depth and quantity. *The Nation* and *New Republic,* both of which were once vigorous outlets for literary commentary, now publish at the most one or two substantial reviews of imaginative work an issue. *Harper's* has abolished its review section completely, and *Saturday Review* and *The New York Herald Tribune Book Week* suspended publication years ago. At the *New York Times Book Review,* which is the sole remaining really large-circulation review medium, a disturbing change of another kind has occurred. Until fairly recently, a professional critic might occasionally be asked to review a book and even given sufficient space to discuss it at some length, although as a rule the books assigned him would be literary criticism or biography rather than new poetry or fiction. But the *Book Review* appears lately to have abdicated the critical function altogether and now routinely assigns such works to other writers of poetry and fiction, most of them contemporaries and often friends or writers conference associates of the authors under review. The result is that the assessments given are nearly always laudatory or carefully neutral and, therefore, quite meaningless except as free publicity.

My own endeavors in the field have over the years benefited greatly from the fact that I was able to function for a long time before these changes occurred, and I had what now seems the scarcely believable good fortune to be allowed by various editors to write as I wished about books and literary topics without being bound by the usual restrictions of length and critical approach. Where most reviewers are seldom allotted space much beyond eight hundred words in the more prominent periodicals, I have had the privilege of working very often in the longer form of the essay-review, in which, with three or four thousand words at one's disposal, it is possible to develop a coherent argument and place the new work of an author in some significant relation to his previous productions.

For about ten years before its demise—a sad event to which I prefer to think I did not contribute—*Saturday Review* provided me with the opportunity to do a fair number of essay-reviews, many of which are reprinted here. The editors of *Harper's, Commentary,* and *The Chicago Tribune Book World* were from time to time equally generous, and I wish to thank them all for enabling me to do for pay what I would have been pleased to be allowed to do for nothing.

Acknowledgments

The essays on Henry James, T. S. Eliot, Ford Madox Ford, Edmund Wilson, Ernest Hemingway's *Islands in the Stream*, Henry Miller, Louis-Ferdinand Céline, John P. Marquand, Robert Penn Warren, William Gaddis, the first essay on Norman Mailer, Saul Bellow, and little magazines appeared originally in *Saturday Review*.

The essays on William Faulkner, John Steinbeck, Nelson Algren, James T. Farrell, James Gould Cozzens, and James Jones appeared originally in *The New York Times Book Review* and are reprinted by permission. Copyright © 1978, 1979, 1983, 1986, 1989 by The New York Times Company. The essay on *Catch-22* first appeared in part in *The New York Times Book Review* and was later published in full in *The Michigan Quarterly Review*.

The essays on Joseph Heller's *Good as Gold* and William Styron's *Sophie's Choice* appeared originally in *Harper's Magazine*.

The essays on Evelyn Waugh and John Barth and "A Mailer Masterpiece" appeared originally in *The Chicago Tribune Book World*—the Barth essay in much shorter form.

The Sun Also Rises—Sixty Years Later appeared originally in the *Sewanee Review* 94 (1986), copyright © 1986 by John W. Aldridge.

The essay on Malcolm Cowley appeared originally in *The Michigan Quarterly Review*.

"Afterthoughts on the Twenties" appeared originally in *Commentary*.

The essay on Donald Barthelme appeared originally in *The Atlantic*.

The essay on Robert Coover appeared originally in *Chronicles*.

"The Death of the Lions" appeared originally in *The Devil in the Fire*, Harper's Magazine Press, © 1972 by John W. Aldridge.

The essay on Wright Morris appeared originally in *Conversations with Wright Morris: Critical Views and Responses,* edited with an introduction by Robert E. Knoll, copyright © 1977 by the University of Nebraska Press.

I wish to thank the editors of these publications for permission to reprint the above mentioned materials here.

Classics & **Contemporaries**

The Erotic Passion of Henry James

Ever since the appearance of the first volume in 1953, one could be confident that Leon Edel had in progress the definitive life of Henry James. Now, with the publication of *H. J.: The Master*, the fifth and final volume, it is clear that Edel has in fact produced something far more remarkable—not only a major biography but one of the truly distinguished works of creative scholarship of our time, perhaps of all time. The sole contemporary work with which it can legitimately be compared is Richard Ellmann's *James Joyce*, and of the two Edel obviously had the harder task, the more difficult subject, a much more complicated problem of coordinating the imaginative processes of the artist with the physical facts of the artist's life.

Joyce was an excellent illustration of Eliot's statement that "the more perfect the artist, the more completely separate in him will be the man who suffers and the mind which creates." One is struck again and again by how completely Joyce, living in exile, was able to transmute the often merely squalid or irritating experiences of his early life in Dublin into the materials of great art through the mythologizing powers of his imagination. James may, as Eliot also famously said, have had "a mind so fine that no idea could violate it." But he was the very opposite of Joyce in the sense that throughout his life his mind was constantly being violated by experience, and it was directly from the quality of that experience, often overwhelming in its complexity and sheer abundance, that he derived his fictional materials. The process in his case was not so much one of imaginative inflation as of finely critical distillation. Eliot called James the most intelligent man of his generation. He may, in fact, have been the most intelligent man who ever wrote in the novel form, and the defining feature of his intelligence, "untouched," as Eliot remarked, "by the parasite idea," was that it was touched by absolutely everything else with an intensity that would undoubtedly have reduced a lesser mind to madness.

Any biographer who hopes to deal adequately with James must, therefore, be prepared to approach him on at least three levels simultaneously. He must cope with a man who had an extremely complicated creative intelligence, who led a hyperactive emotional and social life, and who recorded his responses to that life in some of the most intricately imagined fiction ever written. And these formidable materials must finally be presented in some sort of coherent, interacting relationship with one another. Edel has managed from the beginning to do all this with particular skill, and in this concluding volume with astonishing success, for he covers that rich but multiform final period, the years from 1901 to 1916, when James reached his full artistic maturity, produced the great novels of his career, and brought out the New York edition of his complete works with the critical prefaces. At the same time he was living in the most precarious state of psychological balance, deeply depressed by the death of his brother, William, and several close friends, as well as troubled by the symptoms of his own advancing age, his sense that his best work had failed to win him adequate recognition, and the outbreak of World War I, which he described as "the plunge of civilization into this abyss of blood and darkness," the collapse of that whole brilliant culture he had spent his life shaping to the varied forms of his art.

Edel offers an account of James's development through these years that is both a triumph of biographical reportage and the subtlest kind of psychological portraiture. The suffering man and the creative mind are beautifully integrated; large masses of information are given their appropriate meaning through being placed within the context of James's emotional torments; and the result is not only a new creation of James, the most complete and satisfying we are likely to have, but a fresh interpretation of mysteries that have often led to serious misunderstandings about the character of his life and work.

One of the oldest and most tenaciously coveted of these misunderstandings is that James was a writer who, by some process of imaginative chicanery, was able to create great literature while living an arid emotional life and a public life of singular isolation and social impoverishment. This view was rather gleefully promulgated by certain of his contemporaries—jealousy among literary rivals having been at the time as potent a motive for ill-will as it is today. Arnold Bennett expressed doubt as to whether James "ever felt a passion, except for literature," and H. G. Wells, in his infamous *Boon* attack, called James "the culmination of the superficial type," then went on to document the charge in what is surely one of the cleverest wrongheaded critical statements to be found in literature:

> The only living human motives left in the novels of Henry James are a certain avidity and an entirely superficial curiosity.... It is like a church lit but without a congregation to distract you, with every light and line focused on the high altar. And on the altar, very reverently placed, intensely there, is a dead kitten, an egg-shell, a bit of string.
> Having first made sure that he has scarcely anything left to express, he then sets to work to express it, with an industry, a wealth of intellectual stuff that dwarfs Newton.... And all for tales of nothingness ... it is leviathan retrieving pebbles. It is a magnificent but painful hippopotamus resolved at any cost, even at the cost of its dignity, upon picking up a pea which has got into a corner of its den. Most things, it insists, are beyond it, but it can, at any rate, modestly, and with an artistic singleness of mind, pick up that pea.

In *The Pilgrimage of Henry James* Van Wyck Brooks elaborated this argument into an indictment of what he saw as the adverse creative effects of James's prolonged self-exile from America. With an obtuseness equal to Wells's but less cleverly expressed, Brooks insisted that the great novels of the mature period, *The Ambassadors, The Wings of the Dove,* and *The Golden Bowl,* are devoid of human and emotional content because James cut himself off from the nourishment of his native materials—which gave vitality to his earlier work—and had remained isolated from English society. Even such a sensitive reader as Edmund Wilson appears to lend a certain credence to this view of James's "emotional starvation" while arguing very effectively against Brooks's low assessment of the later novels.

A great deal of this sort of misunderstanding is the result not only of the seeming tenuousness and overcerebration of James's mature style but of the mystery that until now has obscured his personal life. James never married, and for all anyone knew, he never had, could have, or wanted to have physical relations with a woman. In 1861, when he was eighteen, he suffered what he obliquely described as a "horrid even if an obscure hurt," which may, as Edel suggests, have been a sacroiliac strain or some incapacitating sexual injury. As a result of this, it has been widely assumed that he was forced into the celibate life, could have had no direct knowledge of sexual passion, and, therefore, wrote novels that were pristine of eroticism and fastidiously evasive about most of the central realities of emotional experience.

That this was a preposterous assumption will be obvious to anyone in the least familiar with James's work. From his very first novel, *Watch and Ward*—which contained such crude, if unconscious, sexual imagery that brother William later urged James to be more cautious—through the great novels of the late period, his dramatic situations are charged with eroticism. In fact, the eroticism deepens as the art matures. There is nothing more implicitly sexual than the relationship between Strether and Maria Gostrey in *The Ambassadors* or, for that matter, between Olive Chancellor and Verena Tarrant in *The Bostonians*—to say nothing of the several works in which overtly physical love affairs are at the very center of the action. *The Other House,* which was first performed as a play in London in 1969, is as sexual as anything by Tennessee Williams and infinitely more intelligent. But the point, of course, is that because in the bulk of James's work the consummation of passion is usually rendered impossible by personal scruples or social convention, the erotic element is most strongly felt as generalized tension, a continuous building to narrowly averted climax, and it is finally inseparable from the whole elaborate moral and psychological interplay that gives the characters their vitality.

Sexual frustration or inhibition in fact worked for James as not only a dramatizing but a thematically liberating force; it enabled him to explore the full complexities of relationships, short of the sexual, that exist between highly organized people, in particular those fine nuances of feeling experienced but left unexpressed or sublimated into a passion of intellectual sensibility. In witness of this, one has only to imagine what *The Ambassadors* would have been like if Strether and Maria had felt free to make love. Clearly, it would have been a far different novel and a far less satisfactory one—except perhaps for Strether and Maria—because, in effect, it would have climaxed at a level of melodrama far beneath the level created by the psychological implications of the plot. And if the conventions of Woollett, Massachusetts, had not dictated that Chad Newsome and Madame de Vionnet ought not, even in Paris, to be having an affair, there would have been no novel at all. James recognized, whether by wisdom or by prudery, that what he called "the great relation" between men and women is carried on most interestingly, perhaps even most passionately, when the parties involved cannot or dare not take each other to bed. In our present preoccupation with the purely sexual, we have lost sight of this truth. So many of our novelists since James seem to believe that when they have brought their characters to orgasm, they have fulfilled their function, forgetting that the news of orgasm has long since reached us. The inexhaustible mystery, the drama that is forever refreshed because it is nowhere ever the same, is to be found in the nature of the people in the relationship being consummated.

As he grew older, James's sense of the erotic became stronger and found increasingly explicit expression in his work. About the reasons for this, Edel provides some rather startling new information that should settle once and for all any questions concerning the quality of James's personal life—in particular, his capacity for close emotional involvements with men and women. Edel explores in considerable detail his relations with a number of women—most notably, the American novelist, Constance Fenimore Woolson, with whom he seems to have had something like a serious, if platonic, love affair— and with three attractive young men: the sculptor, Henrik Andersen, the novelist, Hugh Walpole, and a sporting Irishman named Jocelyn Persse. James's feelings for these men would now be recognized as decidedly homoerotic. At least his amorous declarations in his letters to them would seem suggestive of something more intimate than simply avuncular sentiment. But if certain codes of behavior were stricter in James's time, those governing the expression of affection between men were far more liberal than they are today, and there seems to be no reason for supposing that his passion ever took overt physical form. The question in any case is of no particular importance. What interests Edel and should interest us is the effect James's involvements had on the quality of his work.

One of Edel's major contributions toward a revised and humanized image of James is that he is able to connect James's awakening to erotic feelings for these people with the richer eroticism of the later novels. Edel even suggests that this awakening was directly responsible for a crucial revision which James made in *The Portrait of a Lady* when he was preparing the later New York edition. In the original version of the kissing scene between Isabel Archer and Casper Goodwood, the kiss is described in a single sentence: "His kiss was like a flash of lightning; when it was dark again she was free." In the New York edition the scene is extended to a paragraph in which Isabel's response takes on distinctly orgasmic overtones:

> His kiss was like white lightning, a flash that spread, and spread again, and stayed; and it was extraordinarily as if, while she took it, she felt each thing in his hard manhood that had least pleased her,

each aggressive fact of his face, his figure, his presence, justified of its intense identity and made one with this act of possession. So had she heard of those wrecked and under water following a train of images before they sink. But when darkness returned she was free.

Edel says that "the earlier Isabel was incapable of this kind of feeling," and so, it would seem, was the earlier Henry James. But we are reminded that in the last great novels, *The Wings of the Dove* and *The Golden Bowl,* there is abundant further evidence that James in his maturity was able to confront erotic relations between men and women with an honesty about the erotic element he had never displayed, evidently because he had never consciously possessed it before. Edel believes that the involvements with Andersen, Persse, and the others were primarily responsible for this development, that James emerged from them as a person who, in Stephen Spender's phrase, "after overcoming great inhibition, has accepted the *idea* of people loving . . . after a lifetime of deep human understanding, has arrived at a stage where in suffering and pity he could accept the physical fact of love."

Surely, one can conclude that if James was actually rendered impotent by the injury he suffered in his youth, he was not, as has so often been supposed, rendered emotionally sterile. In fact, it is possible that the injury was the most fortunate event of his life, for in liberating him from localized phallic sexuality, it may have enabled him to create in his work an image of the erotic that, just because it transcended the limits of the copulative act, became symbolic of the most universalized passion operating at every level of human loving and consciousness.

Another major misunderstanding about James is that his public life was as isolated and arid as his emotional life was supposed to be impoverished, and here again Edel provides important corrective evidence. The fact is that James led one of the most vigorous social and literary lives any writer has ever enjoyed. Not only was he almost ludicrously social during his years in England (at one point in his notebooks he remarks with evident amazement that he had somehow managed to dine out 107 times in a single London winter), but he traveled extensively, especially during his early and middle years, in France, Italy, and Germany, made several trips back to America, and established friendships with almost everybody worth knowing in the international world of arts and letters. Just as his philosopher father had been a friend of Emerson, Thoreau, Carlyle, and Thackeray, so James at various periods of his life knew Dickens, Flaubert, Turgenev, Tennyson, Browning, Trollope, and George Eliot as well as more immediate contemporaries such as Conrad, Meredith, Mark Twain, Stephen Crane, Kipling, Wells, Ford Madox Ford, Pound, Howells, and Edith Wharton. He had, in addition, the most incredible and complex connections with that whole vast society of great families who contributed so much to the intellectual culture of the period, and with some of whom James maintained relations from earliest childhood to the end of his life. In America there were the La Farges, Nortons, Fullers, Higginsons, Lowells, Adamses, Wisters, Vanderbilts, Fullertons, Holmeses, and Perrys—to name only the most distinguished. In England, in addition to a host of socially prominent people, mostly single women, there were the du Mauriers and the Leslie Stephenses, one of whose daughters was Virginia Woolf. Families of this kind formed a society that was remarkable for its combination of wealth, artistic and intellectual talent, and the most highly civilized taste, and from his association with it James derived not merely social stimulus but some of his richest literary materials—at just the time when he was supposed to be dying creatively because he had dared to live abroad and so isolate himself from the vital literary resources of his native land. James may have had a great gift for making much out of little. That, at least, was the standard complaint against him during his lifetime. But it is evident that he suffered not from a paucity of experience but, if anything, from an excess, and the wonder is that he was able to process such abundance and subdue it to the coherence of major art.

Yet even as he was giving it enduring life in his fiction, that society was dying, and James knew it was dying. When he made his last visit to America in 1904, the places he remembered from his childhood were haunted for him because they were associated in his mind with so many dead friends and because the changes that had occurred during his years abroad had in some cases transformed them beyond recognition. On one occasion in Boston he returned to Ashburton Place, the house where he had lived during the last two years of the Civil War and where he had heard the news of Lincoln's assassination, the end of the war, and the death of Hawthorne. The place held, as he later wrote, old secrets and old stories, "a maturation of life as closed together and preserved in it as the scent lingering in a folded pocket handkerchief." Yet when he came back a month later for a second look, the house was gone, every brick of it—"the brutal effacement, at a stroke, of every related object, of the whole precious past."

But the climactic stroke, not simply of effacement but of wholesale devastation, was the outbreak of World War I, occurring at a time ten years later when James, already very near the end of his life, was in failing health and mentally depressed over the commercial failure of his New York edition. It was characteristic of him that he was able to assess very precisely the meaning of the war, to see it in his imagination of disaster in terms of the darkest apocalypse. As he wrote to his friend, Rhoda Broughton: "Black and hideous to me is the tragedy that gathers, and I'm sick beyond cure to have lived to see it. You and I . . . should have been spared this wreck of our belief that through the long years we had seen civilization grow and the worst become impossible. . . . It seems to me to *undo* everything, everything that was ours, in the most horrible retroactive way."

Yet it was also characteristic of him that when Henry Adams during the same period wrote him a deeply despondent letter, James should have replied with a reaffirmation of the one faith that even the cataclysm of war could not bring him to question:

> *Of course* (he said) we are lone survivors, of course the past that was our lives is at the bottom of an abyss—if the abyss *has* any bottom. . . . (And yet) I still find my consciousness interesting—under *cultivation* of the interest . . . . You see I still, in the presence of life . . . have reactions—as many as possible. . . . It's, I suppose, because I am that queer monster, the artist, an obstinate finality, an inexhaustible sensibility. Hence, the reactions—appearances, memories, many things, go on playing upon it with consequences that I note and "enjoy." . . . It all takes doing—and I *do*. I believe I shall do yet again—it is still an act of life. . . . There we are, and it's a blessing that you understand.

There, indeed, we are. Art is still, despite everything, "an act of life," and as he said elsewhere, "Art *makes* life, makes interest, makes importance." We have long had the evidence of his art in confirmation of this. We now have the full evidence of his life, the life that made the art possible. It was a life wholly consecrated to art, but it was also a life wholly and richly lived. We may wonder how soon, if ever again, the two will come together in such perfect union in such a monumental talent and exemplary human being.
1972

Notes toward the Definition of T. S. Eliot

T. S. Matthews has written in *Great Tom* the first full-length biography of T. S. Eliot, surely an act deserving of public celebration and, considering the subject, perhaps a special award for valor. Biographical information about Eliot has been for years both hard to come by and in a state of such profound muddlement that any sincere effort to clarify or extend the record must be applauded. The various reminiscences by people who knew him or, in the majority of cases, only imagined that they did, have been notable mostly for their contradictions and dissimulations. Of the two or three book-length efforts, Robert Sencourt's *T. S. Eliot: A Memoir,* published in 1971 and allegedly based on a close friendship extending over thirty-seven years, was irritatingly vague in treating most of those details of Eliot's life about which one is most curious, and rigorously pedestrian about the details with which one was already familiar. Mr. Matthews is far more forthright. He has made an honest attempt to fulfill his responsibility to his subject, yet for reasons rather beyond the range of his responsibility, his book is a good deal less satisfactory than it might have been.

The first and most obvious problem is that Eliot is no subject for an ordinary biographer, and Mr. Matthews, while a competent writer and a man of considerable sensibility, is decidedly not a Strachey, Ellmann, or Edel. But the more immediate difficulty is that during the time he was gathering his materials, Eliot's widow, Valerie, was still determined to honor her husband's wish that no biography of him be written. She therefore declined to cooperate with Mr. Matthews and instructed her friends to do likewise. This is of course a preposterously unfair requirement for any major figure to impose, and inevitably Mrs. Eliot was forced to violate it in order to discourage the increasing numbers of commentators who have been making irresponsible speculations on the basis of inadequate evidence. It now appears that she will appoint an official biographer, although, as she said in a recent interview, "the right person will not be easy to find. He must have a real understanding of the American background, in addition to knowing England and Europe. Ideally he should be able to sympathize with my husband's religious outlook, and, above all, he must have empathy." Mr. Matthews may be forgiven for a certain wryness when he says in response to this: "In short, . . . the official biographer will have to please the family or a committee, may have to smooth over some rough facts, even suppress others. A good many private papers will still not be available, even to him." There are, for example, more than a thousand letters from Eliot to one of his closest women friends, Emily Hale, deposited in the Princeton University Library with instructions that they not be made available to anybody until January 1, 2020, by which time, one can be reasonably confident, those who may now be most concerned about their contents will be beyond either titillation or embarrassment.

    The evidently widespread desire to protect Eliot both during his lifetime and since his death seems to have arisen from a variety of causes, among them the idea securely established in the minds of many of his admirers that he was a saint whose person could not be exposed to the contamination of secular inquiry. Moreover, the self or selves he allowed to be displayed in public must have enforced the impression that there was indeed something about him that needed to be held in sacred trust or that defied mortal understanding. He was a shy, languid, aloof, extravagantly formal and enigmatic man who could strike some people as arrogant, even cruelly contemptuous, others as generously kind and sympathetic, still others as chilly, selfish, rude, and fake-hearty. Edmund Wilson once suggested that Eliot was an accomplished player of parts, all belonging to an extremely clever publicity stunt designed to awe his followers into craven adulation and at the same time distract their attention from the secret premises where the real Eliot resided. Wilson named six roles that Eliot played to perfection: "the Anglican clergyman," "the formidable professor," "Dr. Johnson," "the genteel Bostonian," "the young rascal" who ultimately metamorphosed into "Old Possum," and "the oracle," whose "every tiny poem, every slender pamphlet of an essay . . . will be received," said Wilson, "with profound respect and read with devoted attention. . . . It is all in the timing, the presence, the silence, the timbre of voice. 'Mr. Eliot' is a master of this and has created a solemn hush whenever he has made a pronouncement on the problems of contemporary society." If we add to this the fact that Eliot wrote some of the most enigmatic poetry of the modern age and was largely responsible for making enigma the fashionable mark of the "serious" in poetry, it is not surprising that the task of penetrating beneath the various masks to the real Eliot should seem beyond the power of conceivable human divination.

Faced with the challenge of such massive complexity and obliged to work without access to many sources of undoubtedly crucial information, Mr. Matthews has inevitably been tempted—as have so many other commentators—to draw inferences from the available materials, the published works, letters, and memoirs, which cannot always be justly drawn, and to indulge somewhat too freely in speculations about the possibility of what Eliot *might* have felt, thought, or done on particular occasions where the factual record is obscure. Yet an image of the man does finally emerge, one that has its coherence and psychological consistency, yet offers no suggestion that it fairly represents the "real" Eliot or successfully embodies his manifold subtleties and contradictions.

Most of the materials Mr. Matthews offers us concerning Eliot's family background and early years in St. Louis and at Harvard have already been supplied by Herbert Howarth in his *Notes on Some Figures behind T. S. Eliot.* But Mr. Matthews has the advantage of being able to assess them in relation to the larger context of Eliot's emotional and creative development, his tragically unhappy first marriage to Vivienne Haigh-Wood, and his subsequent decision to become an Anglo-Catholic. One comes to understand how the extreme moral puritanism of his Unitarian upbringing was strongly influential in the formation of the poet and the public personality, how it burdened him with an inordinate sense of guilt, a fear of sex and a horror of women that became a major motif of his poetry, and how sexual disorder seems to have been the destructive element in his marriage to Vivienne at the same time that it contributed in some primary way to his nervous breakdown in 1921, while he was completing *The Waste Land,* as well as to the metaphysical crisis that led to his religious conversion.

That first marriage was perhaps the most impetuous and fateful act of Eliot's life, and one can only ponder whether the grave damage it inflicted on the man was compensated for by its evidently vitalizing effect on his poetry. When he and Vivienne met, presumably early in 1915, Eliot was 26, a student at Merton College, Oxford, and already the author of "Prufrock," "Portrait of a Lady," "Preludes," and "Rhapsody on a Windy Night." In the fall of the previous year he had met Ezra Pound, who was greatly impressed by these extraordinary first poems and later became Eliot's close friend, mentor, and the editorial architect of *The Waste Land.* Eliot at this time seems to have had little or no experience of women and no financial prospects. Moreover, he disliked Oxford and dreaded returning to Harvard where he was expected to complete the requirements for a Ph.D. in philosophy. Given these circumstances, his marriage must appear to have been rather recklessly precipitate. Yet it may well have been so precisely because to a young man of his innocence and, in particular, his ambivalent feelings toward women, only a desperately impulsive act, "the awful daring of a moment's surrender," held promise of shocking him out of his inhibitions and opening him to the emotional experience he must secretly have craved. This is not to suggest that Eliot married for reasons of therapy but rather that he acted perhaps quite deliberately in defiance of his fears and scruples because he recognized that they were suffocating some essential part of himself.

The decision in any case proved to be a disaster. Vivienne was an attractive, very bright, but pathologically sensitive girl with a long history of poor health. Mr. Matthews tells us that "when she was seven or eight she had an operation for tuberculosis of the hand. . . . By then her nerves were so on edge and her hearing so sensitive that any loud noise was painful to her. If she thought someone near her was about to laugh, she would say sharply, 'Don't let him laugh.'" During the early years of the marriage, when she and Eliot were living in circumstances of near poverty and he was working at various teaching jobs while trying to do his writing at night, her condition steadily worsened. She suffered continually from "nerves," severe migraine, insomnia, neuralgia, and colitis and had to be kept for long periods of time under sedation. Pound described her during this period as "an invalid always cracking up, & needing doctors, & incapable of earning anything." The writer Hope Mirrlees said of her: "She gave the impression of absolute terror, of a person who's seen a hideous ghost, a goblin ghost, and who was always seeing a goblin in front of her. Her face was all drawn and white, with wild, frightened, angry eyes. An overintensity over nothing, you see. Supposing you would say to her, 'Oh, will you have some more cake?' she'd say, 'What's that? What do you mean? What do you say that for?' She was terrifying. At the end of an hour I was absolutely exhausted, sucked dry. And I said to myself: Poor Tom, this is enough! But she was his muse all the same."

Apparently, in a queer awful sense she was his muse, rather in the way that Zelda was Scott Fitzgerald's. The agony of Eliot's life with

Vivienne severely damaged his health and drove him into a nervous breakdown but gave to his poetry a demonic edge that was its most striking feature, an effect of violence held under the highest tension of a precariously balanced control, madness just barely restrained by the exertions of a will on the verge of collapse. Eliot himself was one of the first to recognize the extent of his creative indebtedness to his wife. In 1916 he wrote in a letter to his former Harvard classmate Conrad Aiken that Vivienne had been seriously ill, that his friend Jean Verdenal had been killed at the Dardanelles, that he was worried about money and about Vivienne, and that he had written nothing lately—"but I am having a wonderful time nevertheless. I have *lived* through material for a score of long poems in the last six months." These were the first six months of his married life.

It was during this "wonderful" time of intense physical hardship and emotional stress, a period that extended considerably beyond those first months of marriage, that Eliot wrote some of the best poems and most brilliant criticism of his career. The poetry culminating in *The Waste Land* shows the possible influence of Vivienne in its hypersensitivity to the strains of discord, anxiety, sexual conflict, sickness, and emotional exhaustion that, although intensely personal, became objectified in imagery evocative of the general malaise of spirit then afflicting the Western world. It was a poetry that perfectly validated John Peale Bishop's observation that the true artist, "in searching the meaning of his own unsought experience, . . . comes on the moral history of his time." Eliot's unsought experience and the moral history of his time happened by great good fortune to conjoin. As he explored the meaning of the one, he not only discovered the other, but he seemed quite literally to create it so that the qualities endemic to his time and those he attributed to it in his poetry can no longer be effectively distinguished. The waste land is still, for most of us, the modern world.

In his criticism of this same period Eliot was evolving principles that were to revolutionize the reading of literature in this century. Significantly, he affirmed the need for the structures of order—tradition, convention, form, classical objectivity—that were missing from his personal life and the absence of which in modern life his poetry both dramatized and lamented. He also argued that the artist must be able to separate his personal feelings from his imaginative creations: "The more perfect the artist, the more completely separate in him will be the man who suffers and the mind which creates"; "Poetry is not a turning loose of emotion, but an escape from emotion; it is not the expression of personality, but an escape from personality." In view of what we now know of Eliot's life, these statements take on great melancholic significance. Whatever theoretical truth there may be in them must be weighed against their more urgent practical truth as expressions of anguished appeal from an intensely suffering man who was finding it more and more difficult to continue the struggle he saw as the first necessity of the poet—"to transmute his personal and private agonies into something rich and strange, something universal and impersonal."

Just how difficult that struggle became for Eliot is attested to by the noticeable slackening of his creative impulse after 1930 and by a major change in his poetic direction beginning with "Ash Wednesday," developing through "The Four Quartets," and culminating in the later plays. These developments were almost certainly related to, if not the direct result of two extremely important events that occurred in Eliot's personal life: his religious conversion in 1927 and his decision to leave Vivienne in 1932.

Eliot had been aware for a long time that his domestic situation was intolerable. Vivienne's condition had worsened still further; their relationship had badly deteriorated, mainly because of her health but also, according to Mr. Matthews, because of their sexual incompatibility; the strain was having a serious effect on Eliot's own health and ability to work. Yet he could not easily bring himself to contemplate leaving her. She was emotionally dependent upon him to a hysterical degree, and he had come to believe that in marrying her he had done her irreparable harm for which he must continue to bear responsibility. However, as Mr. Matthews tells us, Eliot "finally convinced himself . . . that he was intensifying and prolonging the harm by allowing the marriage to drag on. He was bad for Vivienne; she was ruinous to him. If he was to save them both, or either of them, he must separate from her." Just how much this decision cost Eliot in guilt and self-recrimination is understandably not a matter of public record. But new tonalities of remorse are unmistakable in the later poetry, even as the force of his creative drive appears gradually to wane. In leaving Vivienne he may have released himself and her from an intolerable situation. Yet it was nonetheless a situation that had provided him with a focus for his suffering and the concrete materials necessary to its poetic expression.

Eliot could probably not have survived the last years of his life with Vivienne without the support of the Church, the regular ritual of his attendance at Mass, his prayers, and his ardent efforts to discipline himself to lead a Christian life. In fact, Mr. Matthews suggests that Eliot's conversion was perhaps less a metaphysical experience than an expression of his need for moral authority and reassurance at a time of grave personal stress. In the ceremonies and traditions of

Anglo-Catholicism he found the structures of coherence he had always sought in his life and had made central to his critical conception of literature. Also his conversion had its atavistic aspect. In a very real sense, the Church represented the puritan strength of his family heritage, a source of spiritual discipline to which, for reasons of temperament and upbringing, he was naturally tempted to return. The cleric in Eliot had never been far beneath the surface. The theological preoccupation had been present in his poetry from the beginning, but now it became explicit and doctrinal, a subject matter rather than a thematic motif.

The great continuing debate in Eliot criticism has been over the effect of his conversion on the quality of his poetry. It is possible to argue that the difference between the poems written before 1927 and those written after is a difference of both quality and content, and that the change in content posed a critical problem that Eliot was never able to solve. The early work produced out of his youthful skepticism and, subsequently, the tragedy of his marriage, was grounded in the emotional specifics of experiences closely observed and deeply felt. The narrative voice was that of a complex, overly fastidious sensibility whose revulsion at the shabbiness of modern life, the sterility of the merely secular life, and the ugliness of a merely sexual sexuality was dramatically intensified by the formal restraints imposed by the language and by an imagery that was strikingly concrete and at the same time drily impersonal. The work done after the conversion is abstract, conceptual, and didactically theological. As Bernard Bergonzi has said, the later poems "read like summaries of experience rather than enactments of it," and Mr. Matthews has demonstrated very convincingly that it is possible to print passages of "The Four Quartets" as prose, and, in so doing, separate out "the lodes of poetry" from the heavy layers of "shale in which they lie."

But perhaps the vital difference between the pre- and post-conversion poems is that in the latter Eliot was no longer writing out of his sense of guilt, remorse, and the imperative need for order and belief, but had finally managed to *achieve* order and belief. He was interested now in confronting abstract religious ideas directly, as he might have done in prose, while earlier it was the *experience,* not the matter, of cognition that had preoccupied him. It is also in the nature of theological speculations when used as material for poetry that specific emotional correlatives for them are extremely difficult to discover, unless they exist, as they did for Dante, in relation to a living body of mythic convention and religious symbolism. As Kierkegaard and Kafka well knew, one cannot depict one's experience of

God directly or ever hope to know him. All that can be known is the anguish of the man without God and in search of him.

In defiance of his own dictum concerning Henry James—who "had a mind so fine that no idea could violate it"—Eliot allowed his own perhaps less fine mind to be violated by an idea. He succumbed to a "position," and so began to explore the dimensions of his idea where before he had explored the dimensions of his sensibility. The reduction of a complex perception of life to a theory or doctrine purporting to explain life leads inevitably to an impoverishment of both the perception and the doctrine, whether it is religious, social, or political. In a poet the first sign of such impoverishment is a weakening of the sensory basis of metaphor, an abstracting of experience from its connection with concrete feeling so that it will serve the expression of an idea. One sees this happening in "The Four Quartets" where the theological preoccupation has become paramount and the "poetic" content has been pressed into its service and in the process deprived of integrity and vitality.

A new god is being served in Eliot's later work. It is not an altogether strange god but different from the one served in "Prufrock" and "The Waste Land," a god not of poetic and profane passion but of saintly meditation and beatitude, an entity appointed quite simply to save the sanity and soul of the poet. Eliot in effect gave up being a poet in order to become secure in the universe. And while one may sympathize and understand, this is scarcely the action of the greatest artist, whose allegiance must be, before sanity and soul, to consciousness, the full burden of which he is obliged to carry as best he can for as long as he lives and even, if necessary, into hell.

Eliot may have paid too high a price for his ascension to faith, and he may have paid it too soon. The odds may not have been all that high. There are always more extreme levels of spiritual pain to be endured. We will never know how much he might have been able to endure if the alternative offered by the Church had been less congenial to his temperament. But somewhere inside these questions a future biographer may have to make a final evaluation of Eliot's life and artistic achievement. He will have to begin by trying to understand not only the achievement but its expense, not only the magnitude of the talent but its *possible* magnitude had Eliot not chosen, for reasons that may well have seemed to him unimpeachable, to sacrifice his high investment in it and place himself and his work at the mercy of God.

1974

The Saddest Story of Ford Madox Ford

Until a relatively short time ago, it was fashionable to say that Ford Madox Ford is the most neglected major literary figure of the twentieth century. But in the years since his death in 1939, so many commentators have dedicated themselves to the task of rescuing Ford from obscurity that they have now succeeded in elevating him, if not exactly to notoriety, at least to something like the serious reputation he clearly deserved but never quite managed to achieve during his lifetime.

Beginning in the early fifties with the reissue of his most important novels, *The Good Soldier* and the Tietjens tetralogy, *Parade's End*, we have been experiencing a modest but very genuine Ford revival. Literary scholars and critics have taken him up rather in the way they rediscovered his chief influences, James and Conrad, so that we now have available a body of material relating to Ford's life and work that may soon reach the proportions of a full-scale literature. In addition to various memoirs by friends, enemies, and former mistresses, there are the two earlier biographies by Douglas Goldring and Frank MacShane, this new one by Arthur Mizener, at least a dozen book-length critical studies, and an enormous quantity of articles, mainly analytical readings of *The Good Soldier* and the Tietjens novels. Of the critical books, one of the most valuable is the newly published volume by H. Robert Huntley, *The Alien Protagonist of Ford Madox Ford,* a brilliantly perceptive and coordinated work of textual interpretation and intellectual history.

Mizener, while evidently attempting neither to make exhaustive critical assessments nor to "place" Ford in any very firm relation to intellectual history, has nevertheless written the most comprehensive of the biographies, and offers more detailed information about Ford's character and career than any other commentator to date. If anything, his book suffers from the inclusion of too much detail, particularly in the sections concerning Ford's military service in World War I, his literary and financial negotiations with publishers, and his editorial work on *The English* and *The Transatlantic Reviews.* As a result, Mizener's treatment lacks the tidiness and formal grace of the Goldring and MacShane volumes, both of which provide a more distinct but necessarily narrower impression of Ford, and in Goldring's case, an impression at once biased and humanized by feelings of personal friendship. Mizener has had the advantage of coming to Ford unsullied by sentiments of this kind, and with the additional advantage that Ford's worthiness as a biographical subject—a point of serious issue for earlier commentators—is no longer in question, hence, no longer in need of defense. He has also clearly benefited from the great wealth of biographical and critical materials that have accumulated around the literary period encompassed by Ford's lifetime, a period now recognized as containing the central history of the modern movement in all the arts.

Although Mizener does not make as much use of these materials as he might have, their existence affords him a metaphysical context in which certain assumptions are taken for granted and basic premises need not be redefined. His opinions are, therefore, assured, informed, and highly sophisticated just because he has behind him the full authority of the modernist critical canon. And since he is sufficiently removed from his subject in time, he is able to assess very precisely the relative value of his findings in the perspective not only of Ford's experience while he was alive, but of what, over the long range, we have come to see as his very great and enduring distinction.

Mizener's title, *The Saddest Story,* the phrase used by the narrator of *The Good Soldier* to describe the grim little tale he is about to tell, also accurately characterizes Ford's life, or at least those aspects of his life that relate to his literary and amatory misadventures, his financial difficulties, his physical and nervous disorders, and, above all, his struggle to win recognition as the important man of letters whom, in his more confident moments, he knew himself to be. There is surely no sadder story to be found anywhere in literature, and during the telling of it Mizener provides clues to the reason for the neglect of Ford that, taken together with the clues provided by Goldring and MacShane, make it possible to arrive for the first time at some reasonable understanding of one of the most depressing cases of literary injustice in modern times, and until now probably the most mysterious.

If Ford's many difficulties can be said to have had a single cause, it was very likely his failure to find a focus for his extraordinary creative energies in the kind of work that might have won him important reputation. All his other problems—his frequently abrasive relations with friends, his publicly damaging liaisons with women—seem traceable finally to this one problem of creative diffuseness. Scott Fitzgerald once said, "Most writers line themselves up along a solid gold bar like Ernest's courage or Joseph Conrad's art or D. H. Lawrence's intense cohabitations." But this was a strategy Ford never learned, partly because his true subject eluded him for almost the whole of his creative career, and partly because his literary interests were simply too broad and his skills as a writer too facile. The result was that he wrote during his lifetime more than seventy books of all kinds, and the sheer bulk and variety of his production made it impossible for the reading public to form a clear impression of him, or to perceive in his work the sort of developing design that might have identified him as the maker of a coherent imaginative world.

Ford also did far too much hack work, either for love or money, and he involved himself in a number of projects—such as his well-known collaborations with Conrad and the founding and editing of magazines—which, while they may have seemed, and often were, eminently worth undertaking at the time, not only scattered his energies but left the impression that he was primarily interested in making a career of literary entrepreneurship. He appeared to be so anxious to discover new writers and to arrange for the publication of their work that even his many friends who respected him began to see him as a man who had decided to be the servant of other people's talent rather than the responsible custodian of his own. He seemed much too patly and agreeably to fit H. G. Wells's description of him as "the only uncle of the gifted young."

Yet the whole trouble was that Ford *did* care, and care passionately, about his own talent, and the continual frustration of his efforts to win the recognition he felt he deserved came to have a decidedly unpleasant effect on his personality, just as it may have been partly responsible for his many affairs with women. As Stella Bowen, his second mistress, very perceptively noted: "In order to keep his machinery running, he requires to exercise his sentimental talents from time to time upon a new object. It keeps him young. It refreshes his ego. It restores his belief in his powers. And who shall say that this type of lubrication is too expensive for so fine a machine?"

Ford was extremely fortunate in his choice of mistresses. However badly he may have treated them, however bitterly they may have resented his treatment of them, they all seem to have been in agreement concerning his fineness as a machine. But where his literary friends were concerned, the problem was rather less simple, if only because their loyalty was not always above question. Yet Ford needed and expected from them the same kind of ego refreshment he got from his women, and when, understandably, he sometimes failed to get it, he tended to make extravagant claims for himself, even to become insufferably arrogant and patronizing. It so happened that Ford was in his essential self quite the opposite of the image he projected in public. There is ample evidence that he was kind, considerate, and—toward those he respected—generous at times to the point of saintliness. But because he suffered from an often very accurate sense of being underrated, he was driven to try much too hard and in all the wrong ways to impress people and, as a result, did permanent damage to both his personal relations and his literary reputation.

Inevitably of course, much that people interpreted as arrogance in him was the distorted reflection of his virtue. For example, while he was editing *The English Review,* he alienated certain critics who might have been most helpful to his career because he felt that the work they submitted for publication did not measure up to his standards. He might have done the political thing, but his dedication to literary values was unshakable, and as it turned out, *The English Review,* while it lasted, was distinguished not only for its consistently high quality but for the number of important writers whom Ford introduced through its pages. In the first issue alone he managed to bring together new work by Thomas Hardy, Henry James, Conrad, John Galsworthy, W. H. Hudson, and H. G. Wells, and in subsequent issues he provided D. H. Lawrence, Wyndham Lewis, and H. M. Tomlinson with their first appearance in print.

Yet Ford's public personality seems to have detracted powerfully from the value of his service to literature. A great many people who knew him well, but evidently not well enough, have left to posterity their largely nasty impressions of his public side, while only a relative few have been able to bring themselves to speak in his defense. Richard Aldington once said that Ford gave the appearance of "swanking, bragging, maligning—a village blacksmith of scandal." On the other hand, Stephen Crane replied to the charge that Ford was arrogant by saying, "You must not mind Ford; that is his way. He patronizes me, he patronizes Mr. Conrad, he patronizes Mr. James. When he goes to Heaven he will patronize God Almighty. But God Almighty will get used to it, for Ford is all right." Conrad himself, who, after his initially close friendship with Ford, may have grown tired of being patronized, wrote what must be one of the most meanspirited characterizations a fine writer ever made of another: "His conduct is *impossible*. He's a megalomaniac who imagines that he is managing the universe and that everybody treats him with the blackest ingratitude. A fierce and exasperated vanity is hidden under his calm manner which misleads people. . . . I do not hesitate to say that there are cases, not quite as bad, under medical treatment."

This last is particularly vicious since, as Conrad well knew, Ford had often been under medical treatment for what was then called neurasthenia, and it is obvious that this disorder was partly responsible for his unattractive conduct in public. Yet whether because of neurosis or simple arrogance, Ford always had the greatest difficulty separating his fantasies from reality, and his tendency was to convince himself that his fantasy view of reality was correct, just because he so desperately wanted and, in one part of his mind, sincerely believed it to be. In its most innocuous form, this tendency sometimes caused him to invent the most preposterous falsehoods, most of which were fortunately too outlandish to have a chance of being believed. But Ford also tried on other occasions to govern his life by the dictates of fantasy, and while the effect of this could be merely comic—as when he spent lavishly in expectation of the arrival of nonexistent funds—it could also be both comic and calamitous.

A notable instance was his effort to find some way of divorcing his wife Elsie so that he would be free to marry his first mistress, Violet Hunt. Since Elsie would not agree to a divorce, Ford decided that by going to Germany, his ancestral home, and establishing citizenship, he could eventually obtain a German divorce. After a short stay with Violet in Germany, he somehow convinced himself and her that the decree had been granted and apparently quite innocently announced to the press that he was now married to Violet, who wasted no time in taking his name. The result was a lawsuit initiated by Elsie against certain publications that had referred to Violet as Ford's wife. Elsie of course won the case to the accompaniment of the widest publicity, and the scandal that followed probably had a more destructive effect on Ford's reputation, particularly in England, than any other single event of his life.

The saddest story, indeed, but also one of the most remarkable, even admirable because Ford Madox Ford, in spite of his many difficulties and failures, was a great man and a great literary figure, and he lived a great life. He may have been a disastrously bad manager of his personal relations and his literary career. He may have written far too many books, of which only a very few have any claim to permanence. But of those few, *The Good Soldier* and the four novels of the Tietjens series are among the most distinguished works of fiction of this age because in them Ford was able to engage with enormous imaginative power the one subject that proved to be his one true subject, the collapse of the Edwardian moral empire and the emergence after World War I of what T. S. Eliot once called "the immense panorama of futility and anarchy which is contemporary history." These novels alone are enough to assure Ford the place in literature he did not achieve during his lifetime. Yet his service to literature was almost as important as his personal contribution to it. His career developed through all the major phases of the modern movement, and he was actively involved in all of them. He was born into the fading Pre-Raphaelite world of Swinburne, the Rossettis, and his grandfather, the painter Ford Madox Brown. He was an enthusiastic supporter of the Imagist poets and the Vorticists during the years before the first war. He published in his magazines many of the most original of the new moderns, first in London, then during the twenties in Paris where he was a figure of consequence in the literary life of the American expatriates. In his old age, when financial difficulties forced him to take a college teaching job in this country, he had considerable influence on the younger southern writers of the post-Agrarian period. At various times in his life he knew just about all the important writers it was possible to know: Wells, Arnold Bennett, Stephen Crane, Eliot, Henry James, Lawrence, Hemingway, Pound, Gertrude Stein, Wyndham Lewis, Allen Tate—and most of them had reason to feel greatly in his debt. He gave them friendship, encouragement, good advice, and, most important of all, a renewal of faith in the reality of literary excellence.

It is obvious that Ford was, as Pound once remarked, "a fascinating and, at moments, almost incredible human 'prublum.'" But he was also that rarest of beings, the genuine, wholly dedicated literary professional, very much in the tradition of the Victorian man of letters. It seems possible now that he was the last of that line.
1971

Edmund Wilson's Twenties

Edmund Wilson's personal writings have until now occupied a somewhat peripheral place in relation to his far better-known and more distinguished work in the fields of criticism and literary history. The result is that his considerable gifts as a memoirist and social observer have not been fully appreciated nor the particular qualities of his private mind and personality sufficiently understood.

From the age of thirteen until he died in 1972, Wilson kept copious diaries and journals on which he drew for his two autobiographical volumes, *A Prelude* and *Upstate,* the many personal pieces scattered through his collections of essays, *The Shores of Light, Classics and Commercials, A Piece of My Mind, The American Earthquake,* and *The Bit between My Teeth,* and even for certain materials that he incorporated, often in only slightly disguised form, into his novels, *I Thought of Daisy* and *Memoirs of Hecate County.* By the time of his death he had accumulated forty-one ledger-type copybooks comprising over two thousand manuscript pages, and his friend Leon Edel has now published a lightly edited edition of the journals written during the twenties. Subsequent volumes covering the decades between 1930 and 1972 are scheduled to appear under Edel's editorship at regular intervals over the next several years, and Wilson's widow, in collaboration with Prof. Daniel Aaron of Harvard, will shortly issue a comprehensive collection of Wilson's letters. This massive project when finally completed will unquestionably represent one of the most important literary undertakings conceivable in our time, not only because the abundant records kept by Wilson constitute an invaluable history of American literary and cultural life over the past fifty years, but because they chronicle the intellectual development of a writer whose influence on literary opinion in this country has been greater than that of any other critic of his generation. For Wilson was something far more than simply our best-known and most productive critic. He was also a cultural force of very large size and old-fashioned kind. One thinks of him not so much as the contemporary of Hemingway and Fitzgerald but as belonging to a tradition in which perhaps his closest contemporary is Henry James. In reading these journals one is reminded again and again of James, and not inappropriately, Wilson's editor is also James's official biographer.

James and Wilson both had the singular good fortune to belong to periods in our history when the literary work most urgently needing to be done in their respective forms was particularly well suited to their talents. That work, furthermore, was essentially the same for both. The experience of his time and place, in particular his decision to spend most of his life abroad, gave James the opportunity to internationalize the American novel. Wilson, whose literary standards were formed in large part on the French historical criticism of Michelet and Taine, established his reputation with *Axel's Castle,* a work that might be said to have pioneered the internationalization of American criticism by opening our understanding of the European symbolist movement. Wilson brought to the task an intellectual culture that, like James's, was more European than American, more classical than modern, and a sensitivity to language that not only enabled him to learn several European languages as well as Russian and Hebrew, but gave him a fanatical preoccupation with stylistic nuance and exactitude. Both James and Wilson saw literature as the ultimate vindication of life, and they served it with a priestly dedication, in part because it was their primary and natural mode of connection with the world, but also because it was a means of making coherent and mastering their own troubled responses to the world.

As the earlier entries in these notebooks make clear, Wilson in his youth suffered, as did James, from what the latter called an acute sense of "otherness." James was by turns gratified and oppressed by the feeling that he was a citizen only of the James family, and Wilson seems to have felt similarly ambiguous about the closeness of his own family ties. The Wilsons lived, according to Edel, "in a self-contained world like the Bolkonskys or the Karenins, in relative affluence . . . an assortment of aunts and uncles and cousins who came and went in their particular exclusive corner of New Jersey. The ancestry had been Presbyterian; the Calvinism lingered. There were distinctions of caste and a sense, however powerless, of being 'gentry' in a private universe." Wilson once said that before he entered prep school he had known almost no one but the members of his own family, and when he finished college he felt unable to get on with ordinary people.

Wilson's sense of estrangement from the world beyond his family was aggravated by the peculiar insecurity of his relations with his parents. He had an aloof, strong-willed mother who was made more inaccessible than she naturally was by deafness. His father was a brilliant and successful lawyer but subject to periods of acute depression and often immobilized completely by what at that time was described as neurasthenia. Wilson had nothing to say to his mother even if her hearing had been perfect, and one of the poignant revelations in the early journals is that as a boy he used to take notes on topics about which he might possibly engage her in conversation. Toward his father he seems to have had conflicting feelings of great respect and anxiety that he himself might become emotionally ill and lose control of his life. It is of interest that in 1929 Wilson did in fact have a nervous breakdown, and he was understandably shocked when told that he was then exactly the same age his father had been at the time of the father's first serious breakdown. But like James, who suffered what seems to have been an actual physical injury, his "horrid even if obscure hurt" that may have incapacitated him sexually, Wilson learned to put his frailties to creative use, and he found in literature a means of breaking at least imaginatively out of the confines of otherness and at the same time maintaining his psychic equilibrium. "Books, language, the world of imaginative reconstruction," says Edel, "established some kind of communion with the remote 'outside.' . . . He seemed to have developed a particular meticulosity of mind, cultivated doubtless against chaos."

As he grew to maturity, Wilson was able to involve himself in the world with considerable energy, and his sense of otherness surely intensified his extraordinary powers of observation and his appetite for impressions—much as James, his feeling of personal isolation compounded by the experience of being an expatriated American was impelled with so much curiosity and excitement to immerse himself in the rich social life of England. Both men apparently came to know virtually everybody worth knowing in their respective societies, James the rich, famous, and titled, Wilson for the most part the literary bohemians of the Village, magazine editors, the Algonquin Wits, and the uptown cocktail crowd, along with a great many men and women whom James would have considered wholly disreputable.

A fundamental difference in both taste and the kinds of experience open to the two men is illustrated by the fact that James could reveal with some amazement and pride that he had dined out at various great houses a total of 107 times in one winter. Wilson, product of a less formal age, seems to have done little when not writing except go to parties and travel from bed to bed. He overcame with great success the social and sexual inhibitions of his youth, and he did so in a manner that James might have found sociologically intriguing but assuredly not at all enviable.

Yet the effects of Wilson's early life were never completely eradicated. He seems always to have retained a core of remoteness and emotional rigidity, even while strenuously involved in social life and carrying on his most intense love affairs. Edel observes that when he died in 1972 at seventy-seven, "he had many friends and the admiration of the world . . . but there was to the end something aloof and shut in, as if he were still reaching out from behind obsolete invisible barriers, using the full force of his intellect to establish a truce with mankind."

Evidence for this is to be found everywhere in the journals covering the period of Wilson's early adult life. The entries reveal his incredible sensitivity to the tonalities of character, setting, weather, and spoken language. His reportage of conversations overheard and his mimicry of dialects show him to have had a perfect ear and a fine sense of the ludicrous, whatever in fact is comic, vulgar, or gauche in the speech and behavior of the people he encounters. Yet his innate spectatorial stance as well as some dead or anesthetized area of his psyche causes him again and again to seem obtuse or wooden in relation to his own feelings. He observes himself in emotional situations and at times in the act of expressing emotion. But there is a clinical quality about his descriptions of these occasions and a seemingly nervous embarrassment that makes him want to rush past them as quickly as possible. There is also something particularly distorted and secretive about his treatment of the women with whom he has his most serious relationships. Concerning the two women, Mary Blair and Margaret Canby, who became his first and his second wives during the period, he offers almost no information at all and presents only the most cursory description of the quality of his feelings for them. Yet when he writes of his affairs with other women—and they are almost always the kind he would never dream of marrying—he can be expansive and confessional to the point where at moments the clinician is nearly but not quite vanquished by the lover, and the lover completely disorients the judgment of the writer. He devotes long passages to detailed accounts of exactly how he performed intercourse with these women, what positions they assumed, whether clothes were on or off, what odors were detectable and delectable, and the number of orgasms arrived at by himself and/or his partner after a specified period of effort. He is also capable of so completely giving way to amatory gusto as to offer, with absolute solemnity, passages like the following one, which is surely calculated to sully the appetites of cheese lovers throughout the world: "I held her firm little insteps for a moment in my hands: in pale stockings, her tired and sweaty feet were like two little moist cream cheeses encased in covers of cloth: her body, which seemed now so slight in its pale blue dress, lay as limp as a lettuce leaf soaked by the summer rain." The girl being described served as the model for the character of Anna in *Memoirs of Hecate County,* although the quoted passage was reproduced verbatim earlier in *I Thought of Daisy* and used as a description of the heroine.

For reasons perhaps having to do with his ambiguous relations with his mother, Wilson seems to have been afflicted with a problem not unfamiliar in male chauvinist sexual lore. He was capable of responding passionately and tenderly to women who were waitresses, dance-hall girls, prostitutes or otherwise below him socially. But women who were his equals, who were brilliant, artistic, or independent in love, were mysterious and unattainable, goddesses to be worshipped but not with any ease sexually enjoyed. Wilson's first two wives apparently belonged to this latter category as the poet, Edna St. Vincent Millay, whom he adored, also very clearly did. There is a sad but significant description in the journals of a moment when Wilson and his friend the poet John Peale Bishop, also in love with Miss Millay, are both given permission by her to hold her body—fully clothed of course—at the same time. Bishop sits decorously clasping the top half, while Wilson embraces the bottom half. It is a scene that contrasts interestingly with the one in which Wilson tenderly holds Anna's sweaty feet.

Yet it would be a mistake to assume that the value of these journals consists merely of the insight they afford us into the character of the younger Edmund Wilson. They also have the very greatest importance as documents of social and literary history, and the segment of history they chronicle is one we continue to look back upon with undiminishing nostalgia; however, in comparison with our situation today, it is one we must find more and more difficult to comprehend.

Although Wilson does not himself generalize abstractly about the qualities of the era but rather is consistently descriptive and impressionistic, one cannot help but be struck by the fact that the life he is recording now seems removed from us by at least a century of psychological time. Through his many vivid portraits of people encountered across an extremely wide social spectrum, we are reminded that the twenties were years when the lines of communication among the various classes in America had not yet broken down, and the literary community still had a cohesiveness that made it possible for writers constantly to see one another and at the same time have some chance to associate with the very rich and the very poor, the highly educated and the unsophisticated. This was a decade when artists and intellectuals had a style of life markedly different from that of business and professional people, and there existed a vital relationship between the way they lived and the work they produced. The worlds of literature and publishing had not yet become institutionalized and domesticated as they have today. Writers lived in New York and Paris, not on isolated farms in Connecticut or in university towns scattered across the country.

The period that Wilson recreates so superbly was seemingly crowded with remarkable and individualistic people who were engaged in experimenting with new freedoms, trying on new identities, seeking to create new ways of giving expression to what they sensed were radically changed realities following the end of World War I. Wilson was one of the most distinguished participants in and observers of what we now recognize to have been the revolution that brought the modern age in American society and the arts to its first dramatic flowering. It is an instructive experience to witness the growth of his sensibility in the growth of that remarkable time, to learn what it was like to be alive then, and to recognize how greatly we have since matured, how quickly we have aged, and just how much the process has cost us in excitement and vitality.

1975

Hemingway's Last Big Novel

At the time of his death in 1961 Hemingway is known to have had at least four book-length manuscripts in various stages of preparation. There were the two nonfiction books: *A Moveable Feast*, his collection of Paris sketches published posthumously in 1964, and *The Dangerous Summer,* of which three portions dealing with the Ordoñez-Domingúin bullfights of 1959 appeared serially in *Life* in 1960. In addition, Hemingway had been working on a very long but presumably unfinished novel called *The Garden of Eden* and a book often referred to as the "Land, Sea, and Air Novel" based on his experiences during World War II.

In spite of the quantities of gossip that have accumulated around the Hemingway tragedy over the last nine years, very little has been said about his still unpublished works. According to Carlos Baker, his official biographer, the complete text of *The Dangerous Summer* is now "locked away" at Charles Scribner's Sons and seems a generally mediocre piece of writing. Judging by the quality of the *Life* installments, one would suppose that as a book it would be best kept locked away. Since 1961 it has been impossible to obtain reliable information on either the status or the whereabouts of the two fiction manuscripts, *The Garden of Eden* and the "Land, Sea, and Air Novel," and reports circulated during Hemingway's lifetime were contradictory in the extreme. There is some evidence that he may have worked sporadically on both right up to his final illness and breakdown. But one does not know how far he had progressed or what disposition was later made of them. It may be that they were among the unfinished materials found on his worktable after his suicide. It may also be that they were finished and placed in deposit—as his widow and others have said was sometimes his custom—in bank vaults, at his publishers, or with certain trusted bartenders. In any case, information has been so meager that undoubtedly very few people outside Hemingway's immediate circle of family and friends were even aware that such a work as *The Garden of Eden* existed until Baker referred to it in his biography. The description he gives there is far from complete, and it would appear that he saw only a draft of the work in progress. But if the book is as preposterously bad as he makes it seem, one can only hope that its publication will be delayed until such time as it can safely be offered as a literary curiosity too ancient to be any longer embarrassing. Baker characterizes it as "an experimental compound of past and present, filled with astonishing ineptitudes . . . a long and emptily hedonistic novel of young lovers in the old days of Grau-du-Roi and the Costa Brava: page after page of their talk was filled with inconsequential commentary on the color and condition of their hair, the food and drink they were always consuming, and the current state of their suntanned skins."

This is all we have heard about *The Garden of Eden,* and it would seem to be more than enough. About the original manuscript of the "Land, Sea, and Air Novel," on the other hand, we have heard a great deal for years, but what we have heard has told us very little. In fact, ever since 1949, when Malcolm Cowley writing in *Life* confirmed the many rumors that Hemingway was engaged on a big new book about the war, the "Land, Sea, and Air Novel" has been the most widely publicized literary mystery of the past two decades. Scarcely any of the information released during Hemingway's lifetime contained more than an oblique reference to the book's theme or subject matter. One learned only that the action was supposed to be divided into three parts corresponding roughly to the different phases of Hemingway's experience of the war, first as captain of his cruiser, the *Pilar,* during its service as an improvised submarine-chaser in the waters around Cuba, then as a correspondent with the RAF over France and Germany, and finally with the Fourth Infantry Division during the Allied drive across Europe. Most of the publicity took the form of reports concerning his rate of progress with the book, and these were so contradictory that they served only to deepen the air of mystery surrounding the whole enterprise. They even caused one to wonder whether the book actually existed.

Cowley said that Hemingway began writing it before Pearl Harbor and by 1949 had completed over a thousand pages. But as early as 1946 Hemingway had announced that he had completed twelve hundred pages—a report which, if true, would seem to indicate that in the following three years he made no progress at all. The columnist Leonard Lyons has been quoted as saying in 1954 that "the long novel is finished and is in a safe-deposit box in a Havana bank." But Hemingway apparently had not heard the news, for in July of 1955 he was still apprising the public of his progress. In fact, he seemed actually to have lost ground. The number of pages he said he had completed had dropped mysteriously to nine hundred. Then a year later in a *Look* article he wrote that he had reached the eight hundred and fiftieth manuscript page, evidently having lost another fifty pages in the interval. Finally, more than two years later, his rate of loss having sharply accelerated, he is reported to have told Earl Wilson that he had "finished page six-sixty-seven today."

These contradictions may or may not be important in themselves. They may indicate only that Hemingway was speaking on one occasion of rough-draft pages and on another of finished pages. But they may also indicate that there was some real ambiguity about his progress on the book and perhaps about his imaginative relation to his materials. Surely, there is some ground for suspicion on both counts. If, as Cowley claims, Hemingway actually began the book before Pearl Harbor, he seems to have been sufficiently cavalier in his attitude toward it to be able to interrupt the writing again and again to do other things and even to take on other and, one would think, much less important literary projects. Between Pearl Harbor and 1949, in addition to his Q-Boat operations with the *Pilar,* he had been extremely active as a war correspondent, had produced a large quantity of journalism about his experiences, written several introductions to books, edited the *Men at War* anthology, and had suspended all other operations in 1949 to write *Across the River and into the Trees.* By 1952 the only material remotely related to the "Land, Sea, and Air Novel" that he apparently had ready to publish was *The Old Man and the Sea,* and that book had nothing to do with the war at sea.

Hemingway's desultory progress on his big novel might not by itself have seemed especially disconcerting when one considered his temperamental restlessness and the very wide range of his interests; however, there were certain facts that made it deeply disconcerting. For one thing, it was not at all like him to suspend work on his important books for long intervals. In the past he had followed a carefully disciplined routine and rarely allowed himself to be distracted from the writing of a book until it was finished. Yet now he appeared to be almost frantically seeking distraction and taking advantage of any excuse, however trivial, to avoid full commitment to the big novel. Second, contrary to the statements made by his intimates, it had also not been Hemingway's habit in the past to put finished manuscripts in the bank for extended periods before publishing them. He evidently did not follow this practice in the case of any of his earlier books. One does not know whether the big novel, as originally conceived, was ever finished. But if it was and Hemingway thought it successful, there is little likelihood that he would have postponed its publication, particularly at a time when he is known to have been acutely conscious of the need to bolster his reputation with an important new work. Hence, it would seem either that he was unable to finish the book as he had first planned it, or that he did finish it and was dissatisfied with the result.

He might well have had his doubts, for there was good reason to suppose that he could no longer rely on the absolute rightness of his instincts or work with anything resembling his old energy and endurance. He had apparently been in failing health for quite some time, perhaps even as far back as the war. But the injuries he suffered in the two African plane crashes of 1954 seem to have brought him in the next few years to a condition of virtually complete physical and mental breakdown. It seemed obvious also from the internal evidence of the work published in the fifties that his physical deterioration had been accompanied by a decline in creative vitality. In 1950 he published *Across the River and into the Trees,* surely the poorest of his novels, and even though *The Old Man and the Sea* represented for many people a triumphant recovery, it could also be seen to have a quality of specious attractiveness and efficiency that in fiction so often results from the avoidance of more problems than are confronted and overcome. It was, in short, a safe book in the sense that it was made up of the best of Hemingway's old market-tested materials, stylistic and dramatic effects, which at one time had been arrived at with some real originality and risk through a vital engagement of life, but which were now merely postures and autographs of famous but very dead emotions. The problem was not only that Hemingway was sounding like himself in a manner that seemed synthetic, but it was also that the self he sounded like was not the self he any longer was. Writing for him had apparently ceased to be an act of self-discovery and had become an act of self-resuscitation.

At any rate, as various commentators have indicated, Hemingway originally planned *The Old Man and the Sea* as a coda or perhaps a fourth part to the sea section of the "Land, Sea, and Air Novel." But significantly he chose instead to publish it as a separate short novel. While continuing to work on the big book, he may slowly have revised his original plan to the extent of limiting the action to those experiences relating to the sea only. It may also be, as Carlos Baker suggests, that certain of the materials concerning the war in Europe were incorporated into *Across the River and into the Trees* and presumably were either used up in that way or never completed as a separate section of the projected long work. In any case, Hemingway may have decided—or his widow may have decided after his death—that a publishable novel could be made out of the sea materials alone, and it is this section or surviving version of the big book and not the big book itself (the remainder of which, if it was ever written, is still not accounted for) that has now been published, with some emendations by Mrs. Hemingway, under the title *Islands in the Stream.* In it Hemingway tells the story of a painter named Thomas Hudson—whose circumstances and experiences in some ways very closely resemble his own—during three phases of his life: in the mid-thirties on the island of Bimini where Hudson is living alone after a divorce and is visited by his three sons; a number of years later in Cuba during the war when Hudson is involved in secret antisubmarine activities using his cruiser as a Q-Boat; and a short time afterward when Hudson and his crew set out in search of survivors from a destroyed German submarine, this episode culminating in a gun battle and Hudson's death.

Knowing that this may well be the last new Hemingway novel we will ever see, one approaches it with a mixture of wariness, awe, and considerable anxiety, hoping that through some charity of the gods it will turn out to be very good, but knowing also the chances against its being other than very bad. It would be nice homage to be able to pronounce it a masterpiece; yet there is diminishment for each of us in the possibility that it might prove a disaster. And the worst diminishment of all: if honesty forces it upon us to be equivocal, finicky, and faint, to say, as unfortunately one must, that the book is neither very good nor very bad, but that it is both, in some places downright wonderful, in others as sad and embarrassingly self-indulgent as the work of any sophomore.

In this respect it resembles *For Whom the Bell Tolls* perhaps more closely than it does any of the earlier novels. There are other obvious similarities between the two books, but they are most strikingly similar in the way each brings together in a single narrative—at times within the space of a single page—some of the best and worst features of Hemingway's writing. The interesting thing, furthermore, is that these features relate in both books to the same kinds of material. Those sections that are devoted mainly to the description of physical action are almost invariably excellent. Those sections in which the physical action is interrupted to give Robert Jordan and

Thomas Hudson an opportunity to *think,* to analyze their feelings or to find intellectual justification for doing what they are about to do, are as vapid and pretentious as such passages nearly always are in Hemingway. Luckily, the two kinds of material are not present in equal amounts in either book: the passages describing physical action far outnumber the passages of intellectual analysis in both. But the element that finally saves *For Whom the Bell Tolls* is missing from *Islands in the Stream.*

In the latter there is no coherently formed or sufficiently compressed narrative structure in which the action can take on the intensity or the meaning it would seem potentially capable of developing. There is also no thematic design strong enough to support the weight of Hudson's sagging cerebral muscles or to give his thoughts the kind of relevance to the action that Jordan's can finally be seen to have. Where *For Whom the Bell Tolls* is held together by the rigid economy of the form and the tightly interlocking relationship of the events occurring over a period of a very few days, the new novel is composed of episodes much more widely spaced in time and only vaguely connected by an evolving plot. The result is that such dramatic tension as may be generated in any one of the episodes tends to be dissipated in the lapse of time separating it from the next. The problem is not simply that the book is divided into three parts but that, as a novel, it *disintegrates* into three parts or long short stories, and these are related only by the fact that Hudson is the central, if somewhat opaque, character in all of them.

Yet taken separately as, given the looseness of structure, they must be taken, many of the episodes contain the most exciting and effective writing Hemingway has ever done. There is a marvelous ocean-fishing sequence in part 1, the account of a protracted and agonizing struggle by one of Hudson's young sons to bring in a giant fish. The pathos of the boy's almost superhuman effort—which of course ends in last-minute failure—is brilliantly evoked, and one realizes that here is a dimension of Hemingway one has seen before but perhaps not often enough, that side of his nature that was capable of responding not merely to bluster and bravado but with admiration for bravery in the weak and with tenderness toward weakness in the brave. There are also some nicely comic scenes in a Havana bar that are reminiscent of the better moments of *To Have and Have Not,* and the best sustained piece of writing in the book, the long story of the search for the German submarines ending in the gun battle. This is one of the most impressive descriptions of physical action to be found in Hemingway, and it is comparable to the best of them all, the account of El Sordo's last stand on the hilltop in *For Whom the Bell Tolls*.

In spite of the high quality of individual episodes, one still senses a deficiency in the whole that another comparison with *For Whom the Bell Tolls* may help to clarify. When he wrote that book, Hemingway was still close enough to the values and emotional responses of his early career to be able to use them to give a plausible edge of tragedy to Robert Jordan's story. Jordan was the climactic Hemingway hero and the last of the heroes able to embody convincingly the old attitudes about life, love, courage, and death. But even at that, one saw that the old attitudes were being stretched extremely thin in Jordan. Already the Hemingway style, which had once been not merely a certain choice and arrangement of words but the verbalization of a distinct metaphysical view of experience, showed signs of hardening into a stance. The conviction was already beginning to drain out of it, and it was obvious that Jordan, in those rather maudlin moments of introspection, was struggling hard to keep his old attitudes intact. But one also saw that this very feature of the novel, this element of ideological strain, helped to provide it with its considerable dramatic tension. There was the conflict, never finally resolved, between Jordan's World War I negativism, the rather effete *Weltschmerz* of Jake Barnes and Frederic Henry, and the requirement imposed by his situation that he be positive and idealistic in his beliefs. Jordan had continually to persuade himself that he believed in the Loyalist cause, just as he had to persuade himself that he believed in the war and, with less success, in "Life, Liberty, and the Pursuit of Happiness."

Then there were the other sources of dramatic tension: the conflict between the desires of love and the demands of duty; the difficulties Jordan encountered in trying to convince the guerrillas that they should help him perform a mission in which he himself could not entirely believe; the poignancy of all emotions in the face of danger and the threat of death. There was all that Jordan stood to lose by the action of blowing the bridge. There were Maria and his possible future with her. There were all the experiences of life he had always enjoyed and wished to be able to enjoy again. These elements helped to convert what was in some ways a too heavily melodramatic novel into a work that had some real artistic complexity and truth.

But the situation of Thomas Hudson is very different, and the difference helps to account for what is most wrong with the new novel. Hudson is primarily the product of his past losses, sorrows, and mistakes. He has already lived a long life, and he has been much damaged in the process. He is no longer positively committed to the early

Hemingway values, yet he retains the early skepticism that in him is fast souring into hopelessness. The simple fact is that, unlike his predecessors, he no longer believes in life and no longer enjoys life. By the time he is confronted with his own certain death, he is carrying nothing but grief over the death of his three sons, the failure of his marriages, and all the emotions he is no longer able to feel. Nothing motivates him to take action except a vague stubborn sense of duty. He does not believe in this war or in any wars, and the very idea of Life, Liberty, and the Pursuit of Happiness has become for him a very sad joke indeed. Consequently, he meets his death like an automaton. He has gone through the motions and put on a good show, but he has had nothing to lose from the start. Hence, his actions have had no meaning. When he dies, he is ready to die, not for the cause, not in order to save the girl he loves, but because he is tired to death of life. There is sadness in this but no real tragedy because there is no sense of missed possibility, no conceivable alternative to dying.

It is evident that as he grew older Hemingway came to identify himself more and more explicitly with his fictional heroes and to draw increasingly on his own emotions and experiences in the creation of his heroes. Jake Barnes and Frederic Henry were essentially fantasy projections of what in some secret part of himself Hemingway wished he might be like. But Thomas Hudson and Colonel Cantwell of *Across the River and into the Trees* are realistic projections of the tired, ailing, and disillusioned man he had by then actually become. And as the distance narrowed between himself and his heroes, his writing lost a crucial dimension. He began to try to *live out* his fantasies instead of projecting them in his fiction. The result was that his fiction became devitalized because the real force of his creativity was being expended in living the experience he imagined. It is even conceivable that in the end Hemingway succumbed to the limitations of the philosophy he had for years been developing in his work and endeavoring more and more to practice in his life. For that philosophy was tenable only for a young and healthy man who could afford to be cynical since his hold on life was vigorous, and he could never really believe in the possibility of his own death. Thus, because of age and failing health Hemingway could no longer do the things that made him feel good afterwards. When the eyesight began to go and the legs went bad, and the condition of the liver would not allow him to drink, and it was no longer fun to hunt or fish or make love, then the limitations of that philosophy became intolerable. But by then there was no turning back. There was no way of building another more durable or complex set of values. Hemingway had succeeded in becoming his heroes, and finally he was beginning to die with them.

But art, when everything else failed, was always there. In the past there had always been art, the one dependable source of new hope and self-renewal. The world could collapse and it would not matter so long as you wrote carefully and well and tried always to write an absolutely true book. When he went down into the basement of his house that summer morning and selected the weapon that would end his life, Hemingway evidently forgot about art. It is a pity because if art had saved him in the past, there was still a chance it might save him once again. There was, in fact, an excellent chance. For in spite of its defects, the best parts of *Islands in the Stream* make clear that he had in his last years enough talent left to serve art successfully. If he had been able to recognize this and believe in it, he might have put the shotgun away and gone back upstairs to bed. But all he could believe in was the black emptiness and the pain. Besides, in that moment he had arrived at the kind of despair he had spent his whole life in flight from, the kind he could no longer evade through the killing of big game in Africa or by writing about the death of his heroes in his books. All the heroes were dead now. There was only himself.
1970

A heavily edited version of *The Garden of Eden* was published in 1986 and is exactly as bad as Carlos Baker predicted it would be, but not because of the resolute mediocrity of the writing. The greater problem is that where in his earlier work Hemingway made effective dramatic use of his fantasies of heroism, he here makes embarrassingly fatuous use of his fantasies of bisexual eroticism. David Bourne and his wife, Catherine, are obsessed with their sexual interchangeability and constantly play games in which he becomes girl and she boy. The introduction of a bisexual female playmate makes it possible for all three of them to multiply into infinity the number of different gender roles they are able to play. The effect is uniformly juvenile.

The Dangerous Summer was published as a book in 1985, and it turned out to be much better than the installments published in *Life* seemed to promise. The principal reason may be that extremely drastic surgery performed by the editors at Scribner's reduced what was in early draft a manuscript of 120,000 words to 40,000, the bare essence of the book Hemingway had originally written and clearly the best of it. One might even argue that on the whole it is a more satisfactory book than his classic Baedeker of bullfighting, *Death in the Afternoon*

(1932), because it is less crammed with taurine esoterica and contains none of the sophomoric naughtiness and churlish pontifications that badly flawed that book. Now, with all the fat cut away, the descriptions of the series of bullfights and the trips to and from them, along with the accounts of food eaten and drinks drunk en route, come together to form a clean, almost novelistic narrative line. *The Dangerous Summer* is, in short, an altogether respectable final Hemingway book about Spain.

The Sun Also Rises
Sixty Years Later

As the sufficiently elderly among us may remember, Hemingway, by the time of his suicide in 1961, had become something of a public embarrassment. The trouble began a long time before, somewhere back in the years of his first international success, the years of African safari and *Death in the Afternoon,* when he had already begun to go slack and was indulging in celebrity exploits rather than the writing of good books. *The Old Man and the Sea* was received more with relief than delight because it seemed a sign that the old Hemingway was still alive and sounding like himself. But then it had to be admitted that the book had no insides and was simply a synthetic imitation of Hemingway sounding like himself. *Across the River and into the Trees* had been just as bad as the disenchanted said it was, and it was ominously bad for it proved that the writer could no longer tell the difference between himself and his public personality, undoubtedly because there had ceased to be any. But that of course had become obvious in the same year when that sad and silly Indian-talk interview with Lillian Ross was published.

By 1961, all the signs seemed to agree that the usual posthumous decline in reputation would, in Hemingway's case, be redundant. There seemed to be no room for further decline. But what happened was something quite different and altogether unexpected. After the shortest eclipse ever recorded in recent literary astronomy, the Hemingway reputation began to shine with a brightness it had not displayed in decades, and it appeared that all the bad years and bad work had been magically purged from public memory. One cause was undoubtedly a delayed realization that the poor man had really had a very hard time, had suffered terribly, and could really not be blamed, since he was ill, for the inferiority of his later work. Also, his suicide began to be viewed, at least by some, not as the betrayal and cop-out it initially seemed to be, but as the considered and courageous act of a man who knew exactly when all the things he cared about had ended for him. There was pathos, even a hint of tragedy in this, enough to set in motion a curious process by which a former fine writer become boring buffoon could be transformed in death into a species of martyred saint. Finally, there was a vague something else—a sense that all the returns were not yet in, that there remained further questions as yet unanswered, some tantalizing, perhaps vindicating final truth still to be revealed.

Whatever the reasons, it can now fairly be said, twenty-five years after his death, that of the several gifted writers of his remarkable generation, Hemingway is the one who still, in spite of everything, makes the strongest claim on our interest and curiosity. Critical and biographical studies of Faulkner, Fitzgerald, Dos Passos, and some of the others continue to be produced. But one senses in their case that the fundamental interpretations have been made, the perimeters of essential discussion established, and that very little of much surprise or value remains to be discovered about them.

In the case of Hemingway, on the other hand, discussion not only goes forward but seems since his death to have massively accelerated with no indication of an end in view. Along with a seven-story mountain of critical literature, we now have on public display the biased testimony of just about everybody who ever knew him, was related or married to him, or slept, fished, hunted, or went to war with him. We have the recollections of his literary contemporaries, the opinions of those former friends who sat for their portraits in *The Sun Also Rises,* the memoirs of his siblings, his sons, and his favorite Paris bartenders. We have his letters and his manuscripts and all those photographs—Bwana Hemingway stalking kudu on the plains of Africa, commanding his native gun-bearers in terse Swahili; War Correspondent Hemingway in perilous service with the Spanish Loyalists; Sub-chaser Hemingway at the wheel of the *Pilar,* patrolling the waters around Cuba for Nazis; Task Force Hemingway in big Papa beard and swathed in ammunition belts, leading his ragtag band of irregulars on intrepid sorties behind the enemy lines. And of course the image of him that emerges is protean. Evidently, he was a vital, rude, crude, sensitive, kind, unkind, generous, selfish, jealous, petty, helpful, hurtful, loving, and hating human being who did not care terribly much for anything or anyone except the things that excited and diverted him and the people who amused him, adored him, or encouraged and supported him in his work. The more we know about him, the less we like him, yet the more we find him fascinating. There was never before in our literary history a writer of such force of personality, such public presence, so highly skilled in the complex art of self-manufacture and self-promotion that he created and embodied our very conception of literary celebrity in this age.

Since 1961, the sheer volume of critical and biographical information about Hemingway has reached the proportions of a corporate industry, with branches and subsidiaries spreading across the world into virtually every civilized country where his work has been translated and published. The immediate result has been to inflate still further the already overblown Hemingway legend and to elevate almost everything he wrote, both the best and the worst, to the status of holy scripture, while he himself is securely established as the imperial icon of American literature in the first half of the twentieth century.

The information glut, along with the deification process, has had a curiously ambiguous effect: it has informed us so thoroughly about the life and character of the man that we feel compelled to reexamine the work for evidence of the virtues that would perhaps justify the attention and honor accorded the writer. Yet it has also made it impossible for us to recapture that virginity of mind with which we first read him and were able to appreciate, without the inflammations of awe and reverence, the many excellent features of his artistry. For now we are confronting not a writer but an international literary monument, and the works that once seemed real and alive have become—as Mary McCarthy so admirably said about Salinger's Glass family writings—"the sacred droppings of holy birds." There is much irony in the fact that Gertrude Stein foresaw it all while meaning something else altogether when she observed that Hemingway "looks like a modern and he smells of the museums." And it is in the museum showcases of the world's adoration, among the Egyptian mummies, the ancient relics and artifacts, that Hemingway's works are now forever on public view. To extricate them from the museums and restore them to life is an impossible task. But with a sufficiently vigorous exercise of imagination it may be possible to approach them once again and ask some of the first questions, the kind that, in our virginity of mind, we were once able to answer, and that all the subsequent celebrity has almost caused us to forget how to ask.

What was it then, and what is it now, that makes Hemingway so compellingly attractive as a writer; what is the nature and source of the very great pleasure we take in him when he is at his best, and the pain we feel when he is at his worst? To begin with the obvious and accepting the pretense that we are reading him for the first time, let us say that Hemingway's initially most seductive attribute was and remains his powerful responsiveness to experience. It is an attribute perhaps made more seductive by the fact that most of us since his time have found it to be seriously diminished in ourselves. One reason is that our responses to the infinitely more complex and diffuse experiences of our present world have *had* to diminish if we are to retain our sanity. Another reason is that so few of us today have, or have ever had, access to a clearly defined microcosmic world in which the things one feels, says, and does might take on the sacramental importance they had for Hemingway in the first war, in Paris, and later in Spain. It is as if we had all suffered some brain damage as the price we have had to pay for existence in the second half of the century, a loss of acute responsiveness to the life around us, even as our sense that the vitality of that life has itself declined forces us into a troubled and abstracted self-preoccupation.

One does not easily envy the life of any of our immediate contemporaries—the talent, perhaps, but not the life—as one so easily envies Hemingway's, particularly during the years when his talent was freshest and he was writing at the top of his form in those early stories and *The Sun Also Rises,* his first and, withal, still his best novel. He was young then, as we were young when we first read him. He was living, as we regrettably were not, in the most exotic city in Europe among some of the most remarkable personalities and gifted artists of the post-World War I era. And he brought to it all the highly sensitized perspective of the provincial Midwestern tourist viewing with wonder and delight the hitherto undiscovered riches of foreignness.

He took the greatest pleasure—and gave us, vicariously, the greatest pleasure—in the hotels, bars, and restaurants of Paris, and with his quickly acquired inside-dopester knowingness, he appointed himself the official instructor in where and how to live wisely and well. He could recite the names of all the streets; he knew the exact location of all the good places and the best route to take to get to them; and he was on friendly terms with the best bartenders and waiters who worked in them. He had a wonderful eye not only for quality but for terrain, whether the topography of Paris or the landscape of Spain, and in sharing his knowledge with us, he schooled us in the ways of a world we did not know but desperately wished we did.

He also accomplished something far more significant for us and for literature. If he had not, then Scott Fitzgerald's well-known description of *The Sun Also Rises* as "a romance and a guidebook" might have been all that needed to be said. But in introducing us literally to the life of foreignness, Hemingway at the same time created the illusion that *every* element of life is in fact foreign, hence new and without precedent in the known experience of the past. Every element needs, therefore, to be carefully examined and tested to determine the degree of its authenticity. In order to live an authentic life and produce an authentic fiction, one has to proceed with the greatest caution and select only those experiences, express only those emotions, that have proved their validity because they have been measured against the realities of honest feeling and what one senses in one's deepest instincts to be true. The result in Hemingway's fiction is not a realistic reflection of a world but the literal manufacture of a world, piece by piece, out of the most meticulously chosen and crafted materials.

It is a world that is altogether strange and perilous because it is without moral history and received standards of conduct. Characters, therefore, must move through it as if through enemy-held territory, learning how to live while trying to stay alive. To survive they need all the cunning and expertise they can muster. They must be sure that they know at all times exactly where they are, both geographically and in relation to others. They must also learn exactly how to behave so as to minimize the risk of becoming vulnerable to error and the dangerous consequences of losing self-control. They must fabricate, through constant study and trial, an etiquette that will enable them to know instinctively what is appropriate and what is not, so that they can maintain decorum under stress or siege. They must master the procedure for everything, the correct methods for carrying out their function—whether it is hunting, fishing, bullfighting, or eating and drinking. And above all they must know the cost of everything, not only the cost in money but the physical and emotional cost. To survive successfully is to learn how to get one's money's worth, the right return on the investment; hence, one must be extremely careful to make only the *right* investments, those that will yield honest satisfactions and beneficial emotions rather than lead to the overinflation of specious values and destructive emotions.

The characters in *The Sun Also Rises* might all seem to be morally measurable on the basis of whether or not they are wise enough to get their money's worth. Jake Barnes is one who is constantly preoccupied with cost. He tells us what meals cost in restaurants, how much it is proper to tip waiters and bellmen in order to be assured of a satisfactory return in attentive service, who borrowed how much from whom and whether the debt was promptly repaid (Mike Campbell borrows constantly from everybody and never repays). In Bayonne after the disastrous end of the fiesta Jake is pleased to be back in France because there "everything is on such a clear financial basis. . . . If you want people to like you you have only to spend a little money." Earlier in Pamplona, while indulging in some drunken philosophizing, he concludes, "You paid some way for everything that was any good. I paid my way into enough things that I liked, so that I had a good time. Either you paid by learning about them, or by experience, or by taking chances, or by money. Enjoying living was learning to get your money's worth and knowing when you had it."

Count Mippipopolous has learned to get his money's worth and knows when he has. Robert Cohn does not know because he never understands the rate of exchange. His values have not been submitted to the test of actual experience and cannot be for they have come out of books and romantic fantasy. He is therefore unable to see Brett for what she is, although exactly what she is never becomes altogether clear. Because of the Count's wisdom about money as well as his arrow wounds, Brett identifies him as "one of us," which he may or may not be since he has already learned what she and Jake are still trying to learn, namely, how to live decorously and well. Brett fails from the beginning because Jake's wound prevents her from fulfilling what she believes to be her true love for him. In compensation, she has affairs and she plans to marry Mike, about whom she does not appear to care very much, presumably because he will one day be rich. She has had an interlude with Cohn in San Sebastian, mostly because she was bored at the time, and she comes to despise Cohn because he is so obviously not "one of us" and refuses to believe that the affair did not mean anything.

Such values as Brett has are in limbo through the greater part of the novel and become operative only momentarily and feebly when she decides to send Romero away. There is finally no hope for her because she has been undisciplined and adrift for too long. She has never learned the value of anything, has given up or never taken control of her life, and so has passed into the control of random impulse and boredom. In the ultimate sense of the word, Brett is lost. That is the poignant message behind Jake's closing remark about the prettiness of thinking things might ever have been different between them. Nor will things ever be different between her and Mike. He may inherit a fortune, but one can be sure that neither of them will get his money's worth because neither knows how to.

Hemingway's tight minimalist style, which is displayed in its purest form in *The Sun Also Rises,* is the precise verbal expression of the view of life that dominates and finally evaluates the action of the novel. If Hemingway believed, as he clearly did, that if the right, carefully selected experiences are chosen and only the proper emotions expressed, the result will be an absolutely authentic fictional world containing nothing that will ever ring false, then the language, chosen with equal care, so authentically simple and basic, is the perfect fastidious statement of the morally fastidious world it is designed to create. The vacant spaces between and behind the words, the strongly sensed presence of things omitted, become expressive of all the alternatives and elaborations, all the excesses and equivocations of language, that have been scrupulously rejected in the style's formation. The emphasis given to the individual words and phrases that seem so much larger than they are just because they have escaped rejection makes it appear that a verbal artifact is being constructed or salvaged, word by word, from a junk-heap of redundancy and imprecision. There are no moral or literary precedents to provide the style with foundation or scaffolding. Everything that manages, against great resistance, to achieve utterance is seemingly being uttered for the very first time in human history, is a kind of Ur-statement of primordial truth. It is a method whose ultimate effect is incantatory and catechistic, and what is being prayed to and propitiated is the demon god of flux and excess, that force of anarchy that drives most of the characters toward ruin and that it is the task of the language to redeem and convert into a force of artistic order.

Such a method, composed as it is of a minimum of simple words that seem to have been squeezed onto the page against a great compulsion to be silent, creates the impression that those words—if only because there are so few of them—are sacramental, while the frequent reappearance of some of them in the same or in similar order at intervals through the text tends to give them idiographic value. Thus, "nice" and the phrase, "one of us," become the pervasive but hollow designations of moral judgment in the novel, and the hollowness is perfectly consonant with the theme. In a similar way, some of the characters become idiographs when a certain distinctive feature of their appearance or behavior is established in our minds as their identifying logo or psychological autograph—again because Hemingway describes them so sparingly that what little he does say about them takes on something of the quality of Homeric epithet. Thus, Jake is personified by his impotence, Bill Gorton by his passion for stuffed animals, Brett by her mannish hats and hairstyle, the Count by his arrow wounds, Robert Cohn by his romanticism. In each case, furthermore, the defining detail becomes revelatory of the character's dramatic role and thematic meaning, so that what begins as a novel of manners ends as a moral allegory about people who lack the moral substance even to follow the code of behavior which they profess to honor. Jake is unmanned and Brett is defeminized. Bill Gorton's passion is for things that look like the real thing but are actually dead. The Count has been wounded by arrows, which must make him as anachronistic as his fancy title and tastes supported by income from a chain of sweet-shops must make him ludicrous.

Brett with her title is also an anachronism, as is Mike, the stereotypical wastrel aristocrat with his stereotypical prospects of one day inheriting a fortune. And Cohn's romanticism, which is the central irritant in the novel, is yet another. All represent former sources of value that no longer have value. Cohn's sentimentalized vision of love belongs to that part of the 19th Century that was supposedly killed in the first world war, and its resurrection in the aftermath can only mean trouble for people who are also resurrected casualties, stuffed human animals, to whom any feeling, when aggressively acted upon, is a threat to psychic harmony and the security of nonfeeling.

In his study of American modernism, *A Homemade World,* Hugh Kenner makes the extremely perceptive observation that "Hemingway's achievement . . . consisted in setting down, so sparely that we can see past them, the words for the action that concealed the real action." There is abundant evidence for this everywhere in *The Sun Also Rises.* Jake's strength as a character derives in large part from his capacity for withholding information. We are constantly aware in the novel of the presence of what we are not told, of what Jake refuses to acknowledge and judge because it is too dangerous to make a judgment and thus bring the danger to the surface of consciousness. As Carl Jung wrote in *Psychology and Religion:*

> Consciousness must have been a very precarious thing in its beginnings. . . . Even an ordinary emotion can cause a considerable loss of consciousness. Primitives therefore cherish elaborate forms of politeness, speaking with a hushed voice, laying down their weapons, crouching. . . . Before people of great authority we bow with uncovered head, i.e., we offer our head unprotected in order to propitiate the powerful one, who might easily fall suddenly a prey to a fit of uncontrollable violence.

And Otto Fenichel says in *Psychoanalytical Theory of Neurosis* that "trauma creates fear of every kind of tension . . . because even a little influx of excitement may have the effect of 'flooding' the patient," or, in Jung's terms, causing him to lose consciousness and go berserk.

For the elaborately polite because clearly traumatized characters of this novel, consciousness is so precarious and fragile that any kind of tension is to be feared and, if possible, ignored. One can safely respond to only the barest minimum of sensory stimuli—the look of the landscape, the physical pattern of an action especially when strictly ritualized, what people monosyllabically said to one another. But there must be little or nothing revealed about how anyone really felt, what deeper emotions were aroused by the various conflicts and confrontations. It is part of the magic of the minimalist style that we know almost nothing—and we scarcely miss knowing—about Jake's emotional state throughout the major part of the novel, nor do we know much of anything about the nature of the relationship between Brett and Mike and between Jake and Bill. This information is carefully withheld or we are led to believe that it is revealed in actions that occur in the background or off-stage. But the omissions make a statement that there is some acute unpleasantness here that cannot be directly confronted because it is a threat to psychic equilibrium and might cause a dangerous "flooding" of consciousness.

It has often been said that the dramatic movement of *The Sun Also Rises* is through a series of alternating scenes of conflict and recuperation from conflict. The fishing interlude in Burguette and Jake's holiday in San Sebastian both represent rest and curative periods following the stressful experiences, first of Paris, then of Pamplona. In both, emotional decorum is almost fanatically maintained. Nothing is allowed to occur that might impose a strain or precipitate a crisis, and this is made easier to accomplish, significantly enough, by the fact that in Burguette there are only men without women, and in San Sebastian only one man alone in the good company of himself.

In both, attention is kept focussed on matters of physical procedure: exactly how a fishhook is baited and with what, what kind of box lunch was provided by the hotel, just how cold the wine was, what dinner cost. And we are told just how Jake in San Sebastian went about putting his things away in his room and the movements he made as he went from the hotel to the beach and changed his clothes in a bathing-cabin, put on his bathing suit, and went swimming, then how he came out of the water, lay on the beach until he was dry, then went into the bathing-cabin, took off his suit, sloshed himself with fresh water, and rubbed dry. It is all as meticulously choreographed as the fishing routine in "The Big Two-Hearted River" and for the same reason—because the real situation cannot be confronted, the real story cannot be told.

Gertrude Stein, in one of her famous pronouncements on Hemingway, said that there is in fact a real story to be told about Hemingway, one that he should write himself, "not those he writes but the confessions of the real Hemingway. . . ." Clearly, Hemingway did not write it and could not because the real story was too deeply disturbing to tell, just as the young Nick Adams could not bring himself to enter the shadowy part of the river where it ran into the swamp—because "in the swamp fishing was a tragic adventure." But the remarkable fact is that in telling as much or as little of the story as he did, Hemingway managed through his complex artistry to use words in such a way that we are indeed allowed to see past them and to glimpse the outlines of the mysterious and probably tragic adventure that the words were not quite able to describe but were also not quite able to conceal.

If the thing most feared is barely visible behind the language, the fear itself is barely controlled by the language. Language is a provisional barricade erected against the nihilism that threatens to engulf his characters, the nihilism that is always seeking to enter and flood the human consciousness. Hemingway at his best offered us a portrait that did not need to be painted of a condition we recognize everywhere around and within us, and he gave us as well our only means of defense against it—the order of artistic and moral form embodied in a language that will not, in spite of everything, give up its hold on the basic sanities, will not give up and let out the shriek of panic, the cry of anguish, that the situation logically calls for. That, and not any of the bravura exploits behind his celebrity, constituted his heroism, and that was the lesson in heroism he had to teach. Of his many qualities that was the one that most deserved, and continues to deserve, our admiration and loyalty.

1986

Biographing Faulkner

Following the appearance of Joseph Blotner's massive two-volume biography in 1974, it seemed scarcely conceivable that anything further could or needed to be said about the life of William Faulkner. But now in this nearly as massive new biography Frederick R. Karl has proven that assumption to be false, for he has created a portrait of the man and the writer that is both more complex and a great deal more candid than Blotner was able or willing to attempt.

The problem for Blotner was that as the authorized biographer and a close friend of Faulkner and his family, he was both privileged and burdened. Through the family he was provided with access to an enormous quantity of information that would probably not otherwise have been easily available to him. But because of the trust placed in him he also clearly felt under some obligation not to give too much emphasis to certain facts about Faulkner—such as his affairs with women and his nearly suicidal drinking bouts—that might embarrass the family or sully his own very great admiration for the man. As a result, Blotner produced a sprawling, intricately detailed but on the whole carefully circumspect study that closely chronicles the events of every year of the writer's existence but that portrays him as little more than a kindly, albeit rather eccentric and moody man who lived a respectable, small-town southern life at the same time that he managed to produce several of the most anguished and subversive literary masterpieces of the twentieth century.

While Karl repeatedly acknowledges his large indebtedness to Blotner for biographical details, he does not share Blotner's scruples in his treatment of them. He therefore has been able to write an altogether different kind of book, one that is intended not to sensationalize but to provide a balanced psychological assessment, particularly of those features of Faulkner's character and behavior that Blotner failed to explore in any depth, and that Karl believes contain important clues to the complex mystery of the writer's genius.

Karl bases his approach on the assumption that Faulkner was a tissue of ambiguities that may be seen to possess an underlying consistency of form. He begins with the fundamental paradox of Faulkner's literary position as the foremost American practitioner, at least in the novel, of European literary modernism who, as such, was strongly attracted to violence and subversion, yet who, as a conservative Southerner, had an equally strong desire to preserve decorum and community. The conflict is displayed in his fiction in his use of the most radical modernist experimental techniques to depict a pastoral southern region corrupted at one level by hypocrisy and deceit and at another by every conceivable kind of aberrant behavior—rape, incest, murder, suicide—acts that finally become metaphors for a South ravaged by the forces of another, quite unliterary form of modernism—Northern industrialism and moral anarchy. Yet at the same time there is an undercutting conservative force working in the fiction to rescue and preserve the best elements of the southern moral tradition.

According to Karl, Faulkner saw modernism as a form of anarchism. It represented those negative energies "which swept away the past, destroyed history, and asserted defiance of community and society." Community, on the other hand, represented for him history, custom, tradition, and myth, and it was Faulkner's complex fate to struggle throughout his career to hold—in Scott Fitzgerald's phrase—these two opposing ideas in his mind at the same time and still somehow retain his ability to function. Karl cites as an example of this conflict Faulkner's obsessive effort to restore his house, the antebellum mansion, Rowan Oak, to its former grandeur even while he was writing about a world in which a Rowan Oak was a ludicrous anachronism, and in a language that was far more evocative of dissolution than of restoration. Yet Faulkner spent almost his entire productive life in his home community of Oxford, Mississippi, even as he was describing in his fiction the death of community. And he was not able to function effectively anywhere else.

His existence there was a peculiar and quite sad comedy of paradoxes. As a high school dropout still being supported by his parents, he was a short, rather frail-looking young man without apparent ambition or prospects, seemingly aloof and arrogant, who affected a manner and costumery he fancied to be those of certain impoverished nineteenth-century French symbolist poets, and who was known around town as "Count No 'Count." Since in that time and place real men did not write books or read poetry, he did his writing in secret. Yet he cultivated and perfected what became a lifelong role as a virile good old boy who hunted, fished, and drank corn liquor with mostly untutored cronies who knew and cared nothing about the writer he was.

During World War I Faulkner created another and in this case wholly fraudulent role for himself out of his experience as a Royal Air Force cadet. Although he underwent a few months of flight training in Canada and was discharged at the end of the war without serving overseas, he returned to Oxford wearing an elegant, nonregulation British officer's uniform and carrying a cane. For years he circulated the story that he had been shot down in France, was badly wounded, and wore a silver plate in his head that was worth more than the money he had in the Oxford bank.

A decade after the war when his literary career had begun to be established with the publication of his first three novels, Faulkner married Estelle Oldham who had been his childhood sweetheart but had rejected him for a man who showed greater promise of future success. But after she was divorced and returned to Oxford with two children, Faulkner seems to have decided to marry her largely because years before he had agreed that he one day would. They settled down in Rowan Oak, that noble monument to southern aristocratic tranquillity, to endure a marriage made miserably destructive by the heavy drinking of both parties and Estelle's drug addiction and spendthrift habits. But the same conservative side of his nature that caused him to restore Rowan Oak also make it impossible for Faulkner to face the scandal of divorce. So he remained married to Estelle for the rest of his life and may even have found the relationship perversely stimulating to that other part of himself that craved anarchy—if only because it gave him something to push against and escape from back into the private precincts of his art. There he created his own mythical territory, Yoknapatawpha County, a place tainted by family discord and corruption of every kind but over which he could exercise the absolute control and moral authority he could not bring to his domestic life.

In his detailed analysis of virtually everything Faulkner produced, Karl tries to discover to what extent the writer made use of his personal experience in his fiction. Understandably, the effort is only partly successful because Faulkner derived his materials from many sources and imaginatively transformed much that was personal into the universally human. Yet, as Karl indicates, in such early works as *Soldiers Pay* and *Mosquitoes* there are quite recognizable portraits of people, particularly women, whom Faulkner knew as a young man. Also, in the mature novels of the Snopes trilogy personal elements become visible that were formerly obscured by the elaborate technical experimentation to be found in *The Sound and the Fury* and *Sanctuary*. But the tensions of his relationship with Estelle can be felt everywhere in his fiction, and they surely provided to some forever indefinable degree the vitality of torment that helped to energize its greatness.

Given the state of his marriage and his chronic shortage of funds, it is not surprising that from time to time Faulkner took the opportunity to leave Oxford for fairly lucrative, short-term work as a writer of film scripts in Hollywood. It was there that he had one of a series of affairs he was to have with younger women, in this case with an attractive script girl named Meta Carpenter. In *A Loving Gentleman,* the profoundly sentimental book she later wrote about the relationship, Carpenter describes it as having been so serious and passionate that Faulkner was strongly tempted to ask Estelle for a divorce. But, significantly, he finally declined to do so. Karl convincingly argues that in addition to being the product of his marital unhappiness, these affairs were in part efforts to compensate for the humiliation Faulkner suffered after being rejected by Estelle and other women back when he was young, unattractive, and poor. Now that he was becoming a world-famous writer he seemed much more attractive, and he clearly took full advantage of the fact.

Yet the periods he spent away from Oxford were extremely stressful to Faulkner because they required him to function outside his native environment as a public man and a writer stripped of the anonymity that was so necessary to him. At such times, whether in Hollywood or while visiting his publishers in New York, he tended to experience a disorientation that in its milder form was expressed through his retreat into protracted and terrifying silences at social gatherings and at its most severe could be appeased only through bouts of drinking that were often life-threatening and required him to be hospitalized. It was as if through the silences—which Karl recognizes as expressing "static violence"—and the drinking, Faulkner could dramatize his need to die out of roles he was unsuited to perform and to reaffirm his need for the privacy, even the social oblivion, that throughout his career he had found essential to his creative survival.

In view of this, there is poignant irony in the fact that in the final decade of his life and after receiving the Nobel Prize in 1950, Faulkner began to spend more and more time away from Oxford. He accepted invitations to appear at Princeton and the University of Virginia, undertook cultural missions abroad for the State Department, became involved in the black civil rights movement, granted interviews, and even consented, with some mixture of reluctance and pleasure, to having his portrait painted.

As Karl makes clear in this exhaustingly exhaustive but deeply humanizing study, there were compelling reasons for Faulkner's drastic reversal of habit and principle. He seems to have felt by the midfifties that he had little or nothing further of importance to accomplish as a writer and that the isolation that had once been the medium of his immense creative fertility had become a vacuum. So he went out into the world and took on the function he had formerly so despised, that of highly honored public celebrity. There was anguish in that, but there was also a certain genuine kind of triumph. For one of the rewards of his fame and greatly increased prosperity was the chance to re-create himself one final time in a role foreshadowed by the restoration of Rowan Oak, the compensatory good old boy, and the false legend of the wounded war hero. At the University of Virginia he became the very model of a roistering southern aristocratic gentleman who delighted in dressing up in full fox-hunting regalia and riding to the hounds with a group of wealthy Charlottesville sportsmen. He played this role with much grace until in 1962 a fall from a horse that was too spirited even for him and the massive heart attack that followed brought the performance to an end.

1989

Mailer on Miller

Norman Mailer somehow found the time while working on *Ancient Evenings,* one of the longest and most expensively subsidized serious novels in recent history, to bring together, and prepare critical introductions for, various selections from what he believes to be the best of Henry Miller's writings. Until the early sixties many of them—most notably *Tropic of Cancer, Black Spring,* and *Tropic of Capricorn*—were banned on the ground of obscenity from publication in this country, although they had long enjoyed wide circulation abroad and among American connoisseurs of dirty books.

As a result of the legal prohibitions, Lawrence Durrell's *The Henry Miller Reader,* the most substantial of the earlier collections, was issued in 1959 without excerpts from books that are now generally considered, along with the entirely inoffensive *The Colossus of Maroussi,* to represent Miller's most important work. Hence, Mailer's first motive in offering his collection was to take advantage of the relaxed vigilance of the courts and reprint portions of some of these hitherto contraband books as well as others in the hope that, since they need no longer be read in the febrile atmosphere of the salacious, they may have a chance of being appreciated for the qualities of art he perceives in them. He also wanted to pay tribute to Miller in the year of his eighty-fifth birthday and to use the occasion to argue his case for Miller as one of the major, albeit neglected writers of the literary generation whose greater representatives he had managed to outlive.

There is attractive filial devotion in all this on the part of a younger writer who owes his elder a very large debt of influence and who resembles him in some rather remarkable ways. Mailer may be forgiven for claiming considerably more for Miller than most of us would be disposed to support without hedging our assent with a host of cowardly cavils and self-vindicating discriminations. Yet it is perfectly true that Miller's reputation after all these years of his notoriety is still by no means securely established with either the critics or the general reading public. It exists, as Mailer suggests, in a strange kind of vacuum, and whether for reasons of temperament, the odd fuzziness of his public image, or the several decades during which his books were read for their *extra*literary attributes, Miller remains a mysterious, vaguely appealing, but somehow unenviable quantity in our literature.

This is not, however, at all the same as saying Miller continues to suffer neglect. He has survived the extremely protracted period of his obscurity to see all his books become lawfully available and sources of comfortable income. In addition to the Durrell volume, there now exist three other anthologies containing selections from his work, as well as a good many collections of his letters—to Durrell, Anaïs Nin, and other literary friends. Since the early sixties, at least a half-dozen book-length studies and two substantial volumes of critical essays about him have been published, and according to a recent report, he has been the subject during this same period of eleven doctoral dissertations, to say nothing of a growing number of shorter critiques, reviews, and reminiscences. Still, it must be admitted that as Miller's books have ceased to be controversial, they have not gained in interest, and the scholars, in assimilating him into the canon of standard modern authors, may in fact be applying their particular form of the coup de grace, recognizing that he has at last become respectably historical, if not indisputably eminent, and so is eligible for admission to the hallowed vaults of scholarly entombment.

In any event, it may be possible now after the passage of years and the lifting of censorship to separate the excellent from the dreadful in his work (and there is a great abundance of both) and to arrive at some understanding of the factors that have helped to create the anomaly of his position at this time. First, it should be said that Miller is a writer whose literary quality has been at any moment largely determined by the nature and intensity of his feelings about a particular subject. There is very little, if any, separation in him between the man who suffers or hates, lusts or loves, and the mind that creates, just as there is no effective way of separating Henry Miller, man and writer, from any of his various fictional personae, whether called Henry Miller, Val, or any other name. Thus, when he felt extravagantly and positively, he tended to give way to gush, sentimentality, and pontification—elements that flawed his otherwise quite magnificent book on Greece, *The Colossus of Maroussi.* When, on the other hand, he felt little or negatively, he could be detached, derisive, as cuttingly heartless as a suicidal court jester, and at such moments he was capable of writing like the best who ever wrote.

This is probably why some of his most successful and authentic work is about sex and the Brooklyn world of his childhood. Toward the former he seems to have felt a tremendous cruel hilarity in the face of the grisly horniness of it all, and toward the latter an at times overpowering repugnance that was mitigated, however, by his sense of the pathos of the life led by and foisted upon him by his grim German-Lutheran parents: A mother whose emotional range was precisely defined by her obsession with picking the lint off the clothes of her children, and a father who was driven to seek such meager alternative vitality as he could find in drinking with business cronies through long afternoons of truancy from his tailoring shop. In portions of *Black Spring* and in the incomparable "Sunday After the War" Miller describes these people "who . . . never once had . . . opened the door which leads to the soul, never once did . . . dream of taking a blind leap into the dark," and who, in symbolizing all that he despised about the bourgeois life, helped to create him in the rabidly adversarial role that he defended from then on with a puritan rectitude at least equal to theirs.

Like so many American writers of his generation, Miller formed his artistic premises in the matrix of the subversive, on a fanatical commitment to a doctrine of total personal freedom and the most unsettling honesty about himself and his emotions—whatever, in fact, represented an engagement of life antithetical to the hypocrisies of official society. Also he was, as it seems now, fortunately placed in history to become the sort of man and writer his radical metaphysics required him to be. At a time when, for the provincial American, raw experience in and for itself seemed equivalent to ascension to Godhead, Miller became a supreme cultist and chronicler of the rawest experience conceivable. At a time when the prevailing bigotries deemed it obscene for writers to describe the bodily functions in the language commonly used for them, Miller dedicated himself to becoming the world's first artistically serious writer of pornographic novels. At a time when reason and repression were still the mandatory features of established culture, Miller became a champion of the unfettered libidinous self and treated the sex act as if it were a triumphant dance on the grave of the righteous.

But what is perhaps most striking about Miller is that, in the service of his nihilism, he has been able to reduce himself back to a state of total infantile irresponsibility and to exist in that state not only without the slightest twinge of conscience but with the most astonishing happiness. This more than anything may well be what has helped estrange him from American readers, for he has tended to play far too cheerfully and guiltlessly the complete bastard for us to love him very much. It would seem that we can accept such a man only so long as we have reason to suspect that in some as yet unpolluted part of himself he is conscious of violating principles he knows to be right. The quite honorable French tradition of the flaneur is alien to us, and particularly odious is one who is a professional idler in everything except copulation and the writing of filthy books. We may salivate with the best of them over his descriptions of sex, yet despise him for refusing to treat sex with the requisite moral seriousness and respect. For Miller saw the sex act as one of the funniest routines in the human vaudeville, and he also saw it, in the form of its usual practice in the bohemian world he knew, as one of the most obvious symptoms of the emotional illness of modern culture, which had evolved from a state of miserable repressiveness to a state of moral anesthesia without ever attaining to a genuine revolution of feeling. It is true that he was himself in some large degree a sufferer from the same disability. Mailer correctly observes that Miller could not write about sex with love, for sex finally was copulation, and in the sadly impoverished lexicon of good-old-American-boyism, love was something felt for an ideal woman, a virginal image one worshipped in fantasy, while one copulated with whores who were all other women.

Yet Miller in his best work has always been able to transcend the sordidness implicit in this view. What saves him is his joyfulness in the face of the sordid, his power to find high pleasure in the sexual comedy, and positively to revel in the detritus thrown off by the process of the world's dissolution. Unlike his French contemporary Céline, to whom the ugliness of the bodily functions was a prime indication that life was disgusting, Miller delighted in such ugliness because it was for him an affirmation of the vitality of life at a time when the forces of technology were hard at work regimenting, purifying, and intellectualizing life out of existence.

It is fitting that Mailer in particular should have chosen to reintroduce Miller through this admirable collection to an audience that has not previously responded to him with very much enthusiasm. Mailer and Miller resemble each other in several important ways— in their shared outrage at the totalitarianism of modern machine society, the displacement of instinct by scientific methodology, spontaneous emotion by the calculated determinations of the will, unique individuality by the mass standardizations of the modern egalitarian state. They are also closely similar in their common desire—expressed in formal ideological terms by Mailer, through textual implication in Miller—to foment rebellion against these deadly processes and, partly through the deliberate cultivation of obscenity, to do what they can to restore the integrity and vitality of the subliminal self.

It is also fitting at just this time when we are well advanced into the era of the sexual technocrat, the engineers of the clitoral and the simultaneous orgasm, the programmers of the computable intricacies of oral and digital foreplay that we should be reminded by two of our major writers that an alternative possibility once existed and may yet exist, that the frontier of sexual adventure, mystery, risk, lust, and even spontaneous pleasure may still, for those of us daring and heretical enough, be open to exploration.

1976

The Death of the Lions

The United States during the sixties was a particularly poor country for great men, both young and old, whether they were presidents or writers. Ordinarily, we do not assassinate our writers, perhaps because we do not take them all that seriously. But they die off nonetheless, and in the first years of the decade, some of the best of them died at a spectacular rate.

In fact, we lost during that period nearly all the men whom we think of as forming the classic establishment of modern American letters: our two most famous and gifted older novelists, William Faulkner and Ernest Hemingway, and two of our most famous and gifted older poets, Robert Frost and E. E. Cummings—to say nothing of other poets who may be equally gifted but who are less widely known, such as Wallace Stevens, William Carlos Williams, Robinson Jeffers, and Theodore Roethke. The first four of these writers we perhaps valued almost as much for their physical presence among us as for their work. They seem always to have been there, at least as far back as most of us can remember, as omnipotent and immortal as gods, comforting us with the assurance that we had and *could tolerate* greatness in our midst, that something unmistakably distinguished stood between us and the struggling low eminences and complacent high mediocrities of our immediate contemporaries.

These writers were all distinguished last survivors of what everybody now knows, and knows too well, to have been a remarkable literary generation, one that seems to have had not only the good fortune to be born at exactly the right time, but the bad taste, at least from our point of view, to be triumphantly aware of the fact. It was a time when, as one of their number defiantly said, there was "a great labor of destruction and negation to perform," and when there was also an even greater labor of construction and affirmation to perform, the task quite simply of discovering the experience of modern America when it was first there to be discovered, and of perfecting the vocabulary—the vocabulary, as it turned out, of the distinctively modern American note—through which that experience could be made available to literature and the world.

As a result, these writers had an advantage that, for obvious reasons, fascinates us today perhaps more than any other fact about them, the advantage of an unusual autonomy of consciousness, an unusual concentration of psychic force. Not only do they appear to have known exactly what they wanted to do in art, but their knowledge seems to have been backed by the strongest conceivable sense that what they wanted to do was necessary, right, and finally inevitable. They also appear to have known—and this today is the really remarkable part—exactly what they did not need to do in art. Their position was definite enough and the prospect before them clear enough so that they were able vastly to scale down the possibility of alternatives, above all, the possibility of false starts and dead ends. The main thoroughfares of innovation and discovery lay open before them, and they seem to have led without obstruction or detour straight ahead to new cities of the mind.

Needless to say, the writers of our own unconfident day enjoy no such advantage. The main thoroughfares now seem to be closed or—what amounts to the same thing—much too well traveled. The new cities of the mind are now old cities and overcrowded, depressed by housing shortages. Besides, our elders and betters, all those garrulous old Kilroys, visited them long ago, and their insolent images and signatures chalked up over historical monuments mock us to move on and find new cities, build new monuments, of our own—find and build them if we dare and can.

Our consciousness has been eroded, not only by our self-consciousness about the mocking past and its insufferable simplicities, but more seriously by our derangement of will before the complexities of the present. What we do we understand full well, much too well, and what we understand best is the past and all the ways in which it haunts our work, reduces its range of possibilities, and forces it, against all our knowing and outrage, into parody and repetition. Or we strike out, driving hard, determined to beat the past and what we know, determined also to stay clear of the main route and those well-worn tracks, only to find ourselves bumping around in the dark, sliding into potholes, or taking a wrong turn onto roads that are not worth taking, coming up sharp against a dead end—or, even worse, pushing energetically on, taking the wrong turn on purpose because there at least we feel that no one has been before.

In short, we try too often and too hard to make a virtue of mere originality. We covet too jealously our own little path, hoping that somehow, somewhere, some day, it will lead to a new city of the mind. It is no wonder then that so many of our achievements seem curiously nervous and overwrought, that too many of them strain after every vagrant freshness or work up tremendous acceleration and expectation only to bring us in the end to a dry hole in the desert or a mirage of towers that recede before us on the horizon, consumed in waves of heat and thin air. But perhaps it is our fate just to be symptomatic, to be in that horrible way of textbooks and historical surveys, typical, representative, illustrative, and finally perhaps to be known best for the condition we cannot help but illustrate: the condition of bafflement and talented unease in the chartless, and possibly unchartable, territory of the impotent, the frustrated, and the absurd.

And yet it is a function of criticism to be skeptical, to question, qualify, and disabuse, especially to disabuse itself and its time of a too abject humility before the overshadowing past. It may just be that in the case of this particular past we have all along been worshiping an image that is really the image of our own fear and self-mistrust or simply of our own willful incomprehension of the truth. For we know, or ought to know, that history likes to forget the agony and the cost of great achievement and cherishes only its enduring results. We also know that timid generations will frequently revise history upward to the point where it seems too big to be competed with, so that they can sit righteously in its shadow and lament their littleness.

In envying past writers their massive opportunities, we should not forget the massive liabilities that they overcame and that history so often neglects to record. When we consider Hemingway, Faulkner, Frost, and Cummings we especially should not forget the high price of their achievement in a culture that has never had much time or use for literary greatness. "It is a complex fate being an American," said Henry James (who certainly ought to have known), and these four writers were more than ordinarily aware of just how complex a fate it was. For they were, after all, not simply American but American writers, and that is the most complex fate imaginable.

Let us consider them, then, in terms of that complexity, and in terms of the price they paid for it, a price too high to be paid by anyone not a genius, yet because so high, a price that may sometimes defy men into becoming geniuses just so they can afford to pay it.

All except Frost very late in his life lived out their careers in that peculiar American state of aloof disengagement from the national life, forming their art in secret and keeping their own counsel if only because there was really no one to consult. Hemingway spent the bulk of his most productive years out of the country. Cummings managed to live an extremely solitary life in the very heart of Greenwich Village. Frost had to go to England to win his first recognition as an American poet. Yet regardless of where they lived, at least two of them—Hemingway and Cummings—might have lived just about anywhere else, for where they lived had virtually nothing to do with what they wrote except perhaps to impress them daily with the heavy fact of its colossal irrelevance. Because of that irrelevance, Hemingway, Cummings, and even Faulkner were possibly something less than they might have been, if only because it cost them so much to achieve a sense of what they were—a sense, that is, of what was relevant, what fundamentally did relate to them and to reality, and was not mirage, nightmare, or just people sleepwalking around in a circle. Much of their work was flawed by the kind of idiosyncrasy that breeds in isolation and is the typical product of large talent feeding on itself. It shows, for one thing, the strain of a too deliberate, too desperate attempt to make language take the place of a listening and answering society—or, as in Hemingway's case, it strains too violently toward oversimplification, toward getting down to a basic grammar or baby talk, like that of a man determined on telling the absolute truth to an idiot. Yet in a world in which nothing seems to relate to the self, the words of Hemingway stand as hard little symbols of the few things that do relate—usually insofar as they can be touched, smelled, or tasted—and they are hard at least partly because they have been mined out of the solid rock of a highly resistant cultural experience.

Another result of their sense of isolation from a sympathetic society was that each of these men felt obliged to pretend in public to be something other than what he was. None felt able to engage the public world in his whole person as a writer. Instead, all retreated behind masks of various assumed identities that they supposedly thought would make them acceptable to society. Hemingway became a big-game hunter, fisherman, bullfight enthusiast, and itinerant soldier. In fact, he play-acted a whole series of roles and played them so well that he was finally forgiven for also being a writer. Faulkner prided himself on being merely a farmer and is reported to have received the news of his Nobel Prize award while driving a tractor around a cornfield. Frost was also a farmer, the epitome of the country bard and cracker-barrel philosopher, the kindly wise old rustic from the hills. Whether assumed by accident or shrewd design, the role could be easily assimilated to the American mythology of lovable old character types and so rendered harmless, as harmless and heartwarming, in fact as the cliché it so closely resembled: native American as drawn by Norman Rockwell for the covers of *Saturday Evening Post.* Cummings, however, was perhaps the slyest of them all, for he wore the classic mask of the Bohemian artist-eccentric, which was of course not really a mask at all but a perfect burlesque of his true identity. But because it was mistaken for a mask—and another clearly recognizable, hence, harmless one at that—he was able behind it to be himself and to do exactly what he pleased.

The tragicomic implications of this confusion of roles were rather dramatically impressed upon me the first time I had the privilege of meeting William Faulkner. The great man came suddenly into my life in 1958 on a bright spring day in Princeton. In fact, he literally materialized at the kitchen door, having been brought there unannounced by my wife who, in that odd way of American social encounters, had just happened to meet him on Princeton's Nassau Street and had borne him triumphantly home like a prize cabbage from the supermarket.

The shock of having him sprung upon me in that way was, of course, dreadful. I recognized him at once with that terrible sensation of seeing a historical monument come abruptly to life, and all the blood rushed out of my head, and I came as near as I ever came and probably will ever come to fainting dead away. Luckily for me, my wife was making a good deal of rather aimless talk—I was dimly conscious that she was already calling him Bill—and that gave me time to gain control of myself and to remember that the first thing one did for William Faulkner in an emergency was give him a big drink of bourbon. This was clearly an emergency, at least for me, so I made the drink, taking plenty of time to do it, came back and gave it to him, then realized with genuine panic that I could not think of the slightest thing to say to him. The reason was not nervousness, although heaven knows I was nervous enough. The reason was—and this is the whole horrible and pathetic crux of the matter—that I knew entirely too well what I was not supposed to say. I had read all the stories and heard all the gossip, and one point had been stressed over and over again: Faulkner detested to talk about literature, and what is more, absolutely would not talk about it.

Here, then, was a predicament more nightmarish for me than anything out of Kafka. The man sitting at the moment in my house, drinking my whiskey, and as a matter of fact, flirting with my wife, was undoubtedly the greatest American novelist then alive. Here was I, sitting a few feet away from him, yet forbidden to talk about the one thing that presumably mattered the most to him and that interested me most about him. But I had to remember that this man, however great he may have been as a writer, was not supposed to be a literary person, was not supposed to know anything about books except how to write them, was not supposed, in fact, to think at all. He was, above everything, an American writer, and that meant that his nonliterariness was to be considered a positive virtue, if not positive proof of his creative genius. Yet I was well aware that Faulkner actually did know a great deal about books, even his own books, and was in fact extremely sensitive to literature and literary values. I like to think that he even knew that I knew that he knew. It was just that there had to be this tacit agreement between us that I would respect his pretense of ignorance and accept the fact that it was only his public self, his protective public disguise, that he could reveal to me.

I suppose we might have sat through that strange afternoon in total silence—and Faulkner's silences could be interminable and terrifying—if I had not had a double identity of my own to fall back on, and one that chanced to be exactly the same as his. It so happened that I too had been a farmer once myself, at least I had been brought up on a farm, and a southern farm at that. I therefore knew a little something about crops and growing seasons and even something about the rather complicated psychology of mules, a subject that, I was relieved to learn, interested him immensely. So, while the bourbon flowed, we talked about crops and growing seasons and particularly about mules, and through the whole of that afternoon, the only literary remark I can recall William Faulkner making was that he would some day like to write the real American epic—to be called, he thought very fittingly, *Moby Mule.*

I doubt very much if an incident of this kind could have taken place anywhere except in contemporary America. André Gide could not possibly have understood it, for a fine writer of his time and culture was automatically a literary person and a public literary person, usually of high conversational prowess. If such an incident had occurred to Simone de Beauvoir on one of her visits to America, she would very probably have been charmed by it because it confirmed all her prejudices about the poverty of our literary life. Then she would have gone on to be even more charmed because it was such a perfect illustration of our rugged simplicity and earthiness. Henry James would probably have offered it as a perfect illustration of the sort of thing that caused him to leave America for good.

The pathos of course is in the ludicrous lack of connection between the writer and his public mask and between his person and the surrounding life of his culture. The spectacle alone of William Faulkner wandering around the streets of Princeton is absurd, even pathetic in the extreme, and it is so just because Princeton is an intellectual and cultural center. Yet the spectacle of Graham Greene wandering around Oxford or Cambridge would seem perfectly natural and right. Perhaps it was given only to Henry James, who had the unique advantage of being both American and European, to understand the problem in its full complexity and to see it as a special and specific American phenomenon. At any rate, it is James in his little book on Hawthorne who provides the best description of it to be found anywhere.

> Great things [says James] have of course been done by solitary workers; but they have usually been done with double the pains they would have cost if they had been produced in more genial circumstances. The solitary worker loses the profit of example and discussion; he is apt to make awkward experiments; he is in the nature of the case more or less of an empiric. The empiric may, as I say, be treated by the world as an expert; but the drawbacks and discomforts of empiricism remain to him, and are in fact increased by the suspicion that is mingled with his gratitude, of a want in the public taste of a sense of the proportions of things.

Obviously, everything that James says here with respect to Hawthorne applies equally well to Faulkner. The conditions of the literary life in America may have changed since Hawthorne's time. In many particulars they most certainly have improved. Yet isolation remains the typical condition of American literary art, and the isolated, solitary worker remains our typical literary figure. Faulkner was of course the purest contemporary embodiment of the type, just as he most clearly displays the strengths and weaknesses inherent in it. Except for one brief and apparently unrewarding venture into the New Orleans bohemian world of Sherwood Anderson during the twenties, Faulkner in Oxford, Mississippi, never knew the advantage of the "more genial circumstances" or the "profit of example and discussion" to which James refers. Almost from the beginning of his career he worked alone and in the dark, going to double the pains he might otherwise have had to go to, making perhaps more than his share of "awkward experiments," and suffering all the "drawbacks and discomforts of empiricism."

We can be sure, too, that he was often aware of "a want in the public taste of a sense of the proportions of things." Certainly, after *Sanctuary*, that mostly cheap potboiler which he wrote in three weeks to make money, became the first of his novels to win him fame, he could never again harbor any very exalted illusions about the public taste. He also never harbored any illusions about his own importance, even when late in his life, during the period when I met him, he had finally begun to be "treated by the world as an expert." By then, he had long since learned, and learned the hard way, what it meant—or, more correctly, did not mean—to be a serious writer in America, a land where, as he himself once said, "The writer isn't part of the culture of the country. He's like a fine dog. People like him around, but he's of no use."

He's of no use, we might add, except to himself and to literature, except to the creations of his mind and heart that have been wrung out of the agony of his sense of estrangement. For it is a very real question that I am by no means the first to advance: if Faulkner had in fact been part of the culture of the country, would he have become the great writer he did become? It may be just because he was forced in isolation to go to double the pains that he was able in the end to make double the achievement. It may just be that his uncongenial surroundings had the effect of hurting him into greatness, as mad Ireland, according to Auden, hurt William Butler Yeats into poetry. In a more sympathetic, more interested and responsive society Faulkner might very well have felt far less compulsion to retreat into the dark depths of his genius and there find creative compensation for what the world lacked. If the world had lacked less, he undoubtedly would have suffered less, created less, and less intensely. The world then would have surrounded him and pressed in upon him, flattered him and discussed him, and all that fine sacred rage of his might slowly have been dribbled away in talk or the happier responsibilities of the public man or the production of small, skillful, contentedly minor works like those produced by certain English writers in the somewhat overly fraternal literary society of London—or, as William Styron once half-jestingly remarked, Faulkner might in the end have been corrupted completely and gone into television or written universal ads for Jantzen bathing suits.

But, luckily for us, none of these things happened to Faulkner, or let us say that they began to happen too late in his life to do very much damage. Through his best and most productive years the world remained unfriendly, and Faulkner stayed at home out of the world, suffered, and created a world, appointing himself its Sole Owner and Proprietor. He populated it with some of the most grotesque and memorable characters to be found outside Dostoevsky and Dickens, and he formulated it in a language that, for all its defects, remains one of the most original and autonomous modes of personal expression to be found anywhere in literature.

Its defects are of course very largely the result of its autonomy and personalness. It is irritatingly self-obsessed and often maddeningly complicated, as the method of such a work as *The Sound and the Fury* testifies. It is quirky, knotty, thorny, alternately hard and soft, frequently bloated by the most preposterous swellings of rhetoric, undigested clots of gummy lyricism and philosophy, heavy masses of just sludge and mumble that absolutely will not move. In short, it is the language of a man who got too used to talking to himself, too used to the sound of his own voice, to knowing too well and too easily what he meant, and, above all, to not having someone across the table to say at crucial intervals, "Hold on there. How's that again?"

This is perhaps to say not simply that Faulkner suffered from the defects of his isolation, but that he was distinctly a southern writer, southern in the sense that he used words and sentences in the southern way, as a compulsive talker and spinner of yarns, a man who was only indifferently and rather accidentally an author of novels but superbly a monologist in the language of fictional discourse. Looked at in this way, much of his work can be seen as one long, immensely complicated, immensely meandering tale, a tale that has been divided more or less for convenience into separate books but actually runs on and on almost without pause, spinning out of itself as it moves a thickly tangled fabric of events, past and present, and spreading over the full emotional range of the human condition: from tragedy to comedy, heroism to villainy, nobility to pettiness, pleasure to pain, lust to love, birth to death.

Like the southern mind itself, it is a tale that never really distinguishes between then and now, and moves, it seems, in a timeless, dreamlike, continuous present, for all history is contained in every living moment, and the present is nothing except as it seeks and finds its meaning and vindication in the past. That, for the southern mind and for Faulkner, is what is horrible about the urban, northern, modern age: it is controlled by no sense, no moral memory, of the past. Hence, it possesses no convention or limitation within which human conduct is measurable or even understandable. That is the real horror, too, of the Snopes family in the *Hamlet* trilogy, of Popeye in *Sanctuary,* and Percy Grimm in *Light in August:* The pastless man is also the dehumanized man. Lacking membership in the community of what has been, he is also deprived of membership in the community of what is and is to be. His every move is made in a moral void. It is arbitrary and dangerous, dangerous just because it is arbitrary.

For those, on the other hand, who do possess moral connection with the past, there is a responsibility that is nearly sacred, and that is the responsibility either to take up or, once and for all, to discharge the burden history has laid upon them, to achieve atonement with, and finally absolution from, the whole heavy consequence of what has been and been done. For Quentin Compson in *The Sound and the Fury* the burden is too great and can be discharged only through suicide. For Rev. Gail Hightower in *Light in August* it is also too great, so great that it can never be discharged except in death, not the death of suicide, but the death that comes at last to the man who has died in his heart and soul for many years, and who has waited each day for many years for the merely token, merely posthumous death to overtake his body. For Isaac McCaslin in *The Bear* the burden of the past can be and is discharged in a life of repentance and almost Christlike self-denial.

These are undoubtedly some of the elements people have in mind when they speak of Faulkner as a universal artist, as a creator of truths that have an almost mythic relevance to all men in all places and times. It is odd and wholly remarkable that he himself could have known only one place and time really well, that in many respects he was the most insular and provincial of artists. Yet he had mightily the gift of imaginative conversion, a rare faculty for abstracting the commonplace into the remarkable and for finding not simply the particular truth about his region but the universal truth *in* his region. Working alone down there in that seemingly impenetrable cultural wilderness of the sovereignly backward state of Mississippi, he managed to make a clearing for his mind and a garden for his art, one which he cultivated so lovingly and well that it has come in our day to feed the imagination of literate men throughout the civilized world.

1972

Afterthoughts on the Twenties

The publication back in 1973 of Malcolm Cowley's *A Second Flowering* reopened once again a question most of us might have preferred to leave closed and may have assumed was long closed. Yet even today it continues to preoccupy us like the puzzle of some ancient unsolved crime, and the occasion of this essay may make it appropriate to explore some of its implications still further. Just how important, really, was the generation of writers who are commonly assumed to have produced a renascence of American literature in the twenties; what is the meaning and value of their contribution in the perspective of all that we know about them and all that has happened in our literature since their time?

Mr. Cowley, having spent more than fifty years studying these writers, may be forgiven if, at seventy-five, he was unable or unwilling to offer much more than a reiteration of opinions that over the years have grown habitual with him and have come to represent the official establishment answer to this question. His understandably strong feelings of proprietorship toward the twenties writers have caused him to take it for granted that, in spite of individual shortcomings of which he is well aware, they were, on the whole, the most distinguished literary generation the century has so far produced—the most distinguished, in fact, since the great first flowering of American literary talent in the generation of Emerson and Thoreau. Mr. Cowley has written eloquently in support of his position, and one can scarcely fault him for taking it. He has had a long career as a highly influential critical spokesman for these writers, most of whom were his personal friends. He was on the scene in Paris during the time when they were doing some of their best work, and he was one of the first critics to understand and in *Exile's Return* to explore the significance of the whole artistic phenomenon that so profoundly affected the character of our literature after the first World War. If anyone has earned the right to his biases, Mr. Cowley surely has.

For the rest of us the problem of coming to terms with the twenties writers is considerably more complex. We have existed for years in a state of gross informational surfeit, in which we have become so drugged and bored with knowledge concerning every aspect of their lives and works that the possibility of making new and original assessments of them must strike us as being very remote indeed. Furthermore, their achievement as artists is now effectively inseparable in our minds from the legendry of their lives, and their works are so commonly seen as sourcebooks of gossip and invitations to nostalgia that no balanced view of their literary merits can be maintained for long.

Many of us also have to contend with our own emotional relation to these writers, a relation that cannot be as intimate and avuncular as Mr. Cowley's but is no less affected by sentiment or what, in the case of literary people younger than he, has so often been the most abject kind of filial admiration. After all, the twenties generation were once our very special and personal property. We came to love them long before it became official wisdom to do so, and there are complex loyalties that bind us equally to them and to that part of ourselves that was formed by their influence. For many of us who discovered them at the right (or perhaps exactly the wrong) age, they seemed quite simply the only *real* writers there were, and so they became our proxy writers. They had all the experiences we would have liked to have, and they wrote exactly the books we wished we might have written. It could be fairly said that they were the first and perhaps the only generation of writers to capture our imaginations and to dramatize an image of the literary life with which we could identify because it combined creative achievement with the freedom to explore the fullest possibilities of feeling and being. We may have had the greatest respect for the work of such older men as Dreiser, Mencken, Anderson, and Lewis, but we did not envy them their lives. Their generation seemed grey, remote, and eternally middle-aged. There was something about them that smelled of beer, cigars, pool halls, and the heavy sweat of craft and naturalism. One imagined them going off to the office every morning—potbellied businessmen of letters—carrying their inspiration in a lunch pail. But the twenties writers were a very different breed—elegant, aesthetic, temperamentally gifted rather than soberly skilled, as extravagant and wasteful as young British lords, yet profoundly self-preserving in their function as writers. They were distinguished from their elders, above all, by their dedication to the Flaubertian ideal of the artist, their sense of belonging to an aristocratic fraternity of talent. But they also believed in the interdependence of art and experience, the necessity that literature partake of, even as it transformed to suit its own purposes, the felt realities and passions of the individual life.

They thus embodied for us an adolescent ideal that is deeply rooted in the American mythos but that, in recent years, only Norman Mailer has been able to emulate with any conviction, the ideal of the writer as poet-profligate, our fantasy inheritance from the English and French Romantics and the disciples of Walter Pater that for the first time among the twenties writers became a practical model of conduct for Americans. Hence, they found it possible to live the life of sensation with great vigor and still live the life of literature with great dedication and success. They were able to have it both ways so splendidly, and they made such excellent use of the opportunity, that some of us will probably never manage to see them except against the high coloration of jealousy or adoration.

Another factor obscuring our view of these writers is that they were largely responsible for developing in us the standards by which we might have been able to judge them. For it was on the evidence of their work and that of their European contemporaries that we formed our first impressions of what literary effects were possible to the modern sensibility. No other standards derived from other historical periods seemed quite applicable to them, if only because so much of their significance resulted from their collective belief that they had outmoded the past by confronting a new reality in ways wholly unique to it and to them. Also, in a very real sense, the twenties writers provided the basic assumptions through which we came to perceive, and some of us to express, the experience of the modern world. Their works for a very long time seemed to have done all our essential imagining for us, just as they themselves seemed to have done our essential living, so that we had very little sense of being engaged with life that was not in some way connected with the profoundly seductive images of life with which they first came to dominate our imaginations.

As a result, our view of the literary life of the twenties is a complex mixture of myth and reality, of reality fantasized into myth and myth personalized to the point where it seems like something we ourselves experienced. One does not know, for example, whether the literature created the fantasy or the fantasy found its embodiment in the literary life. But surely a strong attraction of the period for young people was and may still be the fact that it represents their vision of the perfect college literary apprenticeship exported to Paris and prolonged for a decade. The intense, free life of Montparnasse was the idealized equivalent of the intense, free life of the campus literati. There in Paris, happily far away from parents and hometown, it was possible to get drunk as often as one pleased, to stay up all night making love, wander the streets howling into the dawn, be eternally young, sensitive, and promising, do all kinds of experimental work and publish it in the little magazines, be read by an audience of friends who were the perfect classmates, all people of brilliant talent and wit and yet, except for a few, remarkably kind and helpful about one's own work. There too one could enjoy the presence of older teachers and mentors like Pound, Anderson, and Stein, the quintessential writing instructors who were the first to recognize one's gifts and who gave so generously of their advice and encouragement. But perhaps even more important were certain other perquisites of these literary junior years abroad: The advantages of not having to hold down a job because checks were coming regularly from home or a fellowship, not having to be compromised by the bourgeois values of one's parents, not having to worry about marriage and a family, not having responsibilities of any kind except to Art, Truth, and Friendship.

It is not surprising that this image of the Paris literary life should have been embellished in our minds by a cast of personages, both fictional and actual, who have the clarity of outline, the individuality, and the emotional openness that, as a rule, only young people of college age seem to possess. Their appearance and behavior remain with us almost as if recollected from life or recorded in a class yearbook in which we seem to find versions of our own former selves. Nobody will ever be like them again, and nobody will need to be. For these people exist eternally in the roles fixed for them by memory and sentiment—larger than life because they belong to a generation that managed to mythologize its experience while still engaged in the act of having it.

There is the young Jay Gatsby, helplessly in love with the rich and sophisticated sorority girl, holding out his arms to the green light at the end of her boat dock; Amory Blaine proclaiming his valedictory "I know myself but that is all"; Jake Barnes muttering through those bitter, bitter teeth the best line in the senior play, "Yes, isn't it pretty to think so"; Scott and Zelda, the most popular and beautiful couple on campus, behaving insufferably at parties, jumping fully clothed into the Plaza fountain; Hemingway, the most talented boy in the class, writing his first stories at a table in the Closerie des Lilas; good old Thomas Wolfe, a boy who never seemed to stop growing, getting very drunk, waving his arms, and knocking out the electrical system of an entire town. And we remember the others, the people like Harry Crosby, Slater Brown, William Bird, Robert McAlmon, and the Gerald Murphys, who matter only because they were friends of the famous and now belong to history simply because everyone connected, however remotely, with the Paris literary life in the twenties now belongs to history.

The writers whom Leslie Fiedler once called "great stereotype-mongers" have bequeathed us themselves and their characters as clichés, and criticism has made more clichés out of the essential arguments that can be brought against them. Yet the most familiar argument is also the least avoidable. They were a group of highly talented but narrow writers, and their narrowness was most dramatically revealed in the fact that they had one abiding interest—themselves when young, an interest that, in the case of some of them, became the literary preoccupation of a lifetime. Their books had all the attributes of young consciousness. They were lyrical, nostalgic, sentimental, stylish, experimental, and iconoclastic, and they told over and over again the story of self-discovery through the first conquest of experience. We learned from them what it is like to grow up in the small towns of America, how it feels to fall in love, have sex, get drunk, go to war, be an American in Europe, and all for the first time—to be so hungry for life that you want to consume all the food, liquor, and women in the world, or to discover that the system created by adults is capitalistic and corrupt or hypocritical and dull.

Fitzgerald wrote the story of young romance and riotous youth and, remarkably enough, became famous at twenty-four largely on the strength of the fact that he informed the older generation about just how badly the young really behaved. Hemingway's first and best materials were an adolescent's adventures in Europe, his initiation into the mystery cult of foreign sports, bullfighting and big-game hunting, the loss of his innocence through the death of his ideals and his love in European war. Dos Passos found his most dependable subject in the totalitarianism of social hierarchies, whether political, economic, or military, where the integrity of the young was destroyed or severely compromised and the artistic spirit was broken under the grinding pressures of the machine. There are very few people over forty in this literature, and when they do appear, we can usually recognize them by their stigmata of physical ugliness, venality, and hypocrisy. Only the young are truly human. But then the young are doomed to be the victims of the old, to die in their wars, to be tricked by their deceits, and ruined through seduction by their false gods.

It is logical that the qualities we remember most clearly in this literature are those that impressed us when we ourselves were young—the marvelous intensity about people and raw experience, the preoccupation with the self, with love, sex, freedom, time, adventure, the irreverence toward the world of the fathers, the disdain for the adult religion of work, self-sacrifice, expediency, competition, and conformity. It is also logical that so many of these writers were able to function effectively only so long as they could keep alive their youthful responses. A number did not live into middle age. Some died romantically young, others like Fitzgerald died old while still chronologically young. Of those who survived beyond fifty, almost all were engaged in reiterating the experiences of their youth or continued, as did Hemingway, to write out of a fading memory of emotional and intellectual premises established during the time of their first intense engagement of life.

They were, in fact, the first American literary generation to make being young into both a style of life and a state of grace. It is largely because of their influence that so many Americans are unable to perceive experience except as something that happens to one up to the age of thirty, or to understand that life can on occasion be something other than a process of losing the intensities one was once able to feel. At the end of that fateful confrontation between Gatsby and Tom Buchanan in the Plaza Hotel, Nick Carraway suddenly remembers that it is his thirtieth birthday—"Thirty—the promise of a decade of loneliness, a thinning list of single men to know, a thinning briefcase of enthusiasm, thinning hair." Read for the first time at the age of eighteen, the passage seems one of the most poignant in the novel. But then, perhaps years later, we may come to recognize that our sympathies should go not to Nick but to Fitzgerald. It is *his* limited vision of the possibilities of life that is exposed here, even as it is this same limitation that makes Gatsby a convincing and pathetic character.

One reason of course for this preoccupation with youth is that the first world war had the effect of seeming to annihilate past history and the old styles of history. Hence, the generation that had fought in the war felt urgently the need to establish new premises, to redefine the terms of existence. Not only was this necessarily a task for youth, but it placed unique and dramatic emphasis on the responses of youth. Only the young were sensitive and adjustable enough to be able to determine whether a given emotion or experience conformed to the new standards of authenticity produced, at least in large part, by the war. Besides, they were the ones who had "been there," been initiated, had heard all the big words and learned that those words did not describe how they felt or what they had been through. Thus, the literature of the twenties is not merely a narcissistic but—as the example of Hemingway makes particularly clear—a testing literature, one in which the effort again and again is to create an accurate new idiom and at the same time to determine the truth or falsity of a radically new, essentially foreign experience—most often according to the responses of a provisional and existential, inevitably youthful self.

Fortunately, there were elements that worked powerfully to the advantage of these writers. First, there was the fact that their consciousness of being unique and their experience unprecedented was validated by social and moral changes so profound that a literary career might be constructed around the process simply of recording them. These writers were in a position to be among the first to witness such changes, and they were aided greatly by what Frederick J. Hoffman once called their creatively "useful innocence," their small-town sensitivity to forms of conduct that, in spite of their surface sophistication, they could not help judging by the provincial standards they had been brought up on. It is not surprising that some of their best work has the incandescent quality of the astonished spectator, privileged to be on the scene of first encounters involving people who suddenly seem no longer to know by what assumptions they should behave.

Secondly, their prolonged apprenticeship in Europe enabled them to view American life from the perspective not only of distance but of adversary cultural values. They had inherited from their predecessors—most notably Lewis, Mencken, and Van Wyck Brooks—an intellectual arrogance, a disdain for bourgeois society, and a belief in the absolute supremacy of art and the artist that were formed into a metaphysics under the tutelage of Stein and Pound. They became cosmopolitan provincials abroad; they learned to judge America by essentially elitist European standards; and of course they found America provincial. But since they were themselves provincial, their attitudes retained a dimension of ambivalence that helped to humanize their satire and finally made it seem an expression more of regret than contempt.

They had, in short, a strong sense of belonging to, or being able to identify imaginatively with, place, perhaps just because they were physically so displaced—not only from home but from the past represented by home. They may have been creatively stimulated by the experience of living in a dramatic, radically changing present. But they could also feel anxious and uncertain and in need of the structures of coherence and identity they had left behind in the Midwest and South. This undoubtedly accounts for the fact that Hemingway and Fitzgerald were so continuously preoccupied with procedural questions, with the effort to formulate dependable rules of feeling and conduct. Hemingway's works can be read as a series of instruction manuals on how to respond to and behave in the testing situations of life now that the rules have changed and the world has become, in effect, an unknown foreign country. It might also be argued that some of his most dependable instructions are those he was able to reclaim from the past, in particular the American frontier past, the lessons of courage, fidelity, honor, and rectitude that might still have the power to influence human conduct when all other values were being called into question. Fitzgerald's best novels are restatements of Henry James's great theme: the implications of the misuse of power upon those who are innocent and helpless by those who are strong and unscrupulous.

In short, one finds in these writers and in some of their contemporaries a concern with the moral authenticity of certain traditions they might have presumed to be outmoded. It may be expressed only in a nostalgic recurrence to the locales that provided security in childhood—Hemingway's Big Two-Hearted River or Wolfe's Old Catawba. But it may also involve complex loyalties and codes of honor that once gave a human dimension to life—as Nick Carraway discovers through the experience of Gatsby, and Dick Diver through his marriage to Nicole. Both men derived a "sense of the fundamental decencies" from their fathers and so can evaluate and ultimately condemn a society in which such decencies no longer have meaning.

One of the very best of Fitzgerald's stories, "Babylon Revisited," is yet another expression of the desire to reconstitute certain values of moral discipline and self-control after the violent dissipations of the decade that ended in bankruptcy in 1929. Charlie Wales, a battered survivor of the time, returns to Paris in the hope of regaining custody of his daughter. To do this, he must prove to his sister-in-law that he has become a fit and responsible person. He very nearly succeeds in convincing her, but fails at the last moment when two of his old drinking friends reappear and destroy his chances of making a new life. Just as Nick after Gatsby's death wanted "the world to be in uniform and at a sort of moral attention forever," so Charlie felt the need "to jump back a whole generation and trust in character again as the eternally valuable element." But there is no escape from the consequences of his wasted past:

> Again the memory of those days swept over him like a nightmare—
> the people they had met traveling, then people who couldn't add a
> row of figures or speak a coherent sentence . . . the women and girls
> carried screaming with drink or drugs out of public places—
> —The men who locked their wives out in the snow, because the
> snow of twenty-nine wasn't real snow. If you didn't want it to be
> snow, you just paid some money.

The act of moral reclamation may be a necessity for every literary generation. In America we do not so much build on tradition as steal from it those elements we think may help us to understand the always unprecedented experience of our own time. The twenties writers had a singular relation to the problem. They had the strongest sense that their experience was indeed unprecedented, and that the older modes of literary statement were inadequate to describe it. They therefore became excessively preoccupied with their own experience and, in both their writing and their lives, with the innovative and defiant. For reasons of temperament and historical position many became fixated permanently at the level of rite de passage where they were condemned forever to play the roles of rebellious sons and wayward daughters, able to find their identity only in the degree of their opposition to the literary and social conventions of the past.

Yet in reviewing their achievement one is struck by how often their most admirable qualities seem to have been revealed at those rare moments when the writer was able, perhaps by accident, perhaps out of desperation, to transcend the limits of the adversarial stance and define his materials in some clear relation to the sustaining values of an older moral tradition or a newly created artistic convention based on those values. If Fitzgerald and Hemingway experienced such moments, as some of their best work, most notably *The Great Gatsby* and *The Sun Also Rises,* would seem to indicate, they did so only occasionally, in part because the life of their own time absorbed them too completely, and they were so rarely able to see that life in a consistently maintained moral perspective.

All that Dos Passos essentially had to support his intricately panoramic vision of American society were the values of adversarial politics, and it is significant that as he grew older his vision did not deepen, only his politics aged. E. E. Cummings and Hart Crane were, in their very different ways, poetically adversarial. Cummings made a limited kind of artistic convention out of wit and irreverence, while Crane, like Wolfe, sought all his life for a convention that would give shape and significance to the chaotic responses of his personality.

Both poets had the defect of being confined by personality, and Crane in particular existed in that state of psychic nihilism in which, as Allen Tate once observed, "any move is possible because none is necessary."

The examples of Faulkner and, on a less exalted level, Thornton Wilder should serve to remind us that there were alternatives to the more fashionable positions taken by so many of the twenties generation. There were alternatives *if* one possessed, as Wilder did, an intellectual culture broad enough to enable one to draw creatively on the best resources of the Western literary tradition, or *if* one had Faulkner's access to the abundant resources of the southern tradition. But without these advantages, supplemented by talent of very large size, too many of the twenties writers remained locked into their first youthful responses to an experience that was too overwhelmingly intense to serve as very much more than the material of an often brilliant but very personal and limited literature. They may be forever established in our minds as the immensely charismatic personages of one of the most dramatic decades in our literary history. But it is significant that we can never separate them from the image we retain of the life of their time, just as they were unable, except at rare moments, to separate themselves, and in so doing, become larger than their experience, its imaginative possessors and masters, the shapers of those truths it contained that might have made timeless in art what is otherwise lost to history.

1975

Homage to Malcolm Cowley

For as long as most of us can remember, Malcolm Cowley has been the chief historian of the literary generation of the twenties, that remarkable group of writers once fashionably known as "lost" because they led dislocated lives but found themselves in the production of distinguished work. This paradox forms the basis for what is surely the most mesmerizing literary legend of this century. Cowley first wrote about these writers more than forty years ago in *Exile's Return*, his now classic memoir of the Greenwich Village and Paris expatriate years that did more than any other book to popularize their legend even as it was among the first to validate the great importance of the literature that made the legend possible.

On August 24, 1978, Cowley turned eighty, a rare achievement for an American writer and undoubtedly rather perplexing for Cowley since he has now outlived nearly all the writers whose lives and works provided him with his principal subject matter. "Now most of the team is gone," he wrote recently, "and the survivors are left with the sense of having plodded with others to the tip of a long sandspit where they stand exposed, surrounded by water, waiting for the tide to come in." Yet the wait for Cowley, however somber it may be, has also been productive, for it has given urgency to his need to come to some final understanding of just what it has been like to be a member of his generation and whether now in old age he might yet find something further to say about the accomplishments of his literary contemporaries, so very few of whom managed to make it with him to the tip of the sandspit.

In two books published over the last several years, *A Second Flowering* and the very recent *And I Worked at the Writer's Trade*, Cowley has tried to offer some at least tentative answers to these questions. Both books consist of his retrospective evaluations of the major and minor writers of his time, and the second contains autobiographical chapters presenting his account of his personal involvement with them and his impressions of the era in which they lived. His critical perspective is quite naturally influenced by his strong sense of being a last survivor, and that in turn gives his treatment of them a benevolence that in some cases seems unwarranted. Still, the two volumes taken together with *Exile's Return* constitute the most valuable record we are likely to have of the many gifted men and women who helped bring about the second great flowering of American literature after the first of the age of Emerson and Thoreau.

What is perhaps most impressive about Cowley as a literary and cultural commentator is his ability—most clearly demonstrated in his earlier writings—to sense and report the psychic weather, the dominant moods and styles, the subtle forces that shape the collective state of mind of the historical moment very often while the moment is still in the process of being formed and he himself is being formed by it. This is what gave *Exile's Return* its special quality of seeming to be almost magically evocative of his generation's experience at the same time that it arranged that experience into a pattern of tonal and thematic development that was more fictive than historical. One could read it—and a great many of Cowley's younger literary contemporaries did read it—as if it were a first-rate novel or play about imaginary characters who happened to be real people being acted upon by real conditions that somehow also became characters. There were the environmental villains (the war, poverty, drugs, Philistinism, Comstockery, unreceptive publishers). Then there were the victims (Harry Crosby, Hart Crane), many heroes (Pound, Eliot, Joyce, Hemingway, Fitzgerald), and some clowns (Harold Stearns, Tristan Tzara), and they all moved through the narrative in a choreography of self-conscious posture and pretense, large ambition, adolescent romanticism, and a certain holy innocence of spirit toward a denouement prepared for them by history but made thematically meaningful because history and the author's creative perceptions had from the beginning been precisely coordinated.

This essentially dramaturgical sense of their collective experience, of belonging to a company of actors at work in a most unusual performance that they were making up as they went along, was shared by more than a few of Cowley's contemporaries—most notably by Hemingway, Dos Passos, and Fitzgerald whose early novels could be read as companion volumes to *Exile's Return.* But although Cowley had something of Dos Passos's historical perspective and wrote a prose that at times uncannily resembled Hemingway's, he was most like Fitzgerald in seeing his personal experience as a sort of microcosmic version of what had happened to them all, as emblematic of their common fate and fortune.

Cowley did not arrive at this perception after making a house-to-house survey or sending out questionnaires—as he most certainly would have felt obliged to do today—but by consulting his own very sensitive but altogether unscientific antennae. He has, therefore, been faulted by some critics on the ground that the experiences he sees as typical of his generation were actually typical only of himself and his friends. There may be some small justice in the charge. But the history of any age or generation will inevitably be cast in the form created by those who have been most active and prominent within it or who have kept its records most assiduously, and in both roles Cowley has earned excellent credentials.

The fact is evident in so very much they have said and written that Cowley's literary contemporaries did indeed have a remarkable awareness of shared experience, and his own career is in many of its aspects not only representative but almost seismographically reflective of the changes that have occurred in the literary life of his country over the past sixty years. During that time he has lived through nearly all the evolutionary phases of the modernist movement in literature, and he has made his own significant contribution to each. More than any other historical critic except possibly Edmund Wilson, he has been persistently alert to the complex interplay of cultural and intellectual forces that have helped shape the character of modern literature even as they provided the collective history from which his generation of writers derived their strong sense of united creative purpose.

Cowley has said that the sudden end of World War I left the writers who took part in it with an unexpended store of nervous energy that invigorated their creative work for at least the next ten years. But the war and its immediate aftermath also greatly influenced the attitudes expressed in so much of what they later came to write. Not long after the Armistice they began to perceive that Germany and her allies had been defeated only to be replaced by a new enemy, the politicians, government officials, and industrialists who had profited from the slaughter and were now engaged in corrupting the peace. The resulting hostility to exploitative bureaucratic systems became widespread among artists and intellectuals throughout the Western World and provided an adversarial ideological basis for the revolutionary movement in all the arts that followed the war.

Absolute dedication to aesthetic values became both a weapon against corrupt values and the one honorable alternative to them. In literature the search for precisely the right words to express what one really felt and believed, the effort to determine, as Hemingway put it, "the exact sequence of emotion and fact which made the emotion," represented not only an attempt to purge the language of wartime propagandistic falsehoods but a blanket repudiation of comparable evils such as the hypocrisy and piety of Mencken's booboisie, the bigotry that had created Prohibition, and the vapid boosterism of the American small town. One came to Paris because it was a haven of escape from Main Street and Gopher Prairie. But one also came and stayed on to become part of the militant creative action that was to restore the integrity of the language and in the process discover original ways of expressing the spiritual weariness, cynicism, and generalized sense of disaffiliation and betrayal that so many of the postwar writers shared in common and that became the characteristic stance of literary modernism.

In coming to maturity during the most vigorous years of a new literary movement, Cowley's generation enjoyed advantages that, with the passage of time and the shrinkage of fresh creative possibilities, have come to seem more and more enviable. They began their careers when the fundamental materials and themes of modern experience were just becoming visible in their full difference from those of the past and when the methods for dramatizing them in literary form were being perfected. They were thus privileged to make formulations of the most primary and innovative kind about the nature of the new era that was fast evolving around them—in effect, to complete the work of establishing the basic premises of modern American literature. If the war had left them with an abiding distrust of official values as well as a feeling of dislocation from the past, they were also, in an important sense, purged of illusion and freed to define their postwar perspective in relation to the best that might be reclaimed from the past. Their profound need for moral and emotional authenticity, to find a way to recognize and express the exact truth of their own perceptions, led them to make a skeptical and, in many instances, satirical scrutiny of the changes in American life that had begun to occur with such rapidity after the war. Not at all surprisingly, they often came to examine the new manners and morals by comparing them with those that had so recently been outmoded. It was as if by testing the current validity of what had gone into the discard pile, they might penetrate the meaning of what had come into being.

Although Hemingway wrote in *A Farewell to Arms* that the war had made obscene the patriotic language composed of such abstract words as honor, courage, and heroic sacrifice, he found his most dependable dramatic subject in those situations of extreme crisis in which honor and courage become the only resources his often heroically sacrificial protagonists have to draw on for the strength to live and die well. Fitzgerald's great subject was, as Cowley has said, the romance of money, in particular, the conflict between old and new money and the fate of traditional codes of honor in a society where people can be careless and destructive of others just because they are rich. Dos Passos created in *USA* a massive portrait of postwar American society in which the frontier values of individual independence and integrity were being destroyed by a rapacious bureaucratic capitalism seeking only wealth and power.

At the same time other writers were exploring from much the same skeptical and morally reevaluative point of view subjects growing out of their war experience; their own development as writers; their progress from provincial isolation and conflict with small-town bigotry to their indoctrination by the war and subsequent disillusionment; the new sexual freedom; and the new conspicuous consumption culture and its manifold vapidities. Never in our history had a literary generation studied so closely and obsessively the character of American life, and never again would our writers feel that they were discovering *for the first time* the basic truths about modern American life. They would not because the writers of the twenties had made the discovery before them and for them.

The advantage for Cowley himself in being associated with those writers at this time was that they, along with their contemporaries in England and on the Continent, were creating for criticism an abundance of challenging and original materials to be evaluated for a reading audience who were discovering the new writers but needed instruction in how to read them. In fact, twentieth-century American criticism came of age in the elucidation of literary modernism, and both Cowley and Edmund Wilson launched their careers with books that were essentially introductions to the history and accomplishments of the movement while it was still in process of development. Cowley told the story of the American and expatriate contribution, while Wilson in *Axel's Castle* discussed the great modernist pioneers and masters. If the new literature was achieving in those years a powerful authority, it was also enabling criticism to achieve an authority it had never had before and that reached during the fifties a dimension it has never since had. At that time some of the most distinguished literary minds in the country were at work in criticism. Along with Cowley and Wilson there were Allen Tate, John Crowe Ransom, Yvor Winters, R. P. Blackmur, Lionel Trilling, Robert Penn Warren, Cleanth Brooks, and Kenneth Burke, nearly all of them critics who made their reputations through the study of the achievements of modernism.

In view of the present debilitated state of American criticism, it seems remarkable that the work of these men should have been so immensely influential, or that for many years through their regular reviews Cowley in the *New Republic* and Wilson both there and in the *New Yorker* could reach and directly affect the taste of such a substantial portion of the reading public. But it must be remembered that not only was literature discovering modern experience, not only was criticism discovering the literature and educating the public in its meaning, but all the central ideas and issues relating to literature, criticism, and intellectual culture in our time were also being discovered, developed, and excitedly discussed. The great controversies of the twenties over the shaping of new artistic forms and the proper use of new artistic materials; the question of art for art's sake or for the reader's sake; Bohemia versus Main Street, symbolism versus realism; freedom of expression versus censorship were followed by the great controversies of the thirties over the social responsibility of the artist; the difference between art and propaganda; the relation between art and politics; the debates over Humanism, Freudianism, Marxism, Stalinism, and Trotskyism. In the field of criticism there were the fierce quarrels between the Marxists campaigning for a proletarian literature and critics defending the virtues of a bourgeois literature, between historical critics and formalists, between the conservative southern Agrarians and northern liberals. Cowley's essays and reviews published in the *New Republic* between 1929 and 1941 and collected under the title, *Think Back on Us,* testify to the amazing vitality, diversity of interests, and political contentiousness that characterized the American literary life during the period, and even more abundant evidence can be found in two of Wilson's collections, *The Shores of Light* and *The American Earthquake.* One finds Cowley attacking Archibald MacLeish who attacked Laurence Stallings on the question of propaganda and then addressing an admonitory open letter to Granville Hicks concerning the latter's strongly Marxist criticism. One finds Wilson attacking Michael Gold for judging Thornton Wilder unfairly and then attacking Bernard DeVoto for seeming to be judging Mark Twain unfairly because DeVoto was really trying to attack the position taken on the novelist by Van Wyck Brooks.

It is difficult to determine just what caused the breakdown of the sense of close intellectual community that made such spirited disputation possible for Cowley's generation, and how we happened to move into an era in which nobody attacks anybody or seems to care enough about any literary issue to become angry over it. Certainly, World War II, the disillusionment with Communism that became widespread among American writers and critics during the postwar period, and the reign of terror initiated by Joseph McCarthy against former Communists all played an important part. But it might also be said that by the end of the fifties the major ideas of modernism along with the primary critical and political questions raised by them had all been discussed, settled, or shelved, and what remained of an intellectual community had come rather complacently to rest in a liberal orthodoxy with which no significant disagreement seemed either rational or permissible. That may well be why when the activist youth movement of the sixties brought controversy briefly back into fashion, it provoked among liberals far less passion than piety and left in its wake not ideas but sentiments.

It should also be remembered that New York over the last two decades has steadily lost influence as a literary and intellectual center and is no longer the one place in the country where it is mandatory for writers to congregate, argue over ideas, and make their reputations. The old New York cultural community has given way to an aggregate of cultural outposts scattered among universities throughout the land, each with its resident poet or novelist and its cadre of critics teaching what are now the clichés of literary modernism using the thoroughly standardized classroom techniques of modernist criticism. It sometimes seems that almost everybody is or thinks he is a critic now and is as qualified to pass judgment as the next person. There are thousands of educated people today who all seem about equally perceptive and knowledgeable and whose critical responses may all be equally authentic. But their sheer numbers vitiate the authenticity of each response. This perhaps explains why no one critical voice carries the authority that Wilson and, to a lesser extent, Cowley once had, and perhaps it is also the reason there is no greatly influential voice in poetry or fiction. What helped the writers and critics of Cowley's generation to achieve influence was that they were highly individual as well as talented, were relatively few in number, and were addressing a reading audience that was both smaller than it is now and particularly responsive to the quality of individual performance in all the arts, just as the public in general admired outstanding performance in sports, on the stage and in films. It clearly was—as everybody now knows—an age of stars, while ours is an age of bit players lost in a cast of thousands.

Cowley at eighty is one of the few literary stars we have left from that distinguished time. It may be that he is not quite of the first magnitude and that he has lacked the incandescence of some of his contemporaries—the massive erudition of Wilson, the eccentric brilliance of Blackmur and Tate. However, he also has not burned out but has remained a source of steady and dependable illumination, knowing what he knows, which is very considerable, and saying what he thinks. He has lived through the intellectual fashions and fads of many decades. He has witnessed the death of the literary movement that produced him and the decline of the old-style literary life in which he was once so active. Yet he seems not once to have deviated from the firm and honest course he set for himself as a young man. All his work gives the impression of great deliberateness and practical sanity. Every judgment he makes seems to have been thoroughly meditated and then remeditated before it is expressed, and the care appears to be the result not merely of a staunch determination to be accurate but of a certain temperamental caution—as Hemingway would have said, a need to keep the flanks covered at all times. His prose has about it an almost country plainness and solidity, as if it had been carved out of the language with a pocket knife. Yet it is preserved from being commonplace by the poet who is still alive in him and who gives it cadence and a rare kind of subtly elegiac gravity. He has written quite simply some of the finest critical prose of our time.

If now in his old age Cowley cannot enjoy the satisfaction of spectacular triumph, great reputation, or large public accolade, he does have behind him more than half a century of working honorably and successfully at the writer's trade, retaining a devotion to the high calling of literature that is now very nearly extinct in the world, and keeping alive the works and days of his generation whom he now lives on to commemorate and represent.

1979

Céline and the Hateful Horror of It All

Louis-Ferdinand Céline was surely one of the strangest and most fascinating of men, and he may also have been the most important novelist to appear in France during the period between the two world wars. Henry Miller and at one time Sartre thought he was, and more recently Alain Robbe-Grillet, in discussing Céline's powerful influence on the nouveau roman, repeated the claim. Yet there have been relatively few attempts to engage his life and work at book length, and the studies that have so far been made tend more to reflect the distortions and idiosyncrasies of their subject than to illuminate the connections between Céline, the horrendously suffering man, and the savage art that his suffering drove him to produce.

Patrick McCarthy in this new biography has presented the most complete account yet available of Céline's life and career while at the same time avoiding the more serious mistakes of his predecessors. He has not, for example, given way to the pretentiousness of Erika Ostrovsky who, in *Voyeur, Voyant,* created a rather too coyly impressionistic portrait of Céline done evidently in parodic imitation of the literary manner of Céline. Nor has McCarthy been drawn into the politico-psychoanalytical debate which has raged around Céline for years and which flawed the perspective of Bettina L. Knapp's otherwise excellent study, *Céline: Man of Hate.* Yet Mr. McCarthy is, if anything, too detached and surgical in his approach to be altogether authoritative. He is sane to the point of seeming insensitive in his treatment of the more sensational, repulsive, and lunatic aspects of Céline's personality, and he is able to bring himself to risk an act of judgment only in his role as literary interpreter, in which he is at his best, offering the most astute stylistic reading of the fiction that has so far been done. One suspects that Mr. McCarthy may have suffered from something of the same handicap that troubled Carlos Baker in his biography of Hemingway. However much he may have admired his subject's artistry, he could not find it in him to approve or really comprehend the violent temperament and radical vision that lay behind the artistry. Hence, one has reason to doubt whether, beyond his acute responsiveness to Céline's narrative methods, Mr. McCarthy possesses the power of imaginative identification necessary for the making of a definitive biographical statement.

Yet the difficulties confronting any biographer of Céline are enormous and vastly complicated. Everything about the man is blanketed in thick layers of ambiguity, and by the time of his death in 1961, it seemed humanly impossible to entertain an opinion about him that was not contradicted by another opinion one might with equal justice also entertain. Mr. McCarthy discusses several of the reasons why this has been true, among them the fact that so much of the information available on Céline simply cannot be trusted, and so few means exist by which its accuracy can be verified. The great majority of the people interviewed for the biography learned what they knew about Céline largely from Céline himself, and he had long been notorious for distorting or completely falsifying the details of his life, usually in order to wrench them into conformity with his paranoid image of himself as hounded, persecuted, or otherwise martyred by the forces of cosmic malevolence, which he was convinced had elected him as their exclusive victim. In his efforts to validate this image he did not, for example, hesitate to depart completely from what is known to have been true about the character of his parents and his childhood experiences, and he did this not only in his fiction, where it is taken for granted that lies make better reading than the truth, but in his statements to friends and interviewers. He repeatedly described his early homelife as an existence made hellish by poverty, filth, moral degradation, and the most violent parental discord, in which the helpless child Céline (then Louis-Ferdinand-Auguste Destouches) was forced to endure unspeakable humiliation at the hands of a father who was brutish and vulgar, while the mother luxuriated masochistically in the torments engendered by his tyranny. Yet one can infer from such facts as are known and the recollections of witnesses that all this is complete and utterly dismal fabrication. One family friend has said that the senior Destouches, who, as vice-president of an insurance firm, could scarcely have been impoverished, was "a man of honour . . . jovial and very frank, a lover of fishing and sailing," and a devoted father. He and his wife are described as living happily together, "nice quiet people, ordinary and retiring," while Madame Destouches seems to have borne no resemblance whatever to the image her son came to have of her. Anything but a pathetic victim, she was actually a businesswoman of considerable acumen and made quite a bit of money trading in expensive antique lace.

It is entirely possible, however, that for a man of Céline's compulsively infuriated temperament the sins of the parents were precisely their bourgeois virtues, and that what he found most hateful about them was that they deprived him of the psychic advantages of a tragic childhood. Later on and for much the same reasons, his experience of World War I also proved disappointing. Even though he served with distinction, was decorated for bravery and wounded, the war clearly failed him because it did not hurt him grandiosely enough. He therefore created the myth, which he continued to embroider to the end of his life, that in addition to his actual arm injuries, he had suffered a severe head wound and wore a steel plate in his skull that caused him incessant and excruciating pain. His fictional treatment of the war, particularly in his first novel, *Journey to the End of the Night*, is, unlike his portraits of his parents, a superb recreation of the cataclysmic actualities. But it is also an experience rendered with such a gleefully brutal exaggeration of the facts that one cannot help but see it as primarily intended to reinforce Céline's obsessive fantasy of martyrdom.

Ironically, the actual ambiguities of his personality and career are far more remarkable and puzzling than any arising out of Céline's penchant for fabrication. He had, for example, in addition to his highly productive literary life, an entirely separate existence as a practicing physician, a role in which he is said to have been skilled, dedicated, and compassionately attentive to his patients, most of whom were drawn by his choice from the working class. He also had more than ordinary interest in the history and sociology of medicine and produced early in his career three substantial scientific papers, two of which had to do with health conditions in modern assembly-line systems and the responsibility of the medical profession to educate industrial workers in the correct habits of hygiene. His strongly humanitarian concerns were most dramatically expressed in his doctoral dissertation that was devoted to Ignaz Philipp Semmelweis, the nineteenth-century Hungarian physician who was professionally crucified because he dared to insist that cleanliness in the operating room would reduce the extremely high incidence among obstetrical cases of puerperal fever, a disease not at the time considered contagious. Céline's treatment of Semmelweis is charged with anger at the bigotry responsible for his persecution, at the same time that it contains overtones of a typically Célinesque infatuation with the idea of such delicious martyrdom.

But what is especially fascinating is that while Céline the physician displayed both here and in the conduct of his practice the most kindly regard for human frailty and suffering, Céline the metaphysician-novelist projected in almost everything he wrote the bleakest and most profoundly nihilistic view of the human condition to be found in modern literature. It is entirely possible that this view was exacerbated by his long exposure to the wretched deformities and ravagements suffered by his patients. But what the doctor sought with implicit hopefulness to cure or at least alleviate in the individual case, the writer saw in the general case to be hopelessly incurable, and perhaps for just that reason, altogether loathsome.

Like so many literary intellectuals—among them Camus and Beckett—who by nature are fundamentally religious, Céline was a disillusioned absolutist who could not abide human imperfection or the prospect of existence in a universe without God, an existence ending necessarily in a meaningless death. The fear of death can become pathological in those who require some idea of transcendental order or design with which to justify life, and Céline in his fear saw no meaning in life beyond the fact that, as he put it, "man's habitual state is to be dying." The only human comfort is to be found in the self-deceiving cultivation of divertissement, some tranquillizing activity that allows a person to forget for a brief time his doomed condition. "You must choose," says Bardamu, Céline's first protagonist, "either dying or lying," and the efforts of human beings to lie their way out of their consciousness of pointless death is one of the central preoccupations of Céline's major novels.

His personal hatred of lies, at least as expressed in his fiction if not in his conversation, was in fact so extreme that he supposed that truth lay only in despair and in the most ruthless revelation of all that is unspeakable in the human condition. If man was not a god, then he should be exposed as the fraudulent and disgusting creature he was, an insect worthy only of contempt. The hatred Céline felt so powerfully was of course self-hatred, and he dedicated himself as a writer to spreading a doctrine of hate that insured that he would win the hatred of others. When, as frequently happened, his expressions of hatred struck a sympathetic nerve in his readers' misanthropy and threatened to be received with approbation, he simply found a way of being still more outrageously hateful, perhaps in the hope of bringing down upon himself the ultimate retribution reserved in this world for heroes and martyrs such as Semmelweis.

When *Journey to the End of the Night* appeared in 1932, it caused a scandal fiercer, if considerably less ludicrous, than the furor created by the publication of *Madame Bovary* seventy-five years earlier. The more conservative critics found the novel obscene and morbidly iconoclastic. "M. Céline," wrote the reviewer for *Candide,* "expresses with unrelieved baseness the disgust he feels for humanity." Yet there were others who responded with the sort of titillated admiration for the offensive in Céline that, particularly in France, helped to secure the reputations of Baudelaire, Beckett, Genet, and other beloved *provocateurs* of the bourgeois masochism. Céline was also given support, as were these men, by the view that if a work is nasty and subversive enough, it must be art, and at least a substantial portion of his reputation as a major writer is the result of the wide acceptance of this view not only among his then more radical contemporaries but in certain literary circles at the present time. Céline managed, however, with his usual alertness to the danger of not being hated, to produce in his second novel, *Death on the Installment Plan,* a work of such sordidness and maniacal frenzy that even the most passionate champions of the ugly found themselves unable to bear the book, although that response seems in no way to have affected the opinion now so widely held that *Death on the Installment Plan* should be judged, along with its predecessor, as the most important fiction Céline produced.

Between 1937 and the first years of World War II Céline issued three polemical works—*Bagatelles for a Massacre, School for Cadavers,* and *Some State of Affairs*—which were so viciously inflammatory that they seemed guaranteed to bring him the wholesale punishment he craved. Best known for their fanatical anti-Semitism, these pamphlets also contained scarcely less virulent diatribes against the moral corruption, materialism, and indolence of the French, the effeminate weakness of the Allies, and the generalized rottenness of the modern world. All these ills, according to Céline, were creating a catastrophic condition in which Europe was drifting into a terrible war; a fictitious "Jewish conspiracy" was responsible for engineering a crusade against Nazi Germany that the Allies were certain to lose; and the only hope lay in the forming of a Nordic state, a "Confederation of the Aryan States of Europe," in which the Allies and Germany would join forces to exterminate the Jewish "warmongers."

Such views served, not at all surprisingly, as excellent evidence in support of the charges of being a Nazi sympathizer and collaborator that were later brought against Céline. By implication and in countless overt statements, he was arguing with an effectiveness marred only by hysteria for a position that, if it did not provide much concrete assistance to the Nazi cause, did give it moral support at a time when the ideological differences between fascism and democracy were rapidly ceasing to have a merely academic significance. However, it must be remembered that politics for Céline was finally only a dialectical framework for the expression of his psychopathology. Behind his hatred of the Jews, for example, was the tangled ambivalence of his self-hatred and perverse lust for martyrdom. It is obvious that for him Jews were a particular threat because he at once identified with them and saw them as rivals for his claim to being God's chosen victim. They became his scapegoat because he needed to project his self-hatred upon others and in so doing purge himself temporarily of his emotional poisons, and because he was anxious to rid the world of his competition. He was also trying through the writing of the pamphlets themselves to offend the reading public so grievously that he would be assured of having a supply of hostility to nourish his persecution mania sufficient to last him for life.

In this endeavor he was almost but not quite successful. By 1944, and particularly after the Allied landings in Normandy, it became evident that Céline was one of those marked for trial as a collaborator and that he was very probably in some real danger of being executed out of hand by the French Resistance. Accordingly, in July of that year he fled Paris with his wife, Lucette, their cat, Bébert, and twenty trunks. He made his way to Berlin where he applied to the Nazis for a visa to go to Denmark, and while awaiting a decision settled in Sigmaringen, a headquarters for refugee collaborators, which became the setting for some of the fiction he was to produce after the war. Eventually Céline received permission from the Nazis to move on to Denmark and made a phantasmagoric journey through the devastation of Germany, arriving miraculously in Copenhagen after having made twenty-seven changes of train and walking a total of eighteen miles but, one can only suppose, with somewhat fewer than the original twenty trunks. In 1945, however, his luck ran out and, in response to a warrant made out in France, he was arrested by the Danish authorities and imprisoned—as it turned out, for seventeen months spent in solitary confinement.

Mr. McCarthy documents very thoroughly the period from 1945 to 1951 that Céline spent in Danish exile. He devoted much of this time to writing letters to people who might be willing to plead his cause in France, and he supported these appeals with strident but not very convincing public statements assuring the world that he had never been a collaborator. But the atmosphere in France had meanwhile grown steadily less vindictive. Influential people began to speak in Céline's behalf. At his trial held in 1950, excerpts from one of his pamphlets were read aloud and provoked riotous laughter rather than indignation, and in April 1951 Céline was granted a full pardon, allowing him at last to return to France.

He had been hated and hounded and made to suffer, yet his position at the end was considerably less than triumphant. He had in fact been pardoned not merely because of his stature as a writer, but because he was no longer taken seriously as a threat to either the national security or the bourgeois pieties. In the years that were left him after his return to France, he tried in his old manner to provoke and scandalize through his public pronouncements. But he was forced to live with what must have been for him an insupportable irony: no one could be provoked by him any more. People who had been repulsed by his wartime pamphleteering were eager to forget him. Most, however, were simply indifferent and would perhaps have been surprised to learn he was still alive. So he was left with his writing and a public who may have continued to read him but who denied him the one consolation that might have brightened his old age—the assurance that he was everywhere despised.

Céline's importance as an artist will most probably continue to be debated for some years to come. But his reputation will surely increase among readers of English as more of his postwar novels become available in translation and as the stigma of his political views loses force as a deterrent to an aesthetic appreciation of his work. What can be said with most assurance at this time is that Céline is notable for having expressed in the angriest form conceivable that classic disgust with the human condition in all its aspects that has been one of the most characteristic motifs of modern literature. In the service of this disgust he produced a neurasthenic, often more than half insane, surreal, and, toward the end of his career, an increasingly mystical fiction that in its day was revolutionary and proved to be highly stimulating to writers of often very diverse views and talents. There are many parallels between the metaphysical preoccupations of his early novels and those of Sartre's *Nausea*, which was dedicated to Céline, and Camus's *The Stranger*. Henry Miller was heavily influenced in particular by *Journey to the End of the Night* and *Death on the Installment Plan*, and the radical technical experimentation in the fiction of Beckett, Robbe-Grillet, and Michel Butor was undoubtedly encouraged by Céline's introduction into the novel of unconventional stylistic idioms and new modes of impressionistic and fantasy projection. Among other contemporary writers there are Günter Grass and in this country William Burroughs, Thomas Pynchon, John Hawkes, and Joseph Heller, all of whom would probably have written very differently if Céline had never lived.

Mr. McCarthy believes that in his stylistic inventiveness and originality Céline can be compared only with Joyce. Yet one cannot easily imagine two writers who are more dissimilar in every other respect. Joyce tried to create an art that would conform to his aesthetic ideal of stasis, that would arouse neither desire nor loathing, but would embody the subtle soul or epiphany of the experience portrayed. Céline produced a vigorously kinetic art that was the embodiment of his loathing and that aroused loathing, if not desire, in others. Joyce was at all times the master of his subject. Céline was the obsessive servant of his, and he had really only one subject—the hateful horror of existence. That subject locked him in as tightly as it locked out his humanity. If he had been blessed with Joyce's power of self-detachment, he might have found the freedom and the wisdom to see beyond his agony and to make that fundamental assent to life that an artist, with whatever skeptical reservations, must ultimately make before he can be considered qualified for elevation to greatness.
1976

J. P. Marquand, Esquire

John P. Marquand is not exactly in the forefront of literary consciousness at the present time. The young do not read him, and if they did would surely dismiss him as counterrevolutionary. One needs to be at least forty-five to have been sentient enough through the period of his greatest fame—from about 1937 to 1958—to remember the kind of books he wrote and the large impact they had on the reading public of those years. Yet even if one does remember, it is still immensely difficult to bring his image into clear focus.

Part of the problem is that Marquand seems to fit none of the somber categories in which we normally entomb literary reputations for posterity. There is, in fact, more than a faint air of meretriciousness about him. His best fiction seemed too facile to be considered profound, and much of it was far too popular to be taken seriously by the kind of people who might have been in a position to judge how very well written and profound his work could be. He was a disciplined literary professional, and if he had lived in Victorian England, he would undoubtedly have been admired for being just that. But in a country where the usual synonym for literary professional is hack, it has been easy enough for critics to condemn him for his craft and ignore his very considerable substance.

Unfortunately, there was at one time some justice in this because Marquand actually began his career as a hack. In 1922, his first book, a florid historical novel called *The Unspeakable Gentleman* was bought by *Ladies' Home Journal* for the then considerable sum of $2000. Over the next fifteen years he turned out large quantities of slick formula fiction for the *Journal, Cosmopolitan,* and *Saturday Evening Post* and made a reputation of sorts as the author of a series of thrillers about Mr. Moto, a delightful, pre–Pearl Harbor Japanese spy, whose exploits enchanted millions of readers and were recreated in films starring Peter Lorre. Marquand was never entirely forgiven for having become a writer in this way, nor was his cause enhanced by his frequent and evidently quite guiltless assertions that he wrote in those years simply to make money and, what was much worse, that he immensely enjoyed the kind of writing he was doing.

It is not surprising, therefore, that when, very suddenly in 1937 with the appearance of *The Late George Apley,* Marquand began to show symptoms of trying to be a serious novelist, he met with some real skepticism, which may or may not have been tempered by the fact that the novel won him the Pulitzer Prize. Yet in eight more novels published during the next twenty years he persuaded at least some of his critics that he was indeed serious, at the same time that he proved to himself that he could write for art quite as enjoyably as he could write for money—and make much more money in the process. *Wickford Point, H. M. Pulham, Esquire, So Little Time, Repent in Haste, B. F.'s Daughter, Point of No Return, Melville Goodwin, U.S.A., Sincerely, Willis Wayde,* and *Women and Thomas Harrow* were all widely read, several were very large commercial successes, and the best of them were works of genuine depth and artistry. Taken together, they constitute an impressive body of fiction, perhaps the most important series of novels about American society produced during the wartime and immediate postwar periods. Looking back on them now, one cannot help but wonder why they are not remembered as such at the present time.

Surely, some clue to an answer is to be found in the ambiguities that still cling to and obscure Marquand's position in our literature. It is not merely that ultimate questions about his artistic stature were never completely resolved during his lifetime and have not been resolved today. The problem is more exactly that Marquand was a serious writer who, for reasons of artistic intention or temperament, was not serious in most of the ways we have been programmed to recognize. For example, he does not appear to belong to the modernist tradition at all, at least not in any conventional sense, nor does he display the usual stigmata by which we validate our conception of the modern. Even though, remarkably enough, he was only four or five years older than Hemingway, Fitzgerald, and Dos Passos, he seems a century removed from them in both experience and metaphysics. Yet Marquand was deeply and personally affected by World War I, in which he saw as much action as Hemingway. He had a knowledge of the society of the very rich that was more comprehensive and accurate than Fitzgerald's. He had as much understanding of the oppressive structures of the capitalist system as Dos

Passos, and he expressed his understanding without the political dogmatism that marred so much of Dos Passos's fiction. Perhaps of all his contemporaries, the writer Marquand most closely resembles is Sinclair Lewis, whose work he in fact greatly admired. Yet there are grounds for believing that Marquand was in many ways a better novelist than Lewis and had more perceptive things to say about the life of his time. He was certainly a much more effective satirist, particularly in the sense that he was never guilty, as Lewis so often was, of producing caricature when he intended characterization.

But Marquand *was* guilty of seeming to work outside the fashionable styles and philosophical stances that helped to earn for his contemporaries their collective status as spokesmen for a generation. He was not a crusader for sexual liberation or social reform, nor was he to the slightest degree demonic, perverse, shell-shocked, or afflicted with much more than a well-mannered, somewhat wistful anxiety. The note of high apocalypse is missing from his work, as is the note, so characteristic of his age, of psychological nihilism. His writing is not particularly provocative of imitation, and he did nothing experimentally to advance the technique of the novel except to popularize the flashback as the conventional method through which the experiences of the past and present can be brought into dramatic and ironic juxtaposition. It is doubtful if he influenced any of the writers who came after him unless perhaps those who tried to commercialize his kind of materials, without bringing to them his quality of insight, in novels like *The Man in the Grey Flannel Suit* and *Executive Suite*. Marquand, in short, was a maverick and loner without being a literary innovator or rebel, and it may be that he was simply too much of a professional to indulge himself with any of the more modish postures of the avant-garde.

Yet he wrote novels that said as much in their way about the nature of American life as those of his more illustrious contemporaries, and they were just as *modern* in their depiction of the actualities of that life. Their recurrent theme is the defeat of the individual by his particular society, whether it is traditional and overly structured or contemporary and relativistic. In the early novels, and principally in *The Late George Apley,* the repressive force is the patrician world of New England and Boston, controlled by old families, old money, and a Calvinist morality that was admirable in many respects but could also be ruthless in its power to shape a person to serve tradition against his real, if unacknowledged desires. Typically, Marquand's characters are presented at a moment in their lives when they are obliged to confront themselves with the knowledge that the opportunity for personal choice—if it ever existed—has already passed, when they have gone beyond the point of no return, and it is too late to begin again, to defy family and friends in order to marry the socially unsuitable girl one really loves, to strike out for a new life of freedom from corporate business responsibility or an ancestral concept of duty and honor.

The drama of self-confrontation is a standard subject of the modern novel, and Marquand treats it without the cosmic orchestration of a Conrad, Mann, Gide, or Camus but rather with a restrained melancholy appropriate to his sort of characters, who usually in the end arrive at understanding with a rather Jamesian sense of resignation. It is all very sad. Often it is comically and pathetically sad. But it is not really tragic, if only because characters like George Apley know from the beginning that they cannot really escape the obligations imposed by their society and that finally there is no choice except to play the game according to the rules. Their dilemma is also not tragic because Marquand's attitude toward the conflict between individual freedom and social responsibility was always ambiguous, and as he grew older, it became steadily more ambiguous. He persistently saw the predicament of his characters as double-edged. They might feel oppressed by the past, but in struggling to free themselves from its influence, they ran the risk of becoming lost in a contemporary society that, because it had succeeded in obliterating the past, existed in an eternal meaningless present, dehumanized and corrupted by materialism.

Just before his death in 1960, Marquand said that he was "out of the tempo of the times," and there can be no doubt that he was. His novels, in fact, record his deepening sense of alienation from the modern world and his increasing disgust with the cultural changes that were subverting the old humanistic values of decency, self-respect, and communal responsibility, values that, in his view, had helped to make life vital and civilized in the past. But his later novels also make it clear that as time went on he found it steadily more difficult to recapture an understanding of just what those old values had meant and how they might be specifically applicable to the new realities of the present. Hence, more and more his characters register their bafflement and outrage at the deteriorative forces at work in society, yet are unable to evaluate them by the traditional standards—because by now the connections to the past have been completely severed.

For the protagonist of Marquand's last novel, *Women and Thomas Harrow,* life has come to seem nothing more than a "shoddy road, decorated . . . with plastic refreshment booths and overnight motels

... places of temporary respite for temporary indulgence, but no more." And as the narrator of that novel observes:

> The late Dr. Albert Einstein, or others vaguely in the Einstein category, had advanced the theory that time, being immaterial, was indestructible—and perhaps it was.... Yet, granted that the past was indestructible, exactly where was it now? Was it in good order, in keeping with the theories of relativity? He did not believe it was. The past in his experience was a tangled mess like ticker tape.

If Marquand cannot be identified with the modernist movement in most of the usual ways, it is obvious that he was deeply identified with it in at least one vital respect. He shared with many of his contemporaries and classic predecessors an essential mistrust of the ideal of unrestrained liberty, for he recognized that while the moral codes and obligations of the past were often unjustly inhibitory, they were also necessary to human life and gave meaning and purpose to life. Specifically, they directed individual energies into channels that were ultimately beneficial to both the individual and the community. They were, in fact, the structural embodiments of those values that the culture as a whole deemed most crucial to its existence. As a rule, we do not associate this view with the modern because the literature of our time is most commonly recognized by its antirational bias, its tendency to celebrate spontaneous feeling, demonic personality, and the primal forces of the psyche. Nevertheless, whether overtly as in the work of Pound and Eliot or implicitly as in the work of Conrad, Gide, and Joyce, our literature also expresses a distinctly contrary bias, an awareness of the necessity for containing social forms within which human beings must carry on their struggle for personal freedom, and without which neither their struggle nor their freedom would have any significance whatever. This is the ambivalence, the double vision, of modernism, and for Marquand it is at the very center of his perception of American life.

One of the several virtues of Stephen Birmingham's biography, *The Late John Marquand,* is that in it he traces the development of this ambivalence through Marquand's major work and at the same time locates its sources in the circumstances of the novelist's life. Mr. Birmingham's admiration for his subject is evident everywhere but so too is his determination to be as truthful as possible, however unflattering his revelations may be to Marquand's memory. This is undoubtedly the reason why his book is not an authorized biography but was written without the cooperation or approval of the Marquand family and without access to letters and personal papers. These materials have for some years been locked away at Harvard, Yale, and Boston University and are now being made available only to Prof. Millicent Bell, who has been designated as the official Marquand biographer.

Clearly then, Mr. Birmingham was placed at some disadvantage, but at least he was able to make honest use of such information as was available to him, and he did have the cooperation of many of Marquand's friends, of whom perhaps the most helpful was Carol Brandt, Marquand's literary agent, confidante, and mistress. Mr. Birmingham has also drawn on his own recollections of the period when, as a young beginning writer, he was befriended by Marquand and given important advice and encouragement as well as practical help in finding a publisher for his work. He evidently had good reason to feel indebted to his mentor and might even be excused if he had chosen to be somewhat circumspect in his treatment of him.

Yet, even though Mr. Birmingham is at all times fair, the image of Marquand that takes form here—the facts, after all, being what they are—is unattractive enough to make it understandable that the family might have wished to prevent the publication of the book. Marquand apparently had a rather bleak personality and, depending on the state of his emotional weather, could be mistrustful, boorish, capricious, generally bad tempered, and often insensitive to the feelings of others. He had a streak of pettiness in him and was penurious to a degree that seems ludicrous until one allows for the fact that financial insecurity was a nightmare to him during his early life. This same insecurity may also have caused him to be afflicted with all the class snobberies of the New England gentry and to have become an assiduous social climber whose greatest satisfaction seems to have been his election to membership in Boston's most exclusive club, the Somerset. About people in general and women in particular—with the notable exception of Carol Brandt—he seems to have had little judgment, and the story of his two marriages is so pathetically awful that one is hard put to decide whether to feel sorry for him for having been stuck with such clearly unsuitable women or to pity them for having perhaps been made unsuitable through marriage to him.

In justice it must be said, however, that there was a certain logic to Marquand's character and, like all of us, he had reasons, if not perhaps altogether adequate excuses for his perversities. His early life contained a pattern of circumstances not uncommon to writers, particularly the experience of being expelled from a condition of childhood innocence and happiness through tragedy or, as happened in his case, the sudden loss of material fortune, and the consequent effort through literature to redeem oneself from the failures of the father or to create a position of superior judgment from which to study, analyze, and possibly expose the weaknesses of the society one has been forced to abandon.

Marquand's childhood was idyllic in the extreme—until his father went bankrupt. And it was a period, significantly enough, when the Marquand family enjoyed aristocratic privilege and leisure, the sort of beautiful life possible in a time of plentiful servants and elaborate social amenities. Marquand was cast out of this paradise in 1907 at the age of fourteen, and it is scarcely speculative to suggest that the experience confirmed in him his lifelong admiration of the very rich or that his preoccupation with them in his fiction was his way of returning imaginatively to and reidentifying himself with their society. But since he came to suffer the humiliations and snubs of the dispossessed aristocrat, he also viewed the rich with some resentment, which took the form in his portraits of them of a cutting satirical dimension.

Following the collapse of the family fortune, Marquand was sent to live with two of his father's sisters and his great-aunt at Curson's Mill outside Newburyport, Massachusetts. The three spinsters formed an eccentric household: Aunt Mollie was a sweet-faced, happy woman who was known euphemistically as "simple." Aunt Bessie had taken a degree as a Unitarian minister, had preached one sermon, then announced that she had lost the faith. Her favorite recreation was reading aloud, and during Marquand's stay at the Mill, she required him to listen while she read through every play of Shakespeare's, the Bible from Genesis through Revelation, all the classics, and Scott's Waverley novels. Then there was Great-Aunt Mary Curson who had once had a flirtation with John Greenleaf Whittier and been a friend of Emerson, Thoreau, William Ellery Channing, and the abolitionist, Thomas Higginson. Marquand recalled encountering Aunt Bessie and Great-Aunt Mary one summer evening at the Mill walking barefoot in the dewy grass and conversing animatedly in classic Greek.

These experiences gave him rich materials for his later novels—most notably *Wickford Point*—but they also gave him additional reasons for envying the rich. To him his aunts and particularly his Hale cousins, who were frequent summer visitors, seemed extravagantly well off (which, in fact, they were not), while he, by comparison, seemed a pauper. Thus, the elements of his central themes, failure and missed opportunity, may be found in the contrast between his own reduced circumstances and the apparent prosperity of his relatives.

Marquand managed in 1911 to enter Harvard on a science scholarship, but he was made to feel there even more of a social pariah, the principal reason evidently being that he failed to make Porcellian. In fact, he was not elected to any social club. Then, to make matters infinitely worse, he married Christina Sedgwick of *the* New England Sedgwicks, a woman who seems to have been so ethereally vague that much of the time she did not know where she was and who, when she went out, could not always be counted on to find her way home. The Sedgwicks were the lords of Stockbridge. In the town cemetery there was something known as the Sedgwick pie, the family burial plot where the deceased lay in a circle, their heads away from the center, so that when the call to resurrection was sounded, they would all rise and face their ancient ancestor, Judge Theodore Sedgwick, who presumably would have something of moment to say on the occasion.

Marquand's marriage to Christina proved to be disastrous. Her family had no comprehension of what he was trying to do as a writer, which at the time was earn enough money to support his wife in the manner to which her background had accustomed her, and they were wholly contemptuous of the kind of writing he was doing. As a result, he began to seek refuge from his domestic unhappiness in a way that was to become a fixed pattern of his life. He would call on friends such as his agents, Carl and Carol Brandt, or the Gardiner Fiskes and stay with them for days or weeks at a time.

Nevertheless, after finally divorcing Christina, Marquand made an even worse mistake. He married Adelaide Hooker, another woman of old and even richer family. Where he had been dominated and at the same time snubbed by Christina's family, he was now dominated and rather patronized by Adelaide. She was a willful, capricious, and profoundly eccentric person whose social skills seemed to be limited to interior decorating and who in time became physically gross and an extremely messy alcoholic. She and Marquand endured each other for years, and when at last they were divorced, he turned once again to Carol Brandt. Their friendship, which developed slowly into an affair, was the one wholly satisfying element in his emotional life, and it may have given additional force to his preoccupation with lost chances that he did not marry Carol when it might have been possible after Carl's death and before time had run out for him. However, the frustrations of the man as always could be put to creative use by the writer, and Marquand found in his relationship with Carol the materials for *H. M. Pulham, Esquire*, which has adultery as its major theme—adultery of course that finally goes nowhere because the forms at all costs must be preserved. Besides, as Harry Pulham says, "There is some needle inside everyone which points the way he is to

go without his knowing it." The way for Marquand was invariably back to conscience, where freedom and responsibility are held, however precariously, in balance and somehow by their holding provide such consolation as there is for not getting what we want.
1972

Steinbeck's Knightly Little People

Like some other important writers of our time—most notably, T. S. Eliot and George Orwell—John Steinbeck was strongly opposed to having his biography written, and he remained so until his death in 1968. He believed that an artist tries through his work to conceal or compensate for personal weaknesses of which he is ashamed, and that if certain facts about his own character were made public, the image of himself that he had projected in his fiction might be badly sullied, perhaps to the point where his disillusioned readers would cease to buy his books. Nevertheless, as finally happened to Eliot and as is in the process of happening to Orwell, Steinbeck is now biographed (evidently without formal authorization by his widow), and it appears likely that as a result his worst fears may be confirmed.

Thomas Kiernan offers *The Intricate Music* as the first "full-length" Steinbeck biography, but the term is relative and may suggest only that he carries his account of the novelist from the day of his birth to the day of his death. However, Kiernan has decidedly not written a complete or definitive biography, regardless of the considerable admiration and good will he has clearly brought to the endeavor. His treatment is synoptic and often superficial, and one feels throughout that more is being said about the physical events of Steinbeck's life than about their significance in the development of the man and artist.

Part of the problem may well be that Kiernan was working with only such information as he could gather from Steinbeck's family and friends, and it is possible that some of these people were only reluctantly cooperative or may not have known the novelist very well or responded to him very forcefully. But one finally suspects that the major difficulty confronting Kiernan lay in the character of Steinbeck himself. He appears to have been not only aloof, defensive, intolerant, and generally bad-tempered much of the time, but also a man afflicted with peculiar contradictions and limitations of mind and feeling, perhaps weaknesses of the sort that he hoped his work would conceal. However, on the basis of the evidence Kiernan does provide albeit fails to analyze, these limitations seem to have been as much responsible for many imperfections of the work.

As Kiernan portrays him, Steinbeck was a lonely, morose, and immensely confused young man who seems to have looked upon the profession of writing as his one hope of achieving emotional stability and a purposeful life. For years during which neither his family nor his friends could detect in him any particular evidence of literary talent, he spent hours and days in an upstairs room of his family's house in Salinas, California, doggedly composing stories that nobody would publish. When he was not writing, he worked at various odd jobs that, as a rule, he quit shortly after taking, and he devoted many nights to carousing in the less savory bars of Salinas. In his early twenties he was persuaded that the next best thing to being a successful novelist, which it appeared most unlikely he would become, was to go into newspaper reporting where he would at least have a chance to make some kind of living. Accordingly, he entered Stanford, became a student of journalism just long enough to demonstrate his total lack of interest in the subject, kept dropping in and out, until finally in 1925 he quit college for good.

Steinbeck's early interest in writing was stimulated by his wide reading in the classics—to which he was forcibly exposed during marathon educational sessions with a culturally ambitious aunt—and in particular by the enormous impact made upon him by Malory's *Morte d'Arthur*. In fact, it was that work more than any other that confirmed him in his determination to become a writer, and it also had much to do with shaping his vision of human life as a romantic quest by faithful, if rather simple-minded, knights for the grail of holy virtue. This vision provides the allegorical basis for his early novels, *Cup of Gold* and *To a God Unknown,* and is clearly operative in *Cannery Row, Sweet Thursday, The Grapes of Wrath,* and *Tortilla Flat,* in which Steinbeck compares his illiterate, childlike *paisanos* to the knights of King Arthur's Round Table.

Another and ultimately conflicting interest of Steinbeck's youth was biology, which he studied with Edward F. Ricketts, a brilliant marine biologist who for many years operated the Pacific Biological

Laboratory in Monterey and who became Steinbeck's intellectual mentor and closest friend. Ricketts's influence on the novelist's literary development was extraordinarily strong and undoubtedly accounts in large degree for both the qualities in him that at one time won the admiration of the general reading public and those simplifications and distortions of thought that many critics have discovered to be his flaws. Ricketts taught Steinbeck to see existence in terms radically different from those of chivalric romance, as pure animalistic process that is without teleological significance beyond the adaptation of organisms to their physical environment. Ricketts believed that allegory in literature was a form of preaching and that fictional characters should not be treated as symbols but as specimens of biological nature to be studied for their generic characteristics and their adaptive capabilities. He impressed it upon Steinbeck that a good writer must be "a scientist of the imagination" and not an allegorist or philosopher.

It is probably unfortunate that Steinbeck was unable to form himself wholly on Ricketts's teachings, for he might then have produced a naturalistic fiction of some real authenticity and strength and become perhaps a kind of American Zola. As it was, Steinbeck struggled throughout his career to reconcile his need to allegorize with his desire to write with laboratory detachment. As a would-be scientist of the imagination he was attracted to the kinds of characters who could most readily be depicted as biological phenomena, whose individuality was sufficiently limited so they could be easily presented in terms of their common features as a species, and whose intelligence was so minimal that there was little chance they would take any action contrary to the laws of social predictability. Steinbeck found such characters in the inhabitants of Tortilla Flat and Cannery Row and among the migrant Oklahoma farmers who were driven out of their homes by drought during the Depression.

But the philosophical allegorist, the romantic seeker after knightly virtue, consistently betrayed the scientist in Steinbeck. The quest for the holy grail ultimately brought down upon him the curse of sentimentality. As it turned out, the little people could not be viewed objectively at all. They had to be made cutely virtuous or adorably mischievous. They possessed the unsullied innocence of complete worldly failure. They were yokel Lancelots and bumpkin Christs victimized by cruel nature and the evil machinations of the rich and powerful, and in the process they became cartoon figures almost completely subsumed to the moral they were supposed to symbolize. Thus, the scientist took his revenge upon the philosopher: the moral existed without meaning because the characters chosen to represent it were without human life. They were indeed biological phenomena, specimens confected out of an imaginative vision based not on sympathy or compassion but on a sentimental love affair with the piety of feeling. Even when Steinbeck seemed to be trying hardest—as he evidently was in *The Grapes of Wrath*—to convince his readers of his close identification with his characters, they do not become real as people. As Edmund Wilson once observed, they are "animated and put through their paces rather than brought to life," and Steinbeck's *paisanos* "are cunning little living dolls that amuse us as we might be amused by pet guinea-pigs, squirrels, or rabbits."

Surely, this element of sentimental humanitarianism in Steinbeck accounted most for his huge popularity in the thirties and forties, just as it must have been primarily responsible for the award to him of the Nobel Prize for literature in 1962. European readers were confirmed in their most cherished out-of-date prejudices to see America depicted as a land divided between a class of utterly ruthless rich exploiters and masses of sweet, charming, childishly innocent people who were the slaves of capitalism. But it was this same element that caused Steinbeck's work to be devalued in the American literary market as the Depression era receded in history, its pieties lost their urgency, and the country took on a different and far more complex character.

In 1960 Steinbeck came to realize that he had lost touch with his work as well as with the American experience, and he tried to recapture his relationship with both by undertaking the journey he described in *Travels with Charley*. But by that time in his life it was clearly too late. His once appealing vision had ossified into a theory of human life that life as he now encountered it did not validate. It seems a pity—and certainly it was a loss to literature—that he did not make his journey and discover this years before.
1979

The Final Novels of Algren and Farrell

During their lifetimes Nelson Algren and James T. Farrell were often discussed together as two very similar and clearly important novelists of the Depression, although neither was ever considered quite worthy of promotion to first-rank eminence. But they did in fact have a good deal in common besides their modesty of status. Both were committed social realists who at various stages of their careers were in and out of sympathy with the Marxist movement. Both spent most of their lives in Chicago and chose as the central subject of their fiction closely related and at times overlapping areas of urban proletarian experience. Farrell wrote his best novels—the Studs Lonigan and Danny O'Neill series—about the Chicago Irish working class in which he grew up and from which, like Danny, he ultimately managed to escape. Algren had far more flamboyant tastes and became a kind of Rabelaisian bard of the ghetto underworld of drug addicts, prostitutes, pimps, thieves, and con men.

Although both wrote a quantity of books—Farrell fifty-two and Algren almost a dozen—and continued to write into their last years, neither gained significantly in reputation after the success of his early work. Farrell in his prime had a higher standing with the critics and a much larger readership than Algren enjoyed. Yet he remained through most of his career best known for his first books, the Studs Lonigan trilogy, and eventually won a curious kind of respectful infamy for the sheer volume of his production, his seemingly heroic and quite thankless dedication to the task of creating ever so slight variations on essentially the same story in novel after novel after novel. Algren remained forever identified with his third and best novel, *The Man with the Golden Arm,* published in 1949 and made into a famous film. Both men died in their seventies, Farrell in 1979 and Algren in 1981, and their publishers have now brought out their final novels.

It would be pleasant to be able to say that these books bring to an appropriate and honorable conclusion the long and industrious careers of their authors. But that can truthfully be said of only one of them, Algren's *The Devil's Stocking,* which confirms one's impression that Algren was always and remained to the end the better writer. He had far richer verbal gifts than Farrell ever possessed, and he had a much more vital relation with his materials as well as a larger and freer range of imaginative inventiveness. It might even be said, however unkindly, that Farrell really should have stopped writing fiction long ago, for while *The Devil's Stocking* is clearly vintage Algren, *Sam Holman* is just as clearly senile Farrell, a product of played out energies, decrepit ideas, and an evidently compulsive desire to perform the act of writing for its own sake long after there existed anything authentic to be said.

Algren, on the other hand, shows evidence not of having aged but of having matured to the point where he seems as never before to be in firm possession of his subject. His language throughout the novel is precise, controlled, almost entirely free of the lush lyrical excesses of the past, but nonetheless genuinely warm and alive. The story he has to tell, furthermore, is recognizable as belonging in the classic Algren repertoire, is freshly conceived, and is carried forward with the kind of easy assurance that makes one feel that if he had lived, Algren had it in him to write five or six more novels in the same vein.

This one is based on the true-life story of one Rubin "Hurricane" Carter, a small-time middleweight boxer who was tried and imprisoned for murder in what Algren believed to have been a serious miscarriage of justice. But the book is not a true-life novel, at least not in the sense that Norman Mailer used the term to describe what he tried to do in *The Executioner's Song.* For Algren has managed with remarkable success to transform the principal figures of the Carter case into fictive characters with lives that no longer conform to actuality but are freed to serve Algren's imaginative vision of their human and dramatic possibility. Most of the familiar jungle types in his low-life menagerie are present once again—the call girls, petty crooks, gamblers, and sadistic police officers. But the character of Carter himself, who was evidently a man of limited mind and spirit, has been transmogrified into Ruby Calhoun, a protagonist who grows in complexity as the action proceeds until he becomes a fully realized multidimensional tragic person in a narrative that has all the vital signs of having been produced by a writer still fully confident of his inventive powers.

Sam Holman is, by sad contrast, a dull, dead novel, embarrassing in its banality and ponderously earnest in its emptiness. It contains all the faults for which Farrell has always been famous, but here they are unredeemed by the presence of his former virtues. From the beginning Farrell was a peculiarly graceless and tone-deaf writer whose prose often appeared to have been laid on the page with a dump truck and shovel. Yet in the best of his early work one sensed a current of evangelical rage that seemed to be given special authenticity just because it was expressed with such bludgeoning artlessness. Farrell evidently believed that it would be a breach of integrity—if not a task well beyond his powers—to write elegant prose about conditions that he knew to be ugly, and that he was determined to expose as ugly in order to shock the privileged world into doing something about them. In short, his very crudity of style could be interpreted as the measure of his high moral principle, his steadfast refusal to compromise with the bitter truth as he saw it. But over the years the anger died out in Farrell while the compulsion to go on writing continued to drive him. The result is that the features of his work that formerly seemed justified by the anger and were, indeed, appropriate instruments of it became blatantly visible as the serious shortcomings they were.

Sam Holman is glutted with the prose detritus of a perception of life in which feeling and judgment have atrophied. Hence, it is a perception that can be communicated only through dimly remembered and quite stale narrative formulas and utterly lifeless portraits of completely uninteresting people. The problem is deepened by the fact that the story Farrell has chosen to tell is far removed from the only social milieu he seems ever to have found wholly real. He is concerned here not with the materials that formed his most vital subject—the physical and spiritual impoverishment of the blue-collar class—but rather with a small group of minor leftist intellectuals who live and work in New York and lead comfortable colorless lives. Such problems as they have are mostly personal and ideological and trivial. There is nothing about them to arouse indignation or to crusade against, unless it is their consummate vapidity. Farrell is therefore left with no recourse other than to document that vapidity in the most minute detail, but without once indicating that he recognizes it as vapidity. As always, his tone is deadly serious throughout.

The novel has no focus and no discernible theme because there is no coherent authorial attitude behind it. Farrell might be saying, and one fervently wishes he were saying, how naive and childishly idealistic was the involvement of many thirties intellectuals with Communism. He might be but clearly is not offering his protagonist, Sam Holman, as a fine example of the confused and feckless Depression radical who has neither emotional depth nor ideological understanding. But Farrell takes no stand either for or against Holman, preferring instead to go on documenting the barren details of his unilluminated existence.

In a narrative composed mostly of yards and yards of the crassest dialogue we are given an account of Holman oscillating between hollow affairs with various women and equally hollow efforts to make himself into a bona fide card-carrying Communist. Both activities are utterly unreal, and they are supplied with the exactly appropriate accompaniment in the long passages of dialogue, many of which cannot be distinguished from one of those Donald Barthelme satires on the trivialization of modern life, except for the fact that Farrell intends no satire. Here is a representative sample:

> "I like Turgenev," Nobel began, "but of course you can't think of him as you would of the two giants, Dostoyevsky and Tolstoy."
> "I'm not so sure of that," Thomas Lawrence said.
> "Turgenev's form is perfect," Frances Dunsky added.
> And so is yours, my dear, Sam thought.
> "Wasn't Turgenev a friend of Flaubert's?" asked Rita.
> "Yes, they were good friends," Thomas Lawrence told her.
> "And good writers," Rita Moeller added.
> "No, Rita. They were great writers," Frances corrected.
> "Yes, of course."
> Rita knew they were great writers. Why had she said they were good writers? She knew the difference. God, they were all so clever. Did they know it was just a slip of the tongue or would they think she didn't know? She turned toward Nobel. He smiled at her.

This is a dreadful final work by a writer who was once important and who produced some of the most moving fiction we possess about the tragedy of the displaced and defeated in American society. But in his later years Farrell evidently lost, along with his anger, his imaginative connection with that tragedy, and he never regained the talent that was born of the connection. Regrettably, this did not keep him from his work.

1983

James Gould Cozzens
By Writing Possessed

Between 1931 and the early 1960s James Gould Cozzens enjoyed a degree of popular success remarkable for a novelist whose work was intellectually demanding and who made not the slightest concession to public taste. Four of his books became in that time best-sellers. His *Guard of Honor* won him the Pulitzer Prize in 1948 and was widely regarded—even in competition with *The Naked and the Dead*—as the most important novel to come out of World War II. *By Love Possessed,* published in 1957, stayed on the *New York Times* best-seller list for thirty-four weeks, received prominent notices in virtually every major and minor review publication in the country, became the number one paperback best-seller, and in 1961 was made into a popular film.

During the same period Cozzens was held in the highest esteem by such middlebrow critics as Bernard DeVoto, Orville Prescott, and J. Donald Adams, who for years exerted an influence that today seems incredible as moral monitors of the American literary conscience. To them Cozzens belonged to a species of writer fast becoming extinct, the novelist of manners who was also a moralist and so could be counted on to help rescue our fiction from that sordid preoccupation with the unpleasant that dominated the work of so many of Cozzens's contemporaries. Cozzens viewed American society as a broad and complex spectrum of class, power, wealth, and privilege that he clearly accepted as the natural order of things. His characters, furthermore, were not expatriates or decadent aesthetes but decent people trying to cope responsibly with life even as they recognized that they were fighting a losing battle in a time when the values of self-discipline and devotion to duty were fast becoming outmoded.

These critics saw Cozzens as the great novelist of the American upper-class establishment, a most welcome antidote to the often disturbingly morbid offerings of Hemingway, Fitzgerald, and Faulkner. It is, therefore, not surprising that their enthusiastic support, buttressed by the wide distribution provided by the Book-of-the-Month Club, helped to give Cozzens a popularity with the middlebrow reading audience that very few novelists of his quality have since been privileged to have.

Yet in the years since his death in 1978, Cozzens has been all but forgotten by that audience while his former critical supporters have mostly passed from the scene, leaving very few descendants. In fact, Cozzens now seems to have come to rest in that limbo to which writers are consigned when their work has somehow ceased to speak significantly to the times and where they await the moment when, with luck, the shifts of history may cause them to be rediscovered. There is of course nothing especially remarkable about this. It happened to Melville and Henry James, and it happened again, somewhat less drastically, to Hemingway and Fitzgerald. But what is different about Cozzens's case is the suspicion, still widely shared in the literary world, that he was the victim of something more insidious than the usual posthumous eclipse of reputation, that his abrupt descent into oblivion, which actually began almost twenty years *before* his death, was the result of calculated critical sabotage.

Shortly after *By Love Possessed* was published, some of the most influential liberal critics—among them Dwight MacDonald and Irving Howe—launched a brutal attack on Cozzens, in part because they found intolerable the densely convoluted prose style of that novel, but mainly because of the presence in it of certain social and political attitudes which they considered offensively reactionary. The MacDonald essay, in particular, became a famous document in the history of critical demolition, and it was largely responsible for making Cozzens infamous as a writer who should never again be taken seriously by liberal intellectuals.

Matthew J. Bruccoli belongs to an emergent group of academic critics who believe that Cozzens was unjustly treated and who would like to prepare the way for a more balanced view of his achievement. To that end Mr. Bruccoli has previously edited *A James Gould Cozzens Reader* as well as a collection of retrospective essays on the novelist, and he now offers the first full-length biography. In so doing, Mr. Bruccoli demonstrates his faith not only in Cozzens's artistic stature but in the idea that an account of his life and personality will ultimately serve the cause of justice. This unfortunately seems improbable, for in spite of Mr. Bruccoli's best intentions, the portrait of Cozzens that emerges seems more likely to confirm than to dispel the doubts about him that have blighted his reputation for so many years.

The sad truth is that Cozzens was an impossible subject for any biographer simply because he was the kind of writer—fairly rare in this country—to whom life was worth living almost solely because it gave him the opportunity to write. He did very little in his seventy-five years except write, and just about everything he did do was designed, whether deliberately or unconsciously, to protect and promote his writing function. The list of things he *did not* do in his life reads like a catalogue of heroically resisted temptations until one realizes that he had no interest in doing any of them. Mr. Bruccoli states the case flatly and a bit ruefully when he says that he has undertaken to write the biography of "a reclusive writer who for most of his life had no life apart from his work. . . . He didn't associate with other writers. He didn't grant interviews. He signed no manifestoes, attended no cocktail parties, made no speeches, joined no faculties, supported no causes, divorced no wives, courted no columnists, punched no reviewers, advised no presidents. He stayed home and wrote." Hence Mr. Bruccoli's subtitle, *A Life Apart.*

But the question naturally presents itself: what, then, did Cozzens do, what experiences went into the formation of a writer who became, after all, not a Joycean chronicler of the isolated consciousness but a possibly major realistic novelist of American social manners? Mr. Bruccoli's answer is brave but unsatisfactory—"It is instructive to learn how a talent was nurtured, but genius is single and singular." That may very well be, but it is a less than promising thesis on which to build a biography, particularly one intended to clarify the record of a man whose character and work are supposed to have been grossly misunderstood.

The fact is that because Cozzens's life was at least outwardly so uneventful, Mr. Bruccoli actually had very little information to work with, and what little he had does not make much of a case for the kind of major reassessment that he clearly hoped to bring about. We learn from him that Cozzens was early encouraged to become a writer by a doting mother who hoped to fulfill her own thwarted creative ambitions through her son. She also seems to have given him such an inflated sense of self-worth that for the rest of his life he tended to behave with an arrogant indifference to the feelings and opinions of others.

At Kent School he horrified the headmaster, the Reverend Frederick Sill, by proclaiming his loss of belief in God and then imperiously refusing to discuss the matter. At Harvard Cozzens regularly cut classes, became a drinking companion of the rich eccentric, Lucius Beebe, and squandered his mother's money on liquor and expensive clothes. He also wrote at Harvard a very bad apprentice novel, *Confusion*, which unfortunately was published and so confirmed him in poor writing habits that took him years to break. At the end of his sophomore year Cozzens left Harvard and never returned. He drifted for a time, wrote a second bad novel, *Michael Scarlett*, traveled in Cuba and Europe for two years, served briefly as librarian of the New York Athletic Club, and in 1927 he married, appropriately enough, his literary agent, Sylvia Bernice Baumgarten. Concerning his feelings at the time of his marriage, Cozzens later told a *Time* reporter that he supposed "sex entered into it. After all, what's a woman for?"

Except for a period of service in the Air Force during World War II, an experience that gave him the material for *Guard of Honor*, Cozzens spent almost all of his remaining fifty years living with his wife in rural seclusion. During that time they had virtually no social life, let decades pass between visits to the theatre, an art gallery, or a concert. All Cozzens wanted to do was write, and his wife not only gave him financial support but encouraged him in his reclusiveness because she believed that that was the way writers should live.

It was this extreme isolation that helped create the popular image of Cozzens as a misanthrope. But he also gave it credence with such statements as "I'm a hermit and I have no friends"—the undisguised implication being that he needed none. Then there was the fact that he was, or said he was, indifferent to public and critical opinion of his work and profoundly contemptuous of the many readers who bought, yet obviously lacked the brains to comprehend, his best-sellers. But what troubled him most was that he could have written novels with sufficiently wide appeal to become best-sellers, and he dreaded the possibility that he might become so well known and respectable that he would eventually be awarded the Nobel Prize.

In view of all this, it is not surprising that Cozzens should have had the social and ethical convictions of a nineteenth-century Tory aristocrat. Although he saw himself as apolitical, he believed that liberalism was sentimental and the ideal of social reform childishly utopian. He recognized an elite class of the intelligent and privileged, had great respect for social hierarchies and traditions and of course none at all for modern egalitarianism. He once remarked of a liberal friend, "Oh, he's one of those fellows that want equality for Indians," and on the race issue in general he said, "I like anybody if he's a nice guy, but I've never met many Negroes who were nice guys."

Cozzens was himself obviously not a nice guy, and the realization that he was not—based in large part on statements he made in a 1957 *Time* interview—did more, according to Bruccoli, to provoke the hostility of the liberal critics than any explicitly reactionary views they may have found expressed in his work. In fact, what seems remarkable, considering how opinionated Cozzens was, is the absence in his novels of overt doctrinal emphasis, of any perceptible effort to direct the reader toward a specific attitude or emotional response to his materials.

His stance is always aloofly objective and cerebral, even at times quite coldly without compassion, resulting perhaps from his fastidious distaste for sentiment and a fear of the emotional messiness that passionate possession can create. But the conflict between the ethics of duty and the obligations imposed by intense feeling stands at the very center of his thematic interest. And in novel after novel the victory, however muted and ironical it may be, goes to those who, guided by reason, perceive that life is difficult and may offer no satisfactory way of resolving such a conflict, but they must, nevertheless, survive with as much courage and dignity as they can muster. As Colonel Ross says in *Guard of Honor:* "A man must stand up and do the best he can with what there is. If the thing he labored to uncover now seemed in danger of stultifying him, could a rational being find nothing to do? If mind failed you, seeing no pattern; and heart failed you, seeing no point, the stout, stubborn will must be up and doing. A pattern should be found; a point should be imposed."

This may be far too Spartan a view to provide anyone with very much comfort, and there is a real question whether the American reading public—however middle-aged and conservative it may be growing—will ever again find such a view as acceptable as it undoubtedly was back in the time when many people could still believe that America won the war through the vigorous application of "stout, stubborn will." Yet if the Cozzens revival that Mr. Bruccoli and others wish to bring about does eventually occur, one suspects that it will result not from new enthusiasm for Cozzens's conservative ideas or his character but from a belated discovery that he articulated some important truths about the human condition that finally transcend ideology.

Cozzens may, as C. P. Snow once said, have lacked "the flame, the passionate impulse, which all very great novelists have possessed. . . . Yet . . . the value (of his novels) rests in his level, informed, investigatory, trustworthy reports on what individual men look like, say, do

and think." It may be that a future recognition of these and other more profound qualities in Cozzens will serve to revive and sustain his reputation long after the political quarrels that damaged it have been forgotten.
1983

Robert Penn Warren's Legend of the South

*M*eet Me in the Green Glen seems certain to be recognized as one of the most distinguished novels Robert Penn Warren has written since *All the King's Men*. It is far more tightly structured than its immediate predecessors, *Wilderness* and *Flood;* the rhetorical fattiness that has always been characteristic of Warren's fiction has been replaced by a hard texture of language very like his poetry. Yet the book is complex enough to sustain the illusion that there are several kinds of narrative form through which the action is simultaneously developed, each providing a view of the action both complete in itself and indispensable to the completion of the whole. As is the case with most of Warren's novels, the central dramatic situation is a murder mystery. But the book can also be seen as a romantic parable existing with perfect rightness on the levels of melodrama and moral philosophy; a love story that, contrary to current fashion, is finally neither sentimental nor narcissistic; a prose poem remarkable for its lyric intensity; a southern novel in which the characters are both realistically depicted cultural types and personifications of forces so violent and destructive that they seem almost more Elizabethan than contemporary.

The literary qualities of the book are considerable enough to assure it an important place among the serious novels of the last several years. But of perhaps equal interest to admirers of Warren is the fact that he offers here a distillation of themes and materials that have preoccupied him throughout his career but have never before been made visible in quite this concentrated a form. As a result, this novel may help to clarify Warren's position at a time when, in spite of his years of sustained achievement, the size of his critical reputation, and his wide popularity with the reading public, he still projects a rather anomalous image, is still somehow more admired as a writer than accepted as a shaper of consciousness.

Since 1939, in addition to his many books of nonfiction and poetry, Warren has published eight novels, nearly all of them vital and original works that have been respectfully received and, in some cases, commercially very successful. Yet only one, *All the King's Men,* can be said to have made a real impact on the imagination of our time, and it is the only one that has appealed equally to literary intellectuals and to the general public. A possible explanation is that *All the King's Men* is the sole instance in Warren's fiction when he has dealt with contemporary life in terms that were familiar and fashionable to both classes of readers. Although in its setting and many of its central materials the book was specifically southern, it was as a whole less regional than generally American.

It also dramatized the dilemma of the narrator-protagonist, Jack Burden, within a philosophical framework that, on the face of it, seemed modishly existential—the tough-talking young cynic confronting the meaninglessness of his life, the empty relativism of his moral attitudes, at a moment when he is forced to define his responsibility for a series of tragedies that overtake almost all the people he has admired and loved. Jack Burden was the quintessential antihero of the Age of Anxiety, a textbook case of contemporary alienation with whom intellectuals could easily identify. The popular audience, on the other hand, undoubtedly responded almost altogether to the thriller aspects of the novel, and as usual their instincts for separating the glitter from the gold were infallible. There were murders and suicides by the dozen, just enough sex to titillate without really arousing, and the whole story was beautifully cast in the Hollywood mold. Not only were most of the characters stock movie types, but the seemingly effortless and quite successful translation of the novel into film made it clear that the meretricious values of that medium were highly compatible with certain, but by no means all of the values implicit in Warren's materials.

His other novels have, for the most part, lacked these qualities of box office theatrics combined with high philosophical chic, and they have suffered from the additional difficulty that they depend for their significance much more directly upon the southern experience. This in itself would scarcely seem crippling when one considers that for a great many people the southern experience is no less valid and real—and may even be considerably more dramatically complex—than the experience of New York or the Midwest, that it has enjoyed for a good many years the distinction of being a chief source of literary materials for the American novel, and that Warren's treatment of the South is imaginative enough to endow it with a dynamic life and a generality of meaning far larger than that of a merely regional subject matter. But two factors have operated to cause the southernness of his novels to be construed as a limitation. The first is that during the period of Warren's greatest productivity as a novelist, Faulkner had already established himself so securely as the official literary imagination of the South that it soon became almost impossible to think of the South except as a mythical Yoknapatawpha County or to believe that any other writer could possibly have anything new or important to say about it.

Also, over the same period, as a result partly of Faulkner's apparent exhaustion of the southern material and partly of a radical shift of cultural interests, we began to take it for granted that the really central experience of our time is that of the northern urban intellectual, of characters like Augie March, Herzog, and Portnoy, who personify the experience not of the Wasp intellectuals of the thirties and forties—many of whom, significantly, have been both native southerners and Faulkner's and Warren's most vigorous supporters—but of the New York literary establishment. Since urban intellectuals are now the principal shapers of literary opinion in this country, it is only natural that they would promote into celebrity such writers as Bellow, Mailer, and Roth with whom they can identify most closely, and that Warren, writing out of a background they find alien, would seem to them a peripheral and rather parochial figure. This attitude is itself of course extremely parochial, but because it is also extremely influential, it has created the impression that only certain forms of American experience are suitable for literature, only certain writers are qualified to tell the real truth about American life.

Yet the problem is not merely that one kind of regional experience has been accepted as more authoritative than another kind. It is also that, perhaps as a result of this development, we have grown accustomed to a particular metaphysical approach to experience in fiction. We now seem to believe that the only really tenable view for the novelist is the nihilistic view in which events without meaning are seen to occur in a world without standards, and neither author nor characters presume to suggest what standards there may once have been or ought to be. The fictional situation we tend to find most artistically serious and relevant to life is one involving the continuous search for identity among people who have no realization of either the presence of the past or the possibility of the future, and so exist in a state of paralysis or dreary preoccupation with the merely sensational, with violence enacted without motive, sex enacted without passion or love—hence, from which all human meaning has disappeared. The fictional characters who speak to us most convincingly are usually those who become deranged by the anarchy of life to the point where they perhaps retreat, like Portnoy, into compulsive masturbation or, like Augie March, seek in the provisional structures of belief fabricated by others some means of understanding and controlling the anarchy in themselves. The experience depicted in our most respected novels again and again poses the problem described so well by Gide's Michel in *The Immoralist:* "To know how to free oneself is nothing; the arduous thing is to know what to do with one's freedom."

As his novels make clear and *All the King's Men* demonstrates in perhaps too programmatic a form, Warren is fully aware of this problem in its connection with contemporary nihilism. But he differs from most of our novelists in realizing that the question of what to do with one's freedom is unanswerable unless and until we define the limits of our freedom in the beginnings of our responsibility. This is to suggest that Warren brings a morally conservative—albeit politically liberal—vision to the problem of nihilism and reveals a clear understanding of just how men should behave, how they may find, or search for and never find, their salvation through self-knowledge, what standards should be used to measure our fall from standards, in exactly what way we should relate to our history and confront what he calls "the awful responsibility of Time."

If such a view is unfashionable at the present time, it probably is so because the urban liberal mind is unfamiliar with, or finds politically reprehensible, the premises on which it is based. Yet in a nihilistic and dehumanized society there is a massive, if seldom articulated, need of the kind confessed to by Nick Carraway in *The Great Gatsby* for "the world to be in uniform and at a sort of moral attention forever," and Warren gives concrete dramatic expression to this need. For him no contradiction exists between liberal politics and moral conservatism. Both are implicit in his broadly humanistic philosophy, and both are inextricably joined to his subject matter, which is always derived from the southern experience. It is most unlikely that he would be able to dramatize the philosophy without the subject matter, for the South is uniquely a region in which the issues that most profoundly engage his imagination have a living and dynamic basis in social fact.

Warren once wrote that in Faulkner's view "the old order (of the South) . . . allowed the traditional man to define himself as human by setting up codes, concepts of virtue, obligations, and by accepting the risks of his humanity. Within the traditional order was a notion of truth, even if man in the flow of things did not succeed in realizing that truth." The same view might, with minor alterations, be attributed to Warren himself. For him as for Faulkner, the literary value of the South is that it provides cultural and mythic structures against which, since they rest upon an idealistic "notion of truth," human character and conduct can be morally—therefore, dramatically—evaluated amid conditions that are the exact opposite of those prevailing in the urban North. In fact, one of the central themes of the southern novel is the conflict between an established humanistic tradition, with its inherited "concepts of virtue," and the forces of materialism, relativism, and opportunism that typify the modern South and the modern world. This is the sort of conflict that is exemplified in Faulkner by the opposition between his Compson-Sartoris and Sutpen-Snopes families. Historically, if not at the present time, the South has existed, or sought to exist, as the metaphysical antithesis of scientific rationalism. Warren has spoken of the tendency of science to create a division between intellect and emotion, between head and heart knowledge, which he calls "the terrible division of the age." Jack Burden's problem is that he cannot reconcile the teachings of his head and heart. By temperament he is a romantic and an idealist. He wants to love, have faith in and give his assent to life. But his cynical intelligence causes him to see people as stereotypes—The Boss, The Brass Bound Idealist, The Scholarly Attorney—and the process of existence as simply biological function, "the dark heave of the blood," "The Great Twitch." This divided view results in his nearly fatal separation from those he loves and from himself. It is only through discovering and affirming his identity with the past and accepting his responsibility for having helped to shape it that he can bring together the disparate sides of his nature.

The southern mind has traditionally aspired to this kind of autonomy and relationship, this state of being harmonious with nature, history, and the flow of life, and it has attempted to exist by concepts of fidelity and responsibility intended to preserve both individual and communal order. The cavalier code of manly honor and feminine virtue is one such concept. It is an aspiration to ideality at the same time that the forces at work against it in southern society have always been of the strongest potential violence, self-destructiveness, and racial and sexual guilt. Unlike New England and the Midwest, where a long puritan history has led to the repression of so much of the demonic in human nature, the South has existed in a state of constant dialectical tension between a romantic urge for absolute purity and the most sensuous appetite for corruption. Hence, it provides a moral situation in which the issues of guilt and responsibility can be concretely dramatized because both the decorums of virtue and the potential for their violent overthrow are concretely present in the social scene.

In addition, the South has provided and continues in many areas to provide factual verification for the idea that past and present are closely interrelated, that there is an observable connection between past actions and present conditions. It is still quite common in the South for people to be born and spend their whole lives in the same community, to know the histories of their own and one another's families in intimate detail, and to live every day with the results of the deeds and misdeeds of their ancestors. Thus, experience confirms the truth of Warren's belief that "the world is like an enormous spider web," and, as Amantha Starr says in *Band of Angels,* "You live through time, that little piece of time . . . is yours, but that piece of time is not only your own life, it is the summing-up of all the other lives. . . . It is, in other words, History, and what you are is an expression of History, and you do not live your life, but somehow your life lives you, and you are, therefore, only what History does to you."

The need to confront one's true nature within history, to live by an ideal of responsibility while learning to accept the facts of human existence, both past and present—these are ideas that can be used in fiction only when the writer has available social materials that embody them. As the examples of both Warren and Faulkner make clear, the materials of the southern experience do embody them in great abundance. Hence, it is not surprising that their novels represent the most vital alternative we have to the urban novel of anarchy. Warren's southern contemporary Allen Tate once observed that

> in ages which suffer the decay of manners, religion, morals, codes, our indestructible vitality demands expression in violence and chaos. . . . Men who have lost both the higher myth of religion and the lower myth of historical dramatization have lost the forms of human action. . . . They capitulate from their human role to a series of pragmatic conquests which, taken alone, are true only in some other world than that inhabited by men.

That other world is the one most commonly reflected in the novels of our time.

"A man that is born," said Joseph Conrad, "falls into a dream," and he may remain in a dream for the rest of his life unless some physical or psychic accident, some signal of destiny, forces him awake. The knowledge that he is in fact alive may come with overwhelming force and be destructive. But an acceptance of that knowledge is the only chance he has to confront himself and recognize his fate. For as Warren believes—and the idea is very Conradian—"The end of man is to know." Jack Burden's awakening to life occurs when he hears his mother's scream of anguish over the suicide of Judge Irwin, his real father, and discovers in that scream not only the identity of his father but a mother he can for the first time honor and love.

Nearly all the characters in *Meet Me in the Green Glen* have fallen into a dream, find life unreal and themselves unreal in life, and there are those who exist permanently in the dream state. Others are awakened, some brutally, some with a great and exhilarating sense of liberation, but each is changed and given significance by the manner of his awakening and the truth or lie he awakens to. The catalyzing agent for them all is a young Sicilian, Angelo Passetto, who comes out of nowhere down a road one day in the Tennessee hill country, enters by chance the life of a woman named Cassie Spottwood, who can never be quite sure he is real but who falls in love with him and, like Faulkner's Joanna Burden after becoming the lover of Joe Christmas, is awakened into sexuality and self-recognition. Angelo, however, remains locked in his narcissistic dream. Cassie is unreal to him. He sleepwalks through her life, taking from her, even in his way loving her, but is untransformed. Finally, he leaves her, and she, understanding his need, helps him to leave. Then, understanding for the first time her own need, she murders her husband who has been paralysed and in a coma for many years. Angelo is inevitably accused of the crime and although he is convicted, Cassie rises in the courtroom and proclaims her guilt. But she is taken in charge by her husband's old friend Murray Guilfort, who manages to convince the authorities that she is insane.

The novel is really about Guilfort, the familiar figure in Warren of the man who has never found release from the prison of himself and so has lived his whole life in envy and fear of those who, like Cassie's husband, are or once were in vital possession of themselves and their freedom. His recognition of his failure compels him in the end to suicide but not before he realizes that "*the dream [of life] is a lie, but the dreaming is truth*—not knowing what it meant, but thinking that, if so many people moved across the world as though they knew what it meant, it must mean something."

Taken in terms of the events themselves, nothing could conceivably be more melodramatic and sentimental. Cassie's last-minute courtroom confession is pure Perry Mason, and the story of her affair with Angelo, his conviction for a murder she committed, and the closing image of her huddled semiconscious against the stone wall of the prison after he is electrocuted—all might have come straight from the tear-stained pages of a nineteenth-century ladies' magazine. Yet Warren contrives by some magic to make these bathetic materials not only acceptable but entirely convincing. The melodrama is given appropriateness by the fact that the characters belong to a pastoral milieu in which emotions are felt with an almost aboriginal nakedness and intensity, and as Warren has repeatedly demonstrated in his novels, it is in the extremities of violence and passion that the moral issues of human conduct may be more sharply defined. But he is also vindicated by his choice of form, the parabolic romance, in which the characters are meant to be less true to life than crystallizations of elemental and extravagant attitudes.

In this respect the novel is, as I have said, a remarkably pure poetic distillation of Warren's typical themes and materials. As such, it possesses a coherence at the levels of idea and action that makes it impossible to separate one from the other. There is no conflict here between head and heart knowledge, between philosophical truth and feeling. Warren, if not his characters, has been able to transcend "the terrible division of the age" and to achieve an autonomy that is at once metaphysical and aesthetic. He has done so undoubtedly because he is committed to a holistic vision of human experience and to a kind of literary material peculiarly suited to its dramatic expression. There is reassurance at just this time in seeing him affirm with continued power his belief that a possibility exists for us beyond the prevailing anarchy. But Warren finally offers no program for the rehabilitation of the moral environment. He is fully aware of the fact that life is a dialectical process and that, as he says, "in so far as [man] is to achieve redemption he must do so through an awareness of his condition that identifies him with the general human communion. . . . The victory is never won, the redemption must be continually re-earned." He might have added what his novels seem always to suggest: that the victory is not in the redemption, but in the process of earning and re-earning. That is the process that creates such meaning as we have in history.

1971

The Appalling Diaries of Evelyn Waugh

The infamous Evelyn Waugh diaries have finally been published here four years after excerpts from them were first made public in the London *Observer* and a year following their appearance in book form in England. American readers may well be amused or mystified by the very considerable furor that the *Observer* excerpts in particular provoked among people who felt that they or their friends had been badly maligned by Waugh. This far removed from the home area of impact his more cantankerous pronouncements seem mostly harmless or merely the expressions of passing pique, while he makes only cursory reference to American contemporaries whom he might have offended or whom we might be offended for. It is also probable that we have become used to hearing celebrities say outrageous things about one another and assume that slander is simply one of the more entertaining functions of being a celebrity. But the English, because of their stricter libel laws and the squeamishness common to the sort of exclusive, inbred social circles in which Waugh moved, are likely to remain fixated for some time to come on what they consider to be the unforgivably candid nature of his diaries.

This seems a pity, but it does underscore the American advantage. For to the extent that we are unable to be shocked by what Waugh had to say about the critic Cyril Connolly ("Cyril has an article in the *Sunday Times* that reeks of insanity") or Randolph Churchill ("He is simply a flabby bully who rejoices in blustering and shouting down anyone weaker than himself"), we may be in a better position to appreciate his diaries for the qualities other than the sensational that make them a wholly remarkable chronicle of the life and times of an extraordinary writer who was also a profoundly *human* being.

Unlike the journals kept by most writers including Hawthorne, James, and Gide, the Waugh diaries are not working notebooks. They contain no materials that represent a preliminary sounding of ideas or themes to be given final development later in his fiction (although a great deal of them in one way or another and often in considerably altered form becomes part of the substance of his novels) nor is there discussion of the problems of fictional craft that were so obsessive to James. Waugh seems to have been interested solely in keeping a record of his daily experiences and impressions—of public events and private scandals made public, people known and incessantly dined with, parties attended, his own frequently appalling behavior at them, and monstrous hangovers suffered the morning after. If his portraits of friends and enemies are often harsh, his self-portrait is absolutely uncompromising and presented in strict conformity to his own obnoxious dictum: "Never apologize. Never explain." There were, however, three periods of his life—the years of his scarcely distinguished undergraduate career at Oxford, his brief and very unhappy first marriage, and a nervous breakdown in his early fifties—when he either did not keep a diary or destroyed those he kept, presumably because the experiences of those times seemed to him too painful to preserve. But except for these omissions the record is continuous from the first entries dating from September 1911 when Waugh was seven ("The wind is blowing dreadfuly [sic] I am afraid that when I go up to Church I shall be blown away. I was not blown away after all"), right up to 1965, a year before his death.

The image that emerges from the record is of a man who was willful, proud, pugnacious, vastly temperamental, very confident, greatly gifted, often rude, often charming, a faithful husband, a grumpy but loving father, a complicated personality who had the simplicity to be altogether himself. At the same time he seems to have shared with more than a few of his fellow writers the defect of a certain emotional aloofness, even obtuseness, and his natural role was that of disgruntled observer with a vision unclouded by what he would have regarded as the vulgar sentiment of sympathy. He was by temperament conservative, by firm conviction an unmitigated snob, and because he was cursed with excellent taste, a savage critic of mediocrity, vapidity, and the generalized tackiness that he felt had overtaken the modern world following the collapse of all traditional standards of decency, excellence, honor, and grace. To the extent that he could be said to have had an overriding preoccupation it was with the tragicomic spectacle of order in a state of disintegration, an interest stemming undoubtedly from his very pronounced anarchistic streak. But as is so often the case, this was simply the coin's other side of a profound reverence for ceremony and coherence, which for him were finally achievable in ideal form only in the Catholic church. The tension within him between anarchy and a craving for order of course gave him his most important literary theme. His best novels tend to develop through a pattern in which an initial structure of great security and serenity gives way because of the irresponsibility or moral shallowness of the people charged with its preservation, leaving them at the end adrift in the limbo of those who do not even know that they have sinned, with only an indistinct perception of the gravity of their punishment. Waugh's gift was always for an absolutely cold-eyed satirical assessment of the human condition in its most dehumanized forms, and it was his immense good fortune to have access to a society that provided rich materials for the nourishment of that gift.

This was the society that flourished in England at a peak of fever and frivolity through the years following World War I until well after World War II when it broke down under the weight of income and inheritance taxes and as a result of excess and the collapse of the Empire. The part of it that Waugh came to know best was composed of what were then called the Bright Young People—a decidedly incongruous mixture of old friends from Oxford, men and women of fashion, rank, and fortune, writers and artists, actors and show girls, drunks, adventuresses, playboys, and assorted hangers-on. Unlike the literary salon life of Paris, which was held together by a serious dedication to art, the London haut monde seems to have been dedicated to practically nothing except travel, constant partying and boozing, gossip, sexual intrigue, clever conversation, and interior decoration. It perfectly embodied the Flaming Youth clichés created by the early novels of Waugh, Huxley, Hemingway, and Fitzgerald.

Yet what must seem remarkable and even enviable to us today is that with all its passion for trivia and chaos this society had a strong cohesiveness that made it not only secure in its excesses but ideally suited to the sort of novelist of manners Waugh was. It consisted of an intricate system of interlocking relationships connecting its seemingly disparate members with the better public schools and Oxford, the most exclusive London clubs, the great houses of the rich and titled, the traditions of distinguished families, and the national past. Everybody who belonged to it seems to have known everything about everybody else, or one had been to school with this person, or another's sister was married to the first cousin of that person, who was

Lord Vapid's nephew. During Waugh's service in the second war, when he quickly proved himself to be the most inept novelist-army officer since Fitzgerald, he was saved from disgrace by the fact that almost every unit he was assigned to (and he was constantly being *reassigned*) was either commanded or staffed by Oxford Old Boys who protected him.

Yet it was evident that the great aristocratic structure that made such support possible was in the process of disintegrating and would soon no longer be able to sustain the pretensions and the extravagance of those sheltered within it. The disparity between the character and conduct of the privileged and what one might expect from them because of their position was becoming ludicrously large, and for Waugh, enamored as he was of everything and everyone aristocratic, it was both tragic and masochistically gratifying. The ambiguity of his attitude formed the complex dialectic of his fiction and gave to the best of it a tone of gleeful apocalypse, bitter laughter at the graveside of a world.

1977

World War II and the American Novel

In 1951, when I published my first critical book, *After the Lost Generation,* a study of the younger post-World War II American novelists, the full impact of the war on our literature had only just begun to be felt, and a good many of the novels that dramatized it with the greatest power and subtlety were still to be written. This is to confess that, however precocious it undoubtedly was for a writer in his midtwenties, my book must now appear to have been premature.

If I had waited twenty years to write it, as some of my critics rather patronizingly suggested I ought to have done, I would have written an altogether different book—older, perhaps duller, but surely infused with the wisdom of a much broader historical perspective and, just as surely, less provocative. Not only has my style lost abrasiveness with the palliations of time, but over the decades my brash pioneering sortie into what was virgin territory in 1951 has been followed by a host of more sophisticated explorers who have thoroughly mapped the terrain and cleared it of hazards and mysteries. Such excellent commentators as Paul Fussell, Malcolm Cowley, Ihab Hassan, Marcus Klein, Joseph J. Waldmeir, Peter Aichinger, and the late Charles Fenton have made the study of modern war in its relation to literature as safe and respectable a subject for scholarship as any other analysis of historical influences in the arts.

But the war writers whose work I discussed in my book—and they included Norman Mailer, Irwin Shaw, John Horne Burns, Vance Bourjaily, Merle Miller, Gore Vidal, Alfred Hayes, and Robert Lowry—had had little critical attention by 1951 except in reviews of their individual novels. Most of them were young, unfamous, and had returned from the war, as I had done, with a need to try to understand what had happened to them and their contemporaries. Perhaps they were fueled by the ambition to write the one true book exposing to a stunned world the unspeakable injustices of the military establishment or, at least, giving an absolutely honest account of their war experiences. I know that if I had not come to have more interest in and, I supposed, talent for evaluating the literary works of my generation, I might have written a war novel myself. In fact, Gore Vidal—back in the days when he could be whimsical rather than splenetic in his responses to what I wrote about him—used to find pleasure in describing *After the Lost Generation* as my first *novel* containing characters with improbable names like Norman Mailer, Vance Bourjaily, and Gore Vidal.

In any case, the main point of my argument about these writers was that while some of them seemed unable to extricate themselves from the clichéd fictional situations and responses they had absorbed from the novels of World War I, they lacked the vital advantage that their predecessors shared, the opportunity—ghastly though it may have been—to encounter the horrors of modern warfare for the first time. Hence, the writers of World War II were denied access to the experience that formed the great subject of some of the best fiction as well as poetry produced by the earlier generation—the violent collapse of their romantic illusions about war after they confronted the unbelievably wasteful slaughter of troops in the largely stalemated fighting on the Western Front. I went on to suggest that perhaps because Hemingway, Dos Passos, and E. E. Cummings, along with Remarque in Germany and Wilfred Owen, Siegfried Sassoon, and Robert Graves in England, had completed the process for them, my contemporaries had no romantic illusions about the glories of war to lose and so entered the various services with their minds already made up that what lay ahead of them was an ugly, undoubtedly stupid, but nevertheless necessary business that needed to be concluded as quickly as possible.

This attitude of cynical acceptance made it impossible for them to produce novels and poems possessing the kind of tragic power that is generated by the betrayal of idealistic expectations and by the terrible disparity finally seen to exist between the inflated sentiments expressed in patriotic oratory and the realities that, as Hemingway discovered, rendered the language of such rhetoric obscene. They therefore wrote nothing comparable in revelatory force to *All Quiet on the Western Front* or so elegiacally poignant as *A Farewell to Arms* or conveying the effect of brutal disillusion that can be felt everywhere in the trench poems of Owen and Sassoon.

Yet the writers of World War II seem to have come through their less traumatic experiences with an understanding that the evils that had sabotaged the idealism of their predecessors were finally merely symptoms of disorders endemic to modern society as a whole, and that the moral issues raised by war were far subtler and more complex than the earlier generation had been able to comprehend. As a result, the novels they wrote were preoccupied not merely with the sufferings of the individual soldier in wartime but with problems of much wider scope such as the injustices inflicted by the mindless authoritarianism of the military system and the degradations of the civilian population in countries controlled by a corrupt Allied occupation force. Mailer in *The Naked and the Dead* and Shaw in *The Young Lions* explored the dilemma of the combat soldier as only Dos Passos and Remarque attempted to explore it before them. But what the earlier writers saw in terms of the wartime experiences of small groups of men, Mailer and Shaw saw in terms of entire armies and Western culture as a whole. Hayes, Lowry, Burns, and Bourjaily emphasized in their novels the ugly contrast between our professed liberating intentions in fighting the war and the immoral practices that cost us the trust and loyalty of those we had helped to liberate. For all these writers, the enemy was no longer anything so simple as an opposing army but had become a generalized malevolence of spirit, a sickness that was somehow implicit in all organizations and governments possessing absolute power. And with this perception they anticipated, even as they contributed to, one of the most important developments in the fiction of the next decades, a steadily growing obsessiveness with the idea that there exists some vast but unlocatable conspiratorial system that is diabolically engaged in manipulating the lives of all of us—an idea most often expressed through a vision of contemporary society as a warscape of seemingly arbitrary and purposeless devastation.

In *The Naked and the Dead,* the one novel of World War II that presents an explicitly conspiratorial theory of power politics, General Cummings tells his aide, Lieutenant Hearn, that postwar America will belong to the militant conservatives, of whom Hitler is the wartime symbol and prophet. The highest value men can achieve, according to Cummings, is not ethical or religious, as weak liberals like Hearn want to believe. It is rather to make men the instrument of policy, and to do this, one must control them by hate and fear. "I've been trying to impress upon you, Robert," says the General, "that the only morality of the future is a power morality, [and] you can consider the Army . . . as a preview of the future."

Here the projection onto the postwar era of the military "fear and hate" concept of authoritarian control is made to seem perfectly plausible through Cummings's coldly clinical exposition of it. And surely subsequent political developments such as the Communist witch-hunt of the fifties seem to have given it some brief validation. Yet it is significant that none of our novelists has tried to formulate a realistic vision of the kind of society that might result if such a concept were to become the working basis of government practice. We have so far had no American *1984* or *Brave New World.*

Instead, Joseph Heller in *Catch-22* reverses the prophetic process and projects backward onto the war the paranoid atmosphere of the witch-hunt years. The novel is infused with the deeply embedded but quite unverifiable suspicion that some central authority is in control of everything that occurs. But since the authority cannot be located and the rationale behind it understood, it seems to impose itself arbitrarily and finally, of course, it is subversive of the very appearances of rational order that presumably it seeks to engender. Heller's narrative method—even more deranging than Kafka's—develops on a principle of continuous self-refutation. Every assertion of fact is followed by a nullifying counterassertion of equally incontestible fact. One must be judged insane to be relieved of flying combat missions. But if one *asks* to be relieved, one is clearly making a sane request and so must fly them. "A concern for one's own safety in the face of dangers . . . was the process of a rational mind."

This fundamental concern is not merely the one clear measure of sanity but is also the sole source of coherence in a world where all attempts to create coherence result in meaningless provisional patternings based on the personal whim of those in command or the specious validation provided by personnel files and bureaucratic regulations. Colonel Scheisskopf, seeing his men as inanimate objects, wonders how they might be wired or nailed together to produce a perfect marching pattern. Milo Minderbinder creates a perfectly organized nightmare travesty of the free enterprise system, a massive syndicate involved in the sale of goods to both the Allies and the Axis Powers. For a fee Milo can arrange the bombing of his own men. Because he was entered in the logbook as being aboard a plane that crashed, Doc Daneeka is declared officially dead, even though he is obviously alive. Aarfy rapes an Italian maid and throws her out the window. When the military police arrive, they ignore the dead girl as well as Aarfy and arrest Yossarian because he is not carrying the proper identification papers. Then there is Nately's whore, a figure of completely random violence, who keeps leaping out at Yossarian and trying to murder him.

All the characters in the novel are cartoonographic. Yet they are made believable to the degree that they embody the cold logic of wartime insanity, and they serve to dramatize Heller's hatred of a system that could so easily become diabolical because it views people as things to be manipulated and destroyed for inane reasons or for no reason. This perception, radically generalized, forms the premise of Thomas Pynchon's extremely intricate novels. From the beginning of his career Pynchon has been obsessed with essentially one idea—that the universe, and by implication modern society, is in a state of slow disintegration because of an irreversible loss of energy through the process of entropy, as defined by the second and third laws of thermodynamics.

Against the threat of entropic dissolution, Pynchon raises certain provisional structures of coherence that promise to provide some means of understanding experiences that seem to occur—as they do in *Catch-22*—outside the stabilizing logic of cause and effect. One such structure is founded on the notion of worldwide, perhaps even cosmic, conspiracy—the existence again of a massive and mysterious system that is devoted to the secret manipulation of persons and events. According to Pynchon, humankind has been engaged in creating systems ever since the first men confronted the wilderness and found its apparent formlessness unbearable. The imposition of a concept of order, however specious or exploitative, became the psychic necessity of the race, just as paranoia, the belief in conspiracy, became its dominant psychic disease, one that has reached epidemic proportions in the modern age, particularly with the triumph of electronics technology during and after World War II. Pynchon, therefore, invests malevolent power in bureaucratic organizations that command vast wealth and technology and are directed by scientists and international cartel tycoons—power so invested being for him the prime force of evil in a period of history that has lost all other means of giving moral shape and direction to human existence.

The major characters of Pynchon's three novels—Herbert Stencil in *V.*, Oedipa Maas in *The Crying of Lot 49*, and Tyrone Slothrop in *Gravity's Rainbow*—are all obsessed with the idea of conspiracy and determined to expose the identities of those in control. Their effort to discern the lineaments of coherent plot, to decide whether everything is, in fact, connected with everything else, may or may not be an expression of their paranoia. But the effort provides them with perhaps their only substance as characters and prevents them from lapsing into randomness and antiparanoia (the fate of those for whom nothing seems to be connected with anything) and finally into a state of inertia, in which one becomes an inanimate object or a thing. The elusive V., whom both Stencil and his father endlessly pursue because they believe she is the key figure in a giant conspiracy linking World War I and II, becomes increasingly a creature of prosthetic attachments until by the end of the novel she is more metal and plastic than flesh.

Both John Hawkes and Kurt Vonnegut have been preoccupied with the same alternatives of paranoia and self-protective passivity as perhaps the only tenable modes of survival in an age dominated by what may be either gratuitous or sinisterly conspiratorial violence. Hawkes's first novel, *The Cannibal,* was also the first of the second war in which bomb-devastated Europe—in this case, Germany—is so treated that it becomes a warscape metaphor of twentieth-century existence, a nightmare wasteland of displaced and traumatized people for whom paranoia is the necessary condition of survival. Later, in *Second Skin,* Hawkes tells the story of Skipper, a naval officer recently demobilized after enduring brutal humiliation at the hands of his mutinous ship's crew. In an effort to escape the world of war, Skipper sets out with his daughter on a journey that takes him first to a barren Atlantic island. There he is confronted by seemingly unmotivated hostility from the inhabitants and is persecuted to the point where his daughter is driven to suicide. The novel is constructed between this island of black malevolence and a Pacific island of pastoral serenity to which Skipper flees. There he settles into a gently primitive existence among the natives and serves the populace as an artificial inseminator of cows. In so doing he has passed, in fantasy or in fact, from the war world of violence and death to its idyllic antithesis, a paradise in which the forces of war are neutralized through surrender to the tranquilizing harmonies of elemental life and reproduction.

In *Slaughterhouse-Five* Billy Pilgrim, like Vonnegut himself, survives the Allied fire-bombing of Dresden but suffers so much psychic damage that he is forced to make periodic excursions into fantasy. On one occasion he imagines that he is kidnapped and taken by spaceship to the planet Tralfamadore where he is placed on display before the inhabitants and is soon provided with an earthling companion, the porno-film star, Montana Wildhack, with whom, by the end of the novel, Billy has enthusiastically produced a child. From the Tralfamadorians he learns that all past and future events occurring in the universe exist in a kind of eternal present. Everything always *is,* and everything that happens *has* to happen because the moment is immutably structured that way. In accepting this philosophy Billy is able to put to rest the traumas induced by his war experiences and abandon himself to a serene and blissfully unthinking passivity.

More militant writers like Mailer and Jerzy Kosinski would find this solution wholly unacceptable. For Mailer, as for Hemingway, human existence is perpetual warfare and the violent confrontation of violence the ultimate test of manhood. *Why Are We in Vietnam?* is not only an account of adolescent initiation into manly courage but a parable in which the brutal shooting of animals from helicopters comes to represent the promiscuous slaughter of peasants in Vietnam and, by implication, the deep hostilities that torment the national spirit as a whole. In *An American Dream* Stephen Rojack is haunted by the memory of the German soldiers he killed during the second war, and on the battleground of Harlem he practices psychokinetic bombardment of his enemies with barrages of imaginary darts fired out of his massive hatred. Like so many of the novels of both wars, much of Mailer's fiction derives from *The Red Badge of Courage.* But in Kosinski's novels we move into an imaginative world deriving in part from much more recent and radical antecedents—Kafka, Céline, and possibly the Robbe-Grillet of *In the Labyrinth*—a world populated by enemies where the threat of violence is accepted as the prime condition of life but where, instead of becoming a victim or escaping into passivity, the beleaguered individual becomes the ruthless dispenser of retributive justice.

The experience of Kosinski's first protagonist, the young boy in *The Painted Bird,* established the emotional pattern of all his successors except Chance in *Being There.* They are all scarred and lone survivors whose responses of life have been frozen by the unbelievable horrors of the boy's persecution at the hands of brutish peasants during his years of wandering in Nazi-occupied Poland. Any one of them might have come out of Dachau or Auschwitz—and, indeed, that is the experience to which the boy's suffering is evidently meant to stand as metaphor. But unlike most such survivors they have been infected with a single demonic compulsion: to take revenge upon the human race by inflicting punishment even more gratuitous and terrible than any suffered by the boy.

Since he operates alone, entirely without accomplices, the typical Kosinski protagonist—as he appears in *Steps, The Devil Tree, Blind Date,* and *Cockpit*—must rely on subterfuge and technology to aid him in his deadly work, and he has trained himself to become expert in the use of a wide array of mechanisms, all of which are cunningly designed to maim and destroy without revealing the identity of the destroyer. He will construct a lethal machine for any nefarious purpose, plant a bomb to be electronically detonated on a crowded Alpine cable car, arrange for an uncooperative girlfriend to be exposed to a fatal dose of radiation from the radar system of a military jet, or—without the help of technology—he will have her gang raped by a group of diseased and filthy Bowery bums whom he has carefully recruited for the occasion.

The protagonist performs these actions quite mechanically, seemingly with little satisfaction, and totally without remorse. They appear to be ritual gestures or ceremonial sacrifices made in a social milieu so completely lacking in the public ingredients of ceremony that they seem to carry their own defiant justification—as if through the fact of violence done to others some lost principle of order or rationality were redeemed, as if gratuitous evil, no matter the degree of its horror, were infinitely preferable to the moral nullity in which it is made to occur. Kosinski in his fiction seems constantly to be trying to authenticate Eliot's observation that "so far as we are human, what we do must be either evil or good; so far as we do evil or good, we are human; and it is better, in a paradoxical way, to do evil than to do nothing: at least we exist. . . . The worst that can be said of most of our malefactors, from statesmen to thieves, is that they are not men enough to be damned."

Perhaps it is one of Kosinski's more exemplary intentions to try in his bizarre way to reconstitute the reality of evil and rediscover the terms of moral damnation. But his effort may be representative of the problem confronting so many of the postwar novelists, even as his approach to it through the imposition of demonic individual control may differ radically from theirs. Against their sense of a conspiratorial design operating behind so many bewildering contemporary events stands his realization that there may, in fact, be nothing and no one at all in charge, that Kafka's castle may actually be empty, that there is no crime for which anybody eternally stands condemned, no order behind organization, no system behind bureaucratic structure, no governing principle behind government, that what is happening is happening for no reason, and that there is absolutely nothing to be done about it because the causes responsible cannot be located and the very idea of responsibility may have lost all meaning.

The suspicion that this may indeed be the case is, of course, a central element of the modernist legacy in all the arts. For well over a century, particularly in literature, the question as to whether or not there exists a design beneath the appearance of randomness in human affairs has heavily preoccupied the modern artistic imagination. But the question has been inflated to the dimensions of paranoia by the massive dislocation of reality from sanity, the increasing unreality of events that are at once real and too terrible to seem real, caused in part by the two world wars, the Nazi holocaust, the nuclear devastation that brought the second war to an end, and the threat of wholesale annihilation that at least until recently has so profoundly tormented us.

Much of the serious fiction produced in this country through the fifties and sixties has been divided in its approach to the question and has reminded us that there may be a convincing argument for both possibilities. Our best writers have, therefore, expressed in their work emotions of the most extreme paranoia at the same time that they have tried to make sense of a reality that just may make no sense whatever except in their imaginative possession of it.

1982

James Jones's Men at War

At the time of his death in May of 1977 James Jones had completed all but the three closing chapters of *Whistle,* the third volume of the massive World War II trilogy that he began in 1951 with *From Here to Eternity* and continued with *The Thin Red Line* in 1962. His close friend, Willie Morris, has undertaken to put together, from notes on his conversations with Jones and the novelist's taped dictations, a fairly detailed synopsis of the unfinished chapters, and it is perhaps testimony to Morris's skill at synopsis or to Jones's deficiencies as a writer of recognizable style that one can scarcely tell when the original text ends and the synopsis begins.

Jones says in his "Author's Note" that he began to plan the three novels and to see them as a trilogy as early as 1947 when he was corresponding with his editor, Maxwell Perkins, about his progress on *From Here to Eternity.* But for reasons that now can only be regarded as lamentable, he did not begin work on *The Thin Red Line* until eleven years later, and after finishing it he failed to act on his intention to write the third volume immediately. As the somewhat askew focus of both novels indicates, the passage of all that time did nothing to improve his memory of the experiences on which his materials were based. But the worst consequence was that he devoted a good part of that time to the production of the two most disastrous novels of his career, *Go to the Widow Maker* and *The Merry Month of May,* works which proved beyond all doubt—if in fact the earlier *Some Came Running* had left any room for doubt—that when Jones tried to move beyond his primary subjects, army life and warfare, and deal with civilian society, he revealed not the slightest comprehension of how people who were not in uniform behaved. Deprived of the built-in dramatic tensions of the military world where everything conspired to violate one's virgin integrity or get one killed or wounded, his civilian characters were left to shuffle around in the peacetime malaise with nothing on their minds except sex, the one other activity besides soldiering which Jones found meaningful in human life and which so constantly preoccupied his soldiers that they were barely able to perform their professional functions of fighting wars, beating one another joyously bloody in the barracks, or getting themselves soused on beer down at the PX. Jones's civilians were actually only soldiers on permanent weekend pass. But removed from their natural habitat, they were exposed as products of an imaginative emptiness that could not be filled by even the most remarkable tumescence. All one learned from them was that over the years since he wrote *From Here to Eternity,* Jones's sexual fantasies had grown increasingly sophisticated and had evolved from straight male-female copulation to the quirkier titillations of lesbianism and female masturbation, while of course skirting with good red-blooded macho fastidiousness any hint of male homosexuality.

Military life provided Jones with a subject that exactly suited his energetic but narrow talent. Its dramatic features were obvious and did not need to be imagined, analyzed, or explained. They also did not depend upon elaborate motivation or character development. But perhaps the most compatible element for Jones in the army experience was that most of his perceptions of it were exactly on the level of the average, uneducated enlisted man. The limitation that handicapped him in writing about civilian life became a virtue when he wrote about soldiers. For whatever they said or thought, however bathetic or banal, rang with conviction because Jones believed just as they did. There is no discernible edge of irony anywhere in his portraits of them. When they work up the acuity, as Prewitt does in *From Here to Eternity,* to formulate such leaden insights as, "When you cut with life you had to use the house deck, not your own," one can be sure it is their maker speaking. Their profundity perfectly matches his, and so does their jock-strap philosophy of life.

Fighting is what real men do and in a perverse way enjoy doing, and women are the things they have sex with when they are not fighting. During intervals away from fighting if women happen to be unavailable, one can relax and have one's real emotional life with the good old boys in the platoon or company. Thoughts on the Big Questions of existence can be exchanged with them because they have all suffered through the same experiences and come to share the same values. They believe as one in personal integrity and manly independence, pride in service and the absolute importance of never letting a buddy down.

These values—defiantly upheld in *From Here to Eternity*—continue to be at least nominally operative in *Whistle*. But the debilitating and deranging effects of prolonged combat, which were dramatized with such violence in *The Thin Red Line,* have seriously weakened their power to govern the conduct of men who once saw them as sacred. In fact, what now becomes clear is that the developing theme of the trilogy as a whole is the gradual disintegration of the knightly code of the old peacetime army under the pressures of a kind of warfare requiring for survival a radically altered mode of existence. One cannot be sure that Jones recognized this as his conscious intention, but his instinctual responses to his material everywhere provide evidence for it, even as they testify to his profoundly darkened apprehension of the meaning of the war experience.

One also cannot be sure that Jones understood the implications of another statement he makes in his "Author's Note," but it has the greatest bearing on the problem he faced in trying to form the three novels into a coherently developed trilogy. He says that he had originally intended Prewitt to be the central figure in all three, but since for dramatic reasons Prewitt had to be killed at the end of *From Here to Eternity,* there was no way short of miraculous resurrection that this intention could be fulfilled. Jones felt obliged, therefore, to create in the second and third volumes a Prewitt-like character but called in each by a slightly different name, and to rename the other characters at the same time. Prewitt thus becomes Witt, then Prell; Sergeant Warden becomes Welsh, then Winch; and Mess Sergeant Stark becomes Storm, then Strange.

On the face of it, all this seems odd until one perceives that Jones's intuitions as a novelist were a great deal sounder than his thoughts on novelistic strategy. The fact was that he felt compelled to change their names because his characters, as they undergo the experiences described in *The Thin Red Line* and *Whistle,* are transformed into altogether different people. He might of course still have retained them, except for Prewitt, under their original names and shown this transformation gradually taking place within them, but that would have required a subtler psychological understanding and a better memory of his first conception of them than he possessed. Besides, he appears to have sensed that the old Prewitt, Warden, and Stark had been effectively destroyed, and that their later incarnations did not and could not resemble them because nothing in their past lives had prepared them for, or was relatable to, what had happened to them on Guadalcanal and New Georgia. At the expense of his plans for a coherent trilogy, Jones was therefore required to settle for three separate novels and three different sets of characters. But he did so, whether consciously or not, because he could not violate the logic of his materials or escape the consequences of his own fidelity to their implications. He could not avoid seeing that the war had outmoded the most fundamental moral premises on which his characters had initially been drawn.

In *From Here to Eternity* the issues were concrete and clear-cut, and it was possible for one man of sufficient courage to have a decisive effect upon them. The conflict was between the lone individual fighting to preserve his honor and freedom of choice and the forces of bureaucratic oppression bent on breaking his will. Prewitt refused to become a boxer for his regiment and so was persecuted outrageously; however, nothing that could be done to him weakened his determination to hold out for what he believed. But beginning with *The Thin Red Line* the individual disappears into the bureaucratic collective, and the issue becomes not honor but survival. In combat, questions of personal morality are shown to be meaningless. Courage and cowardice are wholly arbitrary responses dependent upon chance and physical circumstances, the vagaries of the existential moment. Men die in combat for no reason or for absurd reasons. They fight not to win the war or kill the enemy but to keep from being killed, and to achieve this they will commit absolutely any treachery or brutality.

In *Whistle* the enemy is everywhere. It is war itself, the military system, the nation, the world, modern life, the incurable barbarism of the human race. But the individual is powerless to oppose it or to survive in the face of it. The characters, all of whom are combat casualties in mind or body, no longer know what is expected of them or what to expect of themselves. Now that they have been sent back to the States and hospitalized, the communal connections that held them together in the field have grown tenuous, and even though they try hard to preserve them, they do so out of a sense of loyalty that becomes steadily more theoretical and sentimental.

Prell, descendant of the martyred Prewitt and the most severely wounded of the group, fights not to preserve his integrity but to keep the doctors from amputating his shattered leg, is awarded the Medal of Honor for his conduct on a patrol that may or may not have accomplished its mission or been worth the loss of lives, and then is sent on a Hollywood-style bond-selling tour, during which he is beaten to death in a barroom brawl. Sergeant Winch (Warden), through influential old buddies from the peacetime army, obtains a comfortable and important position as a personnel Warrant Officer and tries to use his considerable power to do what he can to protect the men who served with him. But his efforts have little effect because the men have ceased to trust him. As a delayed result of his combat experiences, Winch begins to lose his sanity, becomes obsessed with the noise of the jukeboxes in the post recreation hall, and at the end steals two hand grenades and blows them up. Sergeant Strange (Stark), after leaving the hospital, searches for an assignment that will have some meaning for him but comes to realize that he is lost in a world in which personal meaning and purpose seem to have been destroyed. Finally, he is assigned to an infantry division on its way to England to train for the Invasion. At night on the troopship he slips over the side and wonders as he floats in the water whether he will drown first or freeze.

The melodrama throughout is heavy-footed, the characterization simplistic, and Jones's prose has the defect that was chronic with him of seeming much of the time to have been dumped on the page by an emptier of wastebaskets. Yet in spite of these and other faults, *Whistle* is in its way an impressive and moving statement, and as the last novel we are to have from him, it effectively concludes Jones's assessment of the experience about which he wrote best. It also contains much to indicate that his understanding of that experience had evolved considerably beyond his first adolescent perception of it, as well as beyond the locker-room code of values by which he had formerly tried to measure its significance.

Jones may not be recognized as a literary artist of the first rank, but he was a powerful naturalistic chronicler of certain essential realities of warfare and the responses of men at war, and he had a gift for being absolutely honest about what he felt and thought, however awkwardly or gauchely he may have expressed it in his writing. This is a rarer gift among novelists than one might suppose, and on the evidence of this final novel it would seem to have been very much alive in him when he died.

1978

Catch-22
Twenty-Five Years Later

Looking back today, twenty-five years after it was published, we are able to see that *Catch-22* has had a remarkable, if not altogether unclouded literary history. It has passed from relatively modest initial success with readers and critics—many of whom liked the book for just the reasons that caused others to hate it—through massive bestsellerdom and early canonization as a youth-cult sacred text to its current status as a monumental artifact of contemporary American literature, almost as assured of longevity as the statues on Easter Island.

Yet it is only in fairly recent years that we have begun to learn how to read this curious book and, as is the case with those statues, to understand how and why it got here and became what it is instead of what we may have once believed it to be. The history of *Catch-22* is, in effect, also a significant chapter in the history of contemporary criticism, its steady growth in sophistication, its evolving archaeological intelligence, and above all, its realization that not only is the medium of fiction the message but that the medium *is* a fiction capable of sending a fair number of frequently discrete but interlocking messages, always depending of course on the complexity of the imagination behind it and the sensibility of the receiver.

The truth of this last is attested to in perhaps a meretricious sort of way by the large diversity of responses *Catch-22* received in the first year or two following its publication in 1961. They ranged from the idiotically uncomprehending at the lowest end of the evaluative scale to the prophetically perceptive at the highest, and in between there were the reservedly appreciative, the puzzled but enthusiastic, the ambivalent and obscurely annoyed, and more than a few that were rigid with moral outrage.

The most hysterically negative review was written by Roger H. Smith and appeared in the Winter 1963 issue of *Daedalus*. Mr. Smith seems to have felt personally insulted by the book and so alarmed by its potential threat to the fragile virginity of literature that he tried in every way he knew to annihilate it. In a fierce display of poorly articulated vituperation he denounced the book as being poorly articulated, utterly formless, pornographic, and immoral because so anti-institutional and so indiscriminate in its repudiation of just about everything right-thinking people have been brought up to believe in.

Way over at the other end of the combat zone were those who seemed to have read another book altogether and to inhabit a completely different ontological epoch. Most notable among these were Nelson Algren and Robert Brustein, the former of whom made what became perhaps the most famous pronouncement on a literary subject to be uttered since John O'Hara announced, on the front page of *The New York Times Book Review* back in 1950, that Hemingway was "the outstanding author since the death of Shakespeare." Algren, with far greater precision, called *Catch-22* "not merely the best American novel to come out of World War II; it is the best American novel to come out of anywhere in years."

Brustein, writing in the *New Republic*, was so superbly intelligent about the book that much of the later criticism has done little to improve on his essential argument. He saw at once, for example, that the Air Force setting in World War II is only the ostensible subject of the book and that Heller's achievement lies in his brilliant use of that setting as a metaphor or "a satirical microcosm for many of the macrocosmic idiocies" afflicting the postwar era in general. Brustein also saw and in seeing foresaw what later critics, after considerable equivocation, came to see: That the descent into phantasmagoric horror that occurs in the concluding chapters of the book is not a violation of the comic mode but a plausible vindication of it, since, as he put it, "The escape route of laughter [is] the only recourse from a malignant world."

Finally, following the same (at the time) pioneering logic, Brustein recognized that, given the premises that Heller had established, Yossarian's much-debated decision to desert, far from being a poorly justified conclusion for the novel, is in fact a meticulously prepared for conclusion that represents an act of "inverted heroism . . . one of those sublime expressions of anarchic individualism without which all natural ideals are pretty hollow anyway," if only because it is proof that Yossarian, alone of them all, has managed to remain morally alive and able to take responsibility for his life in a totally irresponsible world. With these insights Brustein clearly demonstrated prophetic power, and every critic who has since written about *Catch-22* is indebted to him for engaging so early and with so much perceptiveness questions about the novel that have proven much later to be the essential questions.

If responses as sensitive and boldly appreciative as Brustein's were a rarity in 1961, one reason may be that most reviewers were locked into a conventional and, as shortly became evident, an outmoded assumption about what war fiction should be. They had, after all, been conditioned by the important novels of World War I and reconditioned by the second war novels of Norman Mailer, Irwin Shaw, John Horne Burns, James Jones, and others to expect that the authentic technique for treating war experience is harshly documentary realism. The exceptions, of course, were the sweetly hygienic productions of Marion Hargrove and Thomas Heggen that were comic in an entirely innocuous way and depicted military life—mostly well behind the combat zone—as being carried on with all the prankish exuberance of a fraternity house beer party.

Coming into this context *Catch-22* clearly seemed anomalous and more than a trifle ominous. It was a work of consummate zaniness populated by squadrons of madly eccentric, cartoonographic characters whose antics were far loonier than anything ever seen before in war fiction—or, for that matter, in any fiction. Yet the final effect of the book was neither exhilarating nor palliative. This was a new kind of comedy, one that disturbed and subverted before it delighted and that was ultimately as deadly in earnest, as savagely bleak and ugly, as the most dissident war fiction of Remarque or Dos Passos or Mailer. In fact, many readers must have sensed that beneath the comic surfaces Heller was saying something outrageous, unforgivably outrageous, not just about the idiocy of war but about our whole way of life and the system of false values on which it is based. The horror he exposed was not confined to the battlefield or the bombing mission but permeated the entire labyrinthine structure of establishment power. It found expression in the most completely inhumane exploitation of the individual for trivial, self-serving ends and the most extreme indifference to the official objectives that supposedly justified the use of power.

It was undoubtedly this recognition that the book was something far broader in scope than a mere indictment of war—a recognition perhaps arrived at only subconsciously by most readers in 1961—that gave it such pertinence to readers who discovered it over the next decade. For with the seemingly eternal and mindless escalation of the war in Vietnam, history had at last caught up with the book and caused it to be more and more widely recognized as a deadly accurate metaphorical portrait of the nightmarish conditions in which the country appeared to be engulfed.

Ironically enough, in the same year that *Catch-22* came out, Philip Roth published in *Commentary* his famous essay, "Writing American Fiction," in which he expressed his personal feelings of bafflement and frustration when confronted with the grotesque improbability of most of the events of contemporary life. In a frequently quoted paragraph he said that "the American writer in the middle of the 20th Century has his hands full in trying to understand, and then describe, and then make *credible* much of the American reality. It stupifies, it sickens, it infuriates, and finally it is even a kind of embarrassment to one's meager imagination. The actuality is continually outdoing our talents."

Roth then proceeded to discuss the work of certain of his contemporaries—most notably, Norman Mailer, J. D. Salinger, Bernard Malamud, William Styron, and Herbert Gold—and to find in much of it evidence of a failure to engage the American reality—an inevitable failure, he believed, because "what will be the [writer's] subject? His landscape? It is the tug of reality, its mystery and magnetism, that leads one into the writing of fiction—what then when one is not mystified but stupefied? Not drawn but repelled? It would seem that what we might get would be a high proportion of historical novels or contemporary satire—or perhaps just nothing. No books."

Roth was, of course, writing out of an era that was particularly notable for unbelievable and often quite repellent happenings. There had been the fiascos of the Eisenhower presidency, the Korean War, the sordid madness of the Joseph McCarthy inquisitions featuring such uncomic grotesques as Roy Cohn and David Schine, to say nothing of McCarthy himself, the Rosenburg executions, the Nixon-Kennedy debates. But then Heller was writing out of the same era, and what makes Roth's essay historically interesting is that nowhere in it does he show an awareness or even imagine the possibility that the effort to come to terms with the unreality of the American reality might already have begun to be made by such writers as William Gaddis and John Barth, whose first work had been published by 1961, and would continue to be made by Thomas Pynchon, whose *V* came out two years later, as well as by Joseph Heller in *Catch-22*.

These writers were all, in their different ways, seeking to create a fiction that would assimilate the difficulties Roth described and convert them into imaginative materials. And they achieved this by creating an essentially new kind of fiction that represented an abdication of traditional realism—a form rendered mostly ineffectual because of those very difficulties—and that made unprecedented use of the techniques of black humor, surrealism, and grotesque metaphorization to confront the unreal and dramatize its unreality, most often by making it seem even more unreal than it actually was.

The complexity and originality of the work these and other writers have produced impose demands upon criticism that have forced it to grow in sophistication and have obviously contributed to such growth in the criticism of *Catch-22*. As evidence of this, we need only observe that most of the questions that perplexed or annoyed critics of the novel in the first years following its publication have now been answered, and as this has occurred, the size of Heller's achievement has been revealed to be far larger than it was first thought to be.

Robert Brustein at least raised the most important of these questions in his pioneering early review. The first to be asked concerned the extent to which the novel could be read as a satirical attack on World War II, and Norman Podhoretz, in his well-known essay, "The Best Catch There Is," based his criticism of Yossarian's desertion on the assumption that Heller intended to make such an attack but, given the impeccable motives the Allies had for fighting the war, could not do so convincingly. Fortunately, that argument has been put to rest and no longer seriously troubles anyone.

Of much greater interest is the continuing debate, which over the years has grown steadily subtler and more sophisticated, over the question of the form of the novel. And it comes as no surprise that the most valuable advance in this area has been the unitary or structuralist approach, in which certain aspects of the novel that were most worrisome to early critics have been shown to be quite adequately prepared for in the development of the action. The credibility of Yossarian's desertion is one example. Another is the ostensibly sudden transition in the closing chapters from hilarious comedy to the blackest evocation of horror. The more sensitive of recent critics have demonstrated that, in fact, that horror has been present throughout the action, but its force has been blunted and, in effect, evaded by the comedy. Through a complicated process of thematic backing and filling, countless repetitions of references and details, foreshadowing flashbacks and flashforwards, a looping and straightening inchworm progression, the moment is finally reached, beginning with the bombing of the undefended mountain village and culminating in the "Eternal City" chapter, when the humor and playful rhetoric are stripped away and the terrified obsession with death, from which the humor has been a hysterical distraction, is revealed in full nakedness.

It has also been demonstrated that this tangled, excessively repetitive, and seemingly self-neutralizing narrative structure is a perfectly convincing formal statement of the novel's thematic content, even of the reiterated double-bind of the central symbol, catch-22, which is, after all, the ultimate expression of sabotaged expectations, the cruel disparity between the humanitarian ideals by which life is supposed to be directed and the manipulative lies on which the bureaucratic system is actually based. The opening figure of the soldier in white, whose fluids are endlessly drained back into him, the soldier who sees everything twice, the constant raising of the number of bombing missions, the fantastically rapid expansion of Milo Minderbinder's empire, the massive incremental enumeration of detail, which is at first nonsensical, as in Cathcart's paranoid compilation of "black eyes" and "feathers in his cap," but by the end is horrifying, as in Yossarian's speculations in the "Eternal City" chapter about the number of victims and injustices there are in life, even the prevailing comic technique of instantaneous refutation and reversal employed everywhere in dizzying excess—all these come together to suggest a world based upon a principle of quantitative valuation in which more is better and most is best, and yet a world in which the accumulated excess of any one element may at any moment be neutralized by the greater accumulated excess of an antithetical element, as the comedy is finally neutralized by the weightier force of terror and death, as the fateful ubiquity of catch-22 finally eclipses all demands for logic and sanity.

Thomas LeClair has observed in a brilliant essay that *Catch-22* and *Something Happened* are connected in the sense that the struggle in the latter novel results in part "from Bob Slocum's mapping the quantitative assumptions of *Catch-22* onto his own consciousness and life." This seems to me an altogether excellent perception and, surprisingly enough, one of the very few examples of a critical effort to find relationships between the two novels. Most commentators have treated *Something Happened* as if it were a completely different kind of book amounting to a fresh beginning for Heller and often as if it were a particularly unfortunate beginning.

Yet there is much evidence to indicate that the two are actually quite closely related. In addition to the imposition of the quantitative value system on Slocum's consciousness and life, there is the fact that he inhabits a world in which the Cathcarts and Korns have clearly won. The malignant institutions of bureaucracy are now in complete control, and there is no longer the possibility, for Slocum or anyone else, of rebelling against or escaping their influence. If one tried, one would just be filed away and forgotten like Martha, the typist, when at last she goes insane. Self-interest promoted by power over others through the imposition of fear and insecurity is the universal value and represents an extension into the postwar civilian world of the military hierarchy of power—a development sinisterly envisioned by Mailer's General Cummings in *The Naked and the Dead.* Individual integrity and belief in justice are at best a memory; in fact, they are among the attributes that have been lost somewhere back in that past when Slocum believes that something terrible happened to him. Everybody, it seems, has sold out to M & M Enterprises. There is no longer a Sweden to escape to, and if there were, it would turn out to be a branch office of the syndicate.

Something Happened is finally about the death of those humane values in the name of which Yossarian deserted, and that death is epitomized by Slocum's unconsciously intentional murder of his son, the honest and sensitive little boy who reminds him of the little boy he once was and unaccountably has lost. After the murder, it follows logically that Slocum is free to embrace eagerly and even proudly the establishment values of the only world he now knows, for both his son and the innocent boy he himself was are dead and so can no longer stand reproachfully in the way of his capitulation.

LeClair believes that *Something Happened* is a better novel than *Catch-22,* and the large body of critical scholarship accumulating around it may well prove his point. Yet it seems unlikely that *Something Happened,* whatever its merits, will become the literary monument that *Catch-22* now is or exert a comparable influence on the life and literature of its time. It is not merely that *Catch-22* added a wonderful new term to the contemporary vocabulary, one that has been shown to have a thousand ironical applications. The novel also indemnified the sense of universal but unspecifiable conspiracy that has become a major psychic affliction of our time, and there can be no doubt of its great influence on such productions as *M*A*S*H, Dr. Strangelove,* and *Apocalypse Now* or of its close affinities with the works of Pynchon, Gaddis, and Vonnegut. Like them *Catch-22* represents a kind of comedy that depends upon the certain expectation of catastrophe and takes the form of a frenzied dance on the brink of the unspeakable.

As is the case with most original works of art, it is a novel that reminds us once again of all that we have taken for granted in our world and should not, the madness we try not to bother to notice, the deceptions and falsehoods we lack the will to try to distinguish from truth. Looking back, twenty-five years after its appearance, we can

see that the situation Heller described has, during those years, if anything grown more complicated, deranging, and perilous than it was in 1944 or 1961. The comic fable that ends in horror has become more and more clearly a reflection of the altogether uncomic and horrifying realities of the world in which we live and hope to survive.
1987

Donald Barthelme and the Doggy Life

The literary movement known as Black Humor or Dark Comedy, which achieved a certain inflated prominence in the early sixties, has lately shown signs of reaching some condition of impasse or exhaustion. The high claims of its initial publicity have not been fulfilled, and although it has attracted talents as diversely original as John Barth, Joseph Heller, Thomas Pynchon, Bruce Jay Friedman, and Donald Barthelme, these writers continue to seem notable more for their potential than for their clearly major distinction. The movement has also been compromised by the accumulation around it of a small army of camp followers, clowns, and pitchmen, who have apparently seen in it a chance to cash in on their mediocrity through emulation of their betters, and who have busied themselves perverting the styles of Black Humor into affectations, and its affectations into platitudes.

From the beginning the movement has had considerably more than its share of critical attention because it appeared to be a development toward imaginative revitalization of a form that had long been moribund, the form of novelistic satire and self-parody, and because it seemed to promise some renewal of relationship between fiction and the actualities of the social world, a relationship which had grown so tenuous in the forties and fifties that vast sectors of the reading public eagerly mistook the erotic voyeurisms of John O'Hara for penetrating insights into the sociology of American life.

But it has gradually become evident that the promises critics discovered in Black Humor were projections more of their own hopes than of creative possibilities actually present in the movement itself.

For just as Black Humor has all along been characterized by enormous chic and a kind of fashionableness achieved without passing through any of the arduous stages of slow arrival and gradual acceptance, so it has quickly ossified into one more cliché of anticliché, one more casualty of the instantly assimilative and accommodative processes of our culture. As has happened with so much post-avant-garde art, there seems to have been only the briefest interval between the time when Black Humor was recognized as an important innovative gesture, and the time when it was absorbed into style and decor and became nearly indistinguishable from the advertising gimmicks and promotional techniques that have so often been the rightful objects of its horror. The pose or stance of the Black Humorist soon became as familiar and predictable and as falsely provocative as the set of a *Vogue* mannequin's thighs. Suddenly, it seemed capable of registering only the histrionics of a ritual Angst, a merely ornamental because creatively unearned Absurdity, a sleek couturier note of Apocalypse.

Yet it was in the nature of Black Humor to be peculiarly susceptible to this kind of debasement. Even at its best it always verged perilously on the Sick Joke, the nightclub wisecrack, the Pop Art slapstick of the comic-strip cartoon. Its characteristic humor was often more blackface than black, and the ubiquitous catch-22 of its satire seemed too flip and feeble, and above all too good-natured a mockery of the insidious workings of bureaucratic conspiracy. In fact, the most crippling weakness of Black Humor was that it cut itself off from the vital sources of effective satire—the close observation of the social and political world—just because it was too easily horrified by the grotesqueness and complexity of that world, and so found it less painful to retreat into cuteness than to endure and create the true dark comedy of contemporary anguish. In its programmatic preoccupation with the sickness, the absurdity, the incomprehensibility of events, it abdicated its responsibility to deal coherently with events. The result was that except in a very few cases, such as Barth's *The Sot-Weed Factor* and Friedman's *Stern,* the prime requirement of successful satire was never fulfilled by Black Humorist writers: the living reality of the object or condition being satirized was too obliquely suggested in their work or was altogether missing from it.

It has often been argued in defense of Black Humor that fiction in our time has lost the possibility of making this social connection because the events of the social world have become themselves fictitious. Life not only imitates fiction but assimilates to itself the fiction-making functions, so that the happenings reported on any day in the newspapers will in effect out-imagine the creative mind and thus cheat it of its revelatory and prophetic powers. But this would seem to suggest that fiction is best produced in dull ages or in sane, orderly, and uneventful ones, and the history of literature indicates that just the opposite is true. Rather, it seems to be the case that contemporary experience has so worked upon us, has so anesthetized us to the impact of grotesque and appalling occurrences, that we no longer believe they can have any connection with, or any power to influence, the course of individual destiny or the drama of our hermetically personal consciousness. We have suffered a paralysis or eclipse of imagination before the nightmare of history in this age. Hence, we cannot imagine a fictional rationale in which events might be interpreted meaningfully in relation to the self. Our only recourse seems to be to fantasize the feelings of dislocation that obsess the self, or project images that convey, however incoherently, our sense of moral and emotional trivialization in the face of events.

Of the Black Humorist writers whose work represents some expression of, or adjustment to, this dilemma, Donald Barthelme is in many ways the most interesting because he has the talent and intelligence occasionally, but only occasionally, to overcome its worst effects. There are a few stories in both his first volume, *Come Back, Dr. Caligari,* and in *Unspeakable Practices, Unnatural Acts,* which brilliantly demonstrate the power of sheer creative imagination to make the vital connection between satire and the social world that is so very difficult to make at just this time. Barthelme's recurrent theme is precisely the trivialization of contemporary life and consciousness, and at his best in these few stories he is able to dramatize his sense of that trivialization, as well as his satirical comment upon it, within the context of living fact and event which created it. But there is a vast distance between the stories which succeed in this way and the many others, unfortunately the majority of both volumes, which are victimized by the fallacy of imitative form, in which dislocation is expressed through dislocation and trivialization through trivia, to the amusement and edification of nobody. These stories strike one as exercises in free association and automatic writing or as descriptions of bad dreams jotted down in the middle of the night for the benefit of one's analyst, and some of them sound as though they had been begun in the hope that of their own accord, through the sheer act of being written, they would eventually discover their subject and meaning.

Reading them is like finding oneself adrift in a sea of orbiting psychic garbage. Punctured beer cans, potato peelings, gnawed apple cores, squashed toothpaste tubes, stringy hanks of some dubious-looking viscous material float around and seemingly through one, always in the same fixed relation to oneself and everything else, and always somehow impenetrable because one is so completely penetrated by them. The stories are in fact quite literally verbal immersions in dreck, the evacuated crud and muck of contemporary life, and they very effectively dramatize the sensations of being suffocated and shat upon and generally soiled and despoiled in soul and mind which accompany our daily experience of contemporary life. But they do not dramatize the cultural, political, or historical circumstances that give rise to these sensations, nor do they end in a satirical, or even a specific thematic formulation. Everything is offered in deadpan and with the mechanical iterativeness of items recited from a grocery list. Everything is offered, but somehow finally nothing is given.

The effect is actually very much like that of some of the New Wave films which introduce the viewer to an experience through a process of such total saturation in trivial details that it is often impossible to tell which detail or episode is supposed to be more important than some other, hence, impossible to detect the thematic principle that finally binds the details together into meaning. One always suspects the artist of suggesting that he does not really know what he intends the depicted experience to mean, and so will leave it to us to decide for ourselves. By putting in all the details, he has supposedly absolved himself of the obligation to select the significant ones. In such a case, we are obliged, as Virginia Woolf once said, to do the artist's imagining for him, and while that may be a kindness to him, it is no help whatever to the cause of art.

Barthelme appears to be indictable on the same charge. Over and over again in his stories, he seems to be inviting us to take on the job of bringing into focus some idea or meaning that has eluded his powers of imaginative resolution. For example, in *Unspeakable Practices, Unnatural Acts* there is the story called "Edward and Pia," which apparently has to do with an American expatriate and his Scandinavian mistress and the emptiness of their existence in Europe. The characters move apathetically through a horizontal succession of experiences, none of which are distinguished from any other in the slightest way, presumably because they all have exactly the same meaning and value, or are equally without meaning and value. We learn that Edward and Pia went to Sweden, that Pia was pregnant, that in London they had seen the *Marat/Sade* at the Aldwych Theater, that Edward walked out to the wood barn and broke up wood for the fire, that Edward and Pia walked the streets of Amsterdam and that they were hungry, that they went to the cinema to see an Eddie Constantine picture and that the film was very funny, that on Sunday Edward went to the bakery and bought bread, that Edward and Pia went to Berlin on the train, that Edward received a letter from London, that Edward looked in the window of the used radio store and it was full of used radios, that Edward put his hands on Pia's breasts, that the nipples were the largest he had ever seen. Then he counted his money. He had two hundred and forty crowns. And so on and on and on.

All this is undoubtedly heavily redolent of the trivialization of life in our time, and it may well be an attempt to say something important about the form of spiritual death that accompanies the atrophy of all sane responses to life and all hopes of finding causal relationships within experience. But it comes through most clearly as an example of imagination succumbing to the trivia that is its very material. There may even be some justice in the thought that such benumbed recitations of apparently meaningless detail are intended to be viewed as if they were being enacted under the outraged eye of the cosmos, and we are meant to hear rumbling behind it all the distant thunder of the archangelic armies advancing to bring down upon us the terrible wrath of God. But as Auden saw, even during such a cosmic occurrence as the Crucifixion, dogs go placidly on with their doggy life, and "the expensive delicate ship that must have seen something amazing," the fall of Brueghel's Icarus into the sea, "had somewhere to get to and sailed calmly on."

It would appear that the cosmic and the apocalyptic, whether in art or in life, cannot be dramatized directly, cannot meaningfully stand alone. They can finally be understood only in terms of their simple and probably ironical relationship to the doggy life and the very real people sailing away on that ship. It is the task of fiction continually to reaffirm this relationship. Or, in an age such as ours, fiction may be obliged to reinvent it. For between the Crucifixion and the doggy life, between our grandiose visions of doom and the specific creature experiences that embody them, there now lies a chasm that only the best talent and intelligence can hope to bridge. It takes little of either simply to say that the chasm is there and then to laugh at its existence. We already know it is there, and the knowledge has long ago ceased to amuse.

1968

No One in Charge

In 1968 I published an essay on Donald Barthelme in which I made certain impious observations about the literary movement known as Black Humor or Dark Comedy, then just passing the peak of its quite meretricious popularity. In the years that have passed since I made those observations, the world has moved on but Black Humor on the whole has not. Its formerly innovative attitudes and artistic devices have been absorbed into the public domain (not just in fiction but in poetry, drama, journalism, and film) and become institutionalized there as part of the official convention of discourse through which we habitually register our bafflement or outrage at the insane discontinuities and seemingly gratuitous malevolence of contemporary life. They are available now, like mass-produced goods in a supermarket, to any artist or social commentator in need of a jar of pickled Angst or instant Doom, and these ingredients had better be abundantly present in any work with pretensions to be taken seriously as an honest statement about the larger unrealities of our time.

But to the extent that the Black Humor approach has substituted buzz words and stereotypical formulations for fresh imaginative insights, it has conditioned us to respond in certain prescribed ways to experience without really providing us with the experience. If one finds the conditions of contemporary life deranging, one can take comfort from the fact that Black Humor has identified derangement as the only sane response to those conditions, has classified it as the prime symptom of entropy, anomie, atomization, and other derivatives of the Second Law of Thermodynamics, and has perfected certain highly stylized modes of dramatizing it in fictional form. Thus, one knows that whenever the characters in a novel do not resemble human beings, it is because they have been dehumanized by the entropic forces that are fast dehumanizing us all. Whenever a fictional landscape seems fragmented or nightmarishly surreal so that it is impossible to tell precisely what is going on, one knows it is intended to function as a metaphor of the disorientation of the psyche when confronted with the bizarre arbitrariness of contemporary events. If the experiences and people portrayed in a novel seem trivial or empty, one can be sure they seem so because they represent the exhausted sensibility of the age.

In short, Black Humor has provided us with a number of analogical or parabolic evocations of the psychological disturbances of contemporary life, evocations that are sometimes so compelling we are almost persuaded that they constitute the only valid representation of contemporary life and that they actually do reveal its reality rather than merely a set of stock responses to it. Yet over and over again in Black Humor fiction the problem is that while the responses may be powerfully rendered, the concrete events and specific social circumstances that induced them are very seldom identified or objectified. That whole vital dimension of fiction that Hemingway once described as comprising "the exact sequence of motion and fact which made the emotion" is almost always missing, leaving the emotion afloat in a causeless void.

It is one of Joseph Heller's several virtues as a Black Humorist that he has been able to avoid this problem and dramatize his steadily darkening vision of contemporary life through an evocation of the experiences responsible for it. In the fiction of Pynchon, for example, or Donald Barthelme, virtually everything and everyone exists in such a radical state of distortion and aberration that there is no way of determining from which conditions in the real world they have been derived or from what standard of sanity they may be said to depart. The conventions of verisimilitude and sanity have been nullified, and the entire fiction becomes a self-contained metaphor of a derangement that is seemingly without provocation and beyond measurement.

Heller, by contrast, derives his materials from the actualities of the observable world, portrays them with much greater fidelity to realism, and achieves his effects through comic exaggeration and burlesque rather than hallucination—which is perhaps to say that he descends from Dickens rather than Beckett. His characters are almost always grotesques, but they are presented as if they were and not as if grotesqueness were the natural and universal state of being. One is always certain, furthermore, precisely to what degree they and their situations are absurd or insane because his narrative point of view is located in an observer with whom we can identify and who is rational enough to be able to measure the departures from rationality in the people and situations he encounters.

Yossarian's problem in *Catch-22* is that he is hopelessly sane in a situation of complete madness, and the high comedy of the novel is generated by the fact that the familiar actualities of military life, when reviewed satirically—which is to say, rationally—become ludicrous and in wartime, malevolent. But there is nothing in *Catch-22* that a person of Yossarian's perpetually affronted sensibility would not have perceived in the same circumstances. The boundaries of the normal and predictable are never exceeded, but they are extended satirically to the point where, as happens in war, all kinds of idiocy, cruelty, obsessive self-interest, and the most inhumane bureaucratic exploitation are made to seem normal and predictable, hence, altogether horrifying and conducive quite sensibly to paranoia.

In his second novel, *Something Happened,* Heller faced the problem that the paranoia of his protagonist, Bob Slocum, is seemingly without provocation, yet it must somehow be dramatically justified. If Slocum has enemies, he can only suspect or imagine that they are out there, but he cannot locate them. The danger, moreover, is not that they will kill him, but that in some mysterious way they will not allow him to discover and lead a meaningful life. In the conventional view Slocum has all the advantages that make for meaning: a secure position with a large corporation; an excellent income; a big house in Connecticut; an attractive wife with whom he has regular and good sex; and at least one child, his elder son, whom he deeply loves. Yet such things do not constitute the sum of his life, and his difficulty—which is also a large technical one for Heller—is that he must locate and make real the sources of his anguish in a situation characterized precisely by the absence of difficulty.

The environment in which Slocum lives and works has, in fact, been quite deliberately engineered by the various bureaucratic agencies of the new mass dystopianism so that it will contain no conflict or contingency, so that it cannot be engaged, affirmed, or denied by anyone within it. This is its achieved character and, by the standards of the prevailing corporate metaphysics, its supreme virtue. It has been created in conformity to the dogma most revered in the technocratic era: that the freedom to take the risks of one's life in an adversarial environment has been abolished in favor of a secure function within an environment that has been happily sanitized of both freedom and risk—the system guaranteeing in return for the dutiful performance of one's function that nothing will happen to anyone ever again.

This inhumanly benevolent situation gives Slocum no comfort whatever. It provokes and at the same time blandly absorbs his anxiety, even as it offers no tangible justification for being anxious. He has been programmed—he thinks in childhood or at some time back before a mysterious something happened to him and to life—to deal aggressively with his environment, while his environment has been programmed not to deal with him at all except insofar as he can be manipulated as a thing. If he resists, it will simply file him away into instant oblivion. He is driven, therefore, to populate his fantasy world with enemies who will serve as objects for the hostility he feels but cannot externalize in any other way. "In the office in which I work there are five people of whom I'm afraid. Each of these five people is afraid of four people (excluding overlaps) for a total of twenty, and each of these twenty people is afraid of six people, making a total of one hundred and twenty people who are feared by at least one person."

Slocum believes this to be true and needs, for the sake of what sanity he has, to go on believing it. He requires conditions of mistrust and competition, whether real or imaginary, in order to feel real to himself and to keep alive the illusion that he is real to others. But he also knows that his efforts to manufacture these conditions are pointless because there is no social context, no environment of human feeling or personal interchange, in which they can be made to exist. And that of course is why his hostility is so excruciating: there is nothing out there to provoke it, hence, nothing on which to discharge it. The result is that Slocum's voice drones in an interminable monologue out of a void in which the only sound is the sound of itself. It ranges obsessively over the past and present, trying to articulate the incomprehensible, seeking always to talk its way out of what is for Heller the ultimate terrifying helplessness—the inability to identify or confront the forces that are destroying one's life and preparing one's death.

This is also the radically deranging perception behind Heller's next novel, *Good as Gold*. In spite of it, he has nonetheless been able to generate what is at times an almost joyous comedy out of the depths of just this kind of derangement and to identify and engage some of the specific social conditions that have caused the vision of derangement to become one of the defining features of contemporary life. Heller has accomplished this through his particularly effective use of two seemingly very different kinds of narrative materials—the Jewish family experience (his first attempt in fiction to draw on this experience) and a wildly phantasmagoric rendition of the Washington political scene. His protagonist, Bruce Gold, is a minor Jewish intellectual, academic, and essayist who plans to write an "abstract autobiography" based on the history of Jewish life in America, a book which is never written but which the novel, in effect, becomes.

Gold moves back and forth between Washington and various dreadful meetings with his relatives in New York, seeing no connection between the two except that Washington promises to be a glamorous escape from the wretchedness of the family. Yet it is one of the central brilliances of the novel that although they are never explicitly paralleled, the Washington and the family experiences can finally be seen to have a portentous similarity. Both in fact represent aspects of the same condition, the dehumanization and derangement of life that follow on the collapse of those values which once made humanity and rationality necessary.

As Heller portrays it, the trashed and decaying environment of south Brooklyn becomes an objectification of the devolving history of Gold's second-generation immigrant family. The neighborhood in which he grew up had once been a kind of community held together by ties of blood relationship, ethnic tradition, and loyalties growing out of the shared experience of struggle and privation. Now the area has become a jungle and a battlefield where teenage gangs roam the littered streets "murdering old people casually in the course of their youthful depredations," boarded-up shops are vandalized, and there seem to be no places left where people can "buy food, have their suits and dresses mended and dry cleaned, their shoes and radios fixed, and their medical prescriptions filled." As Gold drives up Mermaid Avenue, he does not see a single drugstore or Jewish delicatessen. "There was no longer a movie house operating in Coney Island: drugs, violence, and vandalism had closed both garish, overpowering theaters years before. The brick apartment house in which he had spent his whole childhood and nearly all his adolescence had been razed; on the site stood something newer and uglier that did not seem a nourishing improvement for the Puerto Rican families there now." And Gold, like Tiresias brooding upon the wasteland devastation, concludes:

> Every good place has always been deteriorating, and everything bad is getting worse. Neighborhoods, parks, beaches, streets, schools were falling deeper into ruin and whole cities sinking into rot.... It was the Shoot the Chute into darkness ... the plunging roller coaster into disintegration and squalor. Someone should do something. Nobody could. No society worth its salt would watch itself perishing without some serious attempt to avert its own destruction. Therefore ... we are not a society. Or we are not worth our salt. Or both."

Like the old neighborhood, Gold's family once had a communal integrity founded on the need to survive in an environment that was harshly adversarial not because of crime and violence but because times were hard, jobs were scarce, and too many immigrant families were competing to make a life in a new country. Gold's brother and five sisters all made large sacrifices, the brother quitting school early and going to work to help support the family while the father lost job after job. It could hardly be said that they were happy picturesquely toiling together or even that they deeply cared for one another. They were and remained the sort of people who are caring only so long as circumstances require them to be. Now that they are middle-aged and affluent, they have disintegrated into a group of bickering malcontents who come together only because they are tyrannized into it by their maniacal eighty-two-year-old father. At family gatherings their prime concern is to persuade him to cut short his annual visit with them and return to Florida, but he has no intention of doing this because he knows it would give them pleasure. He finds his own pleasure in abusing Gold unmercifully because Gold is an intellectual and writes articles which nobody in the family can understand and which do not make money. All these people have long been displaced from the realities that formed them and gave them some sense of common purpose, and now they have become abstracted into caricatures of hostility and self-interest. Having survived the need to deal aggressively with their environment, they have turned their aggressions against one another, while around them what is left of their old environment is being destroyed by new generations of displaced people to whom it has no relation whatever and whose aggression against it is a means to nothing.

In the Washington sections of the novel this effect of derangement from conditions of order, sanity, and meaningful causality is achieved through a masterful burlesque of government bureaucratic life. The people in these sections are shown to be as divorced from reality as Gold's family is displaced from its original environment. Political figures have lost all sense of the principles, causes, issues, and human interests they have been elected to work for and represent, and the result in their case is not aggression but a kind of psychotic arbitrariness. In the absence of clear and unavoidable imperatives that fix the nature of reality and control one's perception of it, reality can become anything one wishes it to be or decides it is. Titles of official positions have no relation to any specific function, and any office can be filled by anyone since no one knows what qualifications are needed for what office; therefore, any qualifications will do for any office. The language of government is similarly unrelated to the ideas or experiences it is supposed to describe. It is used not to communicate but to obscure meaning because all meaning is provisional and conjectural.

Gold has hopes of being chosen for an important political position in Washington, and in an effort to win favor has written a flattering review of the president's book, *My Year in the White House*. The president, who is a pointedly unnamed successor to Gerald Ford, has evidently spent much of his first year in office writing about his first year in office. "Yet nowhere in the book does he say anything about being busy with writing the book." He is delighted with Gold's review, especially with a phrase from it, "Nothing succeeds as planned," and instructs Ralph Newsome, an old friend of Gold's now serving as an "unnamed source" in the White House, to sound him out about his interest in a government appointment. Newsome offers Gold several possible choices ranging from ambassador to the court of St. James, head of NATO or the CIA, being an unnamed spokesman, Secretary of Defense, the Treasury, HEW, or the country's very first Jewish Secretary of State (Henry Kissinger, according to Gold, has lied about being a Jew and is really a German). Newsome assures him that whichever job he decides to take, he will be able to do anything he wants "as long as it's everything we tell you to say and do in support of our policies, whether you agree with them or not. You'll have complete freedom." When Gold asks for time to think all this over, Newsome tells him that "we'll want to move ahead with this as speedily as possible, although we'll have to go slowly. . . . We'll want to build this up into an important public announcement, although we'll have to be completely secret."

Gold's time in Washington is spent in repeated sessions with Newsome during which they discuss the possible jobs he might want to hold, and in trying to arrange for Gold to meet the president. But it turns out that the president actually never sees anyone and sleeps during his office hours because, as Newsome explains, "He is a very early riser. He is up at five every morning, takes two sleeping pills and a tranquilizer, and goes right back to bed for as long as he can sleep."

As he did in *Catch-22*, Heller tends here to ring too many changes on what is essentially one good joke, and the satire much of the time seems so light-heartedly outlandish that it very nearly neutralizes one's awareness that the kind of insanity Heller makes laughable has also in the real world had the most destructive consequences. Yet there is more than an edge of anger in Heller's portrait of the Washington political scene, just as there are extremely ominous implications in those general qualities of contemporary American life that he has chosen to dramatize. His novel is indeed comic, often

hilariously so, but it is also comedy of the bleakest and blackest kind because it is all about a society that is fast going insane, that is learning to accept chaos as order, unreality as normal, and the horror is that the time may soon come when the conditions Heller depicts will no longer seem to us either funny or the least bit odd.
1979

William Gaddis and the "Ongoing Situation"

In 1955, William Gaddis published his now infamous first novel, *The Recognitions,* a massive and brilliant work so heavily weighted with erudition and thematic ambiguity that for all but a few readers it was totally inaccessible. Gaddis had tried with an arrogance surpassed only by Joyce in *Finnegans Wake* to produce a satirical portrait of no less than the entire modern world, and he had done so through a most intricate 956-page exploration of such arcane matters as art forgery, counterfeiting, false religious rhetoric, ambidextrous sexuality, the fraudulences of political life, and the masquerades of intellectual and artistic society. Predictably, given the nature of the book and the times, *The Recognitions* was reviewed either hostilely or stupidly, and in 1956, when I wrote in its defense, suggesting that it might be comparable in quality to some of the major novels of the twenties and thirties, I knew that I was merely enlarging my reputation for eccentricity. Yet by slow degrees over the next decade the book became something of a *cause célèbre* and acquired an underground reputation sufficiently substantial to persuade various publishers to issue three paperback editions—in 1962, 1970, and 1974.

As is usually the case with abrasively original work, there had to be a certain passage of time before an audience could begin to be educated to accept *The Recognitions.* The problem was not simply that the novel was too long and intricate or its vision of experience too outrageous, but that even the sophisticated reading public of the midfifties was not yet accustomed to the kind of fiction it represented. Curiously enough, even though the most radical experimentation had by then been made respectable by the great modernist masters, there was still a resistance to it when attempted by living novelists. The most authoritative mode in the serious fiction of the fifties was primarily realistic, and the novel of fabulation and Black Humor—of which *The Recognitions* was later to be identified as a distinguished pioneering example—had not yet come into vogue. In fact, the writers who became the leaders of the Black Humor movement had either not been heard from in 1955 or remained undiscovered. John Barth did not publish his first novel until 1956, and Thomas Pynchon, whose *V* seems to have been heavily influenced by Gaddis, did not emerge until 1963. John Hawkes, although already the author of several brilliant experimental novels, was almost as unknown in 1955 as Gaddis was, and he has still not received the attention he has earned. But *The Recognitions* anticipated the interest these and other writers were later to display in the techniques of parody and self-parody, the comic use of fictions within fiction, and in particular the themes of forgery and fabulation. Their work over the past twenty years has created a context in which it is possible to recognize Gaddis's novel as having helped inaugurate a whole new movement in American fiction. Rereading it with the knowledge of all that this movement has taught us about modern experience and the opening of new possibilities for the novel, one can see that *The Recognitions* occupies a strikingly unique and primary place in contemporary literature.

During the years that have passed since 1955, there have been rumors that Gaddis was so discouraged by the poor reception accorded his novel that he more than once announced his intention to give up writing altogether. While a period of silence lasting for two decades may well indicate that he was having his difficulties, he did continue to write and, it now appears, with undiminished confidence and vitality. In fact, his new novel is, if anything, even more ambitiously experimental than its predecessor and almost as massive, and it is perhaps more successful in engaging the vastly complex realities and unrealities of the way of life that has overtaken us in this technocratic age.

The most radical feature of *JR* (and the one that may limit its audience to readers possessing powers of superhuman endurance) is the form in which it is presented. The book consists of 726 pages of virtually uninterrupted monologue and dialogue, an almost continuous outpouring of language embellished scarcely at all by descriptions of character and setting. People by the dozens move back and forth through thick mists of verbiage talking to and at and around and behind one another. Yet somehow nobody really listens or understands quite what is being said. This, as it turns out, is entirely appropriate to the subject, which is the debasement of language as both cause and symptom of the corruption of a society that has been abstracted by technology from the concrete realities of feeling and being, and in which the totalitarian obfuscations of bureaucratese, the gibber and jargon of the computer, and the lying Newspeak of Watergate politics, corporate finance, and multimedia education have severed the connection that is supposed to exist between words and the truths they are intended to describe. It is a society suffering from precisely the sickness Orwell discussed in relation to political language, the decadence of which, in any culture, is a direct reflection of the decadence of thought, the totalitarian need to obscure the meaning of certain politically sensitive ideas by expressing them in pseudo-scientific euphemisms or in dead metaphors that no longer have any specific evocative function. Carried far enough, this kind of semantical perversion ends in the creation of a world of fictions and forgeries in which words can be used to signify anything or nothing or are strung together to form a catechistic mumble of sounds without relation to meaning. Reality, having become whatever one wishes to name it, soon disappears behind the words employed to misname it.

Bureaucratic systems can become, as they have in our time, so intricately complex, their sources of power so diversified and mysterious, and their lines of communication so glutted with the esoteric terminology peculiar to each that they too effectively exist outside reality and cease to need any cause or objective to justify their existence. The language used to describe their operations exists, by the same token, beyond the necessity of meaning, and those who use it, as Watergate so clearly demonstrated, finally lose all sense of the moral significance of honest statement—for language is made to confuse and conceal in a situation where no one may actually know what the truth is, whether anyone anywhere is telling it, or if there is any need to do so. It is this kind of situation that Gaddis depicts with very great ingenuity, the forgeries of language in their connection with the counterfeiting of bureaucratic realities, and his emphasis is on two particular manifestations of the problem—the corporate structures of secondary education and Wall Street finance.

The action in roughly the first quarter of the novel centers in a large Long Island elementary school where several of the characters are teachers and the protagonist, JR, is an eleven-year-old sixth grader. There is very little to indicate that any actual teaching is being done at the school because—as is the case everywhere in Gaddis's surreal projection of contemporary society—the manipulation of method, along with the complicated electronic equipment used to support it and the abstruse terminology used to mysticize it, have become ends in themselves. The function of the institution is primarily the maintenance of the institution. The teaching of students has been all but supplanted by a preoccupation with audio-visual teaching machines, public relations problems, political strategy for obtaining foundation grants, and the allocation of funds to pay for functions that are preposterously irrelevant to the learning experience. The school budget provides $32,670 for "blacktopping the parking lot over to the tv studio," $12,000 for paper towels, $47,000 for damages resulting from vandalism, and $1200 for books for the library—an amount to be used, one character suggests, not for books but for a pegboard. "You need a pegboard in a library. Books you don't know what you're getting into." A problem heavily on the minds of the school administrators is the establishment of friendly relations with the community, and another character suggests how a school-sponsored musical program might be used to this end:

> Tie it in with this culture center, locating it here, bring in your Spring Arts Festival expanded with a few remote specials stressing the patriotic theme, you might even do one on my [bomb] shelter, what America's all about, waste disposal and all, and wrap it all up with the whole in-school television program once that's on a good interference-free closed-circuit system bring in a little Foundation backing and you're on your way.

These discussions are carried on in the verbal mode that has come to dominate almost all social interchange in our time, the serial or collective monologue, and they are couched in the hieratic language of multimedia communications, in which words are used to denote conditions and processes that may be said to exist, if at all, only in the realm of the technological/ supernatural. One teaching method is described as being designed to "tangibilitate" certain materials. Reference is constantly being made to "the ongoing situation," someone's "position activationwise," "motivational resource areas," and "implementing unplanlessness." One instructor says to another: "In simple straightforward terms Dan, you might say that he structured the material in terms of the ongoing situation to tangibilitate the utilization potential of this one-to-one instructional medium in such a meaningful learning experience that these kids won't forget it for a hell of a long time, how's that Whiteback."

Gradually there emerges out of this babble of jargon-demented tongues the perfectly sane, merely obsessive figure of JR, logical end product of the ongoing situation, supreme example of the utilization potential of a meaningful learning experience. A good old American boy from his perpetually runny nose right down to his torn sneakers with the flapping soles, JR has learned his lessons well and knows by instinct how to apply them manipulatively to achieve, in the classic rags-to-riches tradition, the only goals he has been taught to respect: money, fame, and power. The one explanation he gives for his various actions is to say, "But that's what you *do*," that is what the free enterprise system requires if you expect to win, and of course everybody understands exactly what he means.

JR's interpretation of what it is you do to win is as central to our native ethos of self-realization as any form of adroit political or financial chicanery. Like most healthy-minded Americans he is a devout believer in the religion of technique, the *right way* to go about doing what you do that will guarantee success, and he has discovered that you can find out what the right way is by clipping coupons from the back pages of magazines and sending in for free instruction manuals along with samples of various products. In this fashion he accumulates an astounding quantity of materials including dozens of catalogues offering information on how to have meaningful sexual intercourse, how to identify rare and valuable coins, how to build powerful muscles scientifically, how to buy for practically nothing government surplus airplane gas tanks, how to get started in the import-export business, and how to make large profits by knowing the right investments to make on the stock market. A sixth-grade field trip to Wall Street convinces JR that his destiny lies in corporation finance and, after carefully studying various pieces of free literature he has obtained from a brokerage firm, he proceeds to make an entry into the market through the purchase—entirely on paper—of thousands of Army surplus wooden picnic forks. He then becomes involved in the buying up of bankrupt companies that offer tax advantages and eventually, without at all understanding how it happened, he becomes the head of a massive conglomerate with a paper empire that includes film studios, a brewery, a firm that manufactures plastic flowers, an entire New England mill town, and a vast range of other holdings. JR conducts his business operations from a phone booth he has had installed in a corridor of his school. He muffles his voice with his handkerchief or plays a recording of his voice at a slower than normal speed to make it sound deeper. His official corporation headquarters are located in a wretched little tenement apartment on East Ninety-sixth Street in Manhattan where he has installed one of his former teachers, a failed composer named Edward Bast, to pass on his instructions—which Bast cannot comprehend—and to answer the incessantly ringing telephone. The apartment is also occupied by a freaky young girl, who will sleep with absolutely anyone and when not thus engaged spends most of her time getting into and out of the bathtub, and by a weird collection of free samples, piled-up mail, and miscellaneous junk that JR has sent away for. There are, among other things, thirty-six boxes of a mysterious product known as 200-2 Ply, a carton of Wise Potato Chips Hoppin' With Flavor, 24 One Pint Mazola New Improved, 24-7 oz Pkgs Flavored Loops, innumerable cans of film, volumes of Moody's *Industrials* and Thomas's *Register of American Manufacturers,* a radio buried under such a large pile of debris that no one can reach it to turn it off, a kitchen hot water faucet that also cannot be turned off, an electric clock that runs backward, and an electric letter-opener that slices letters in half. At one point a truck driver attempts to deliver a shipment of a hundred thousand plastic flowers but is persuaded to take them back to the sender. Several men arrive with subpoenas to collect the corporation records for a governmental investigation into the legality of JR's activities, but it is by no means certain that he himself will eventually be tracked down and exposed. By the end of the novel, at any rate, he appears to be still undaunted and is last seen enthusiastically trying to con Bast into helping him launch yet another great scheme.

The absurdity of an eleven-year-old boy gaining control of a huge financial empire is the ultimate burlesque expression of an idea dramatized everywhere in this remarkable novel: that in a society such as the one depicted, absolutely anything can happen because no one is effectively in charge and no one can control what is going on. Certain assumptions about the fundamental coherence and value of human existence have somehow been lost. There is simply no discoverable rational structure in anything; hence, nobody makes sense either to himself or in his efforts to communicate with others. The spoken language with its endlessly reiterated ambiguities, its steady dissolution into streams of utterance signifying nothing, stands as the index of the berserk sensibility of the modern corporate state.

It is undoubtedly inevitable that the novel promises at almost every point to fall victim to the imitative fallacy, that it is frequently as turgid, monotonous, and confusing as the situation it describes. Yet Gaddis has a strength of mind and talent capable of surmounting this very large difficulty. He has managed to reflect chaos in a fiction that is not itself artistically chaotic because it is imbued with the conserving and correcting power of his imagination. His awareness of what is human and sensible is always present behind his depiction of how far we have fallen from humanity and sense. His vision of what is happening in our world is profound and extremely disturbing. If it should ever cease to disturb, there will be no better proof of its accuracy.
1975

John Barth
Versions and Reversions

John Barth became obsessed early in his career by an idea about the nature of the cosmos: namely, that no idea about it can be securely held since everything is relative and there are no absolute truths or fixed realities. Each person has only his version or versions of the truth; hence, each can, if he is so inclined, live his life by improvising and playing a seemingly limitless series of roles that may be external public expressions of the various versions of the truth he perceives as he makes his adjustments to new experience.

Barth's first two novels were relatively realistic dramatic expositions of this idea. *The Floating Opera* has to do with Todd Andrews's decision to commit suicide, but then how he changes his mind when he perceives that while there is no rational reason to live, there is also no rational reason to die. It is significant for what it suggests about Barth's quite mechanistic view of human motivation that Andrews presents the evolution of his decision and his change of mind in the form of a series of dialectical propositions:

I. Nothing has intrinsic value.
II. The reasons for which people attribute value to things are always ultimately irrational.
III. There is, therefore, no ultimate "reason" for valuing anything.
IV. Living is action. There's no final reason for action.
V. There's no final reason for living (or for suicide).

These insights are apparently all that Andrews has been able to derive from the experience of his life by which he can justify its continuance or its termination. But then Andrews has lived a life unstructured and unenriched by any imperative except a free-floating compulsion to rationalize. He is almost entirely immune to emotional stimuli and to the perhaps irrational but nonetheless vitalizing human relationships that make existence tolerable for most people. The single compelling need of his life, he insists, is to understand why his father committed suicide. But the only means he has of trying to penetrate this mystery is to put down on paper everything he knows about his father and to infer from the accumulation of data what his father's motives may have been. Of course he fails in the endeavor because all his efforts to fabricate systems and patterns of action turn out to be only possible versions of the truth, and since he himself is so isolated from life, these versions serve only to propel him further away from life and to seal the vacuum of solipsism in which he spends his days—literally in the hotel room where for many years he has lived alone with his infinitely ramifying and self-sabotaging mind.

Barth's second novel, *End of the Road,* explores the human consequences of this philosophical dilemma, just what happens when a person who is victimized by it as Andrews is becomes involved in the lives of other people. Jacob Horner, the protagonist, suffers from periods of catatonic paralysis or what he calls "weatherlessness," in which he is unable to take any action because his psyche is balked by the massive plentitude of possibilities for action. While trying to recover from one of these periods, Horner drifts into a friendship with Joe and Rennie Morgan, a young couple who believe they can live their lives by rules based upon reason and practical sanity. With very little passionate volition on the part of either, Horner and Rennie have an affair that leads not only to the destruction of the Morgan's marriage but to a particularly gruesome death for Rennie while undergoing an abortion. Joe is left in a condition of complete metaphysical breakdown because he is unable to arrive at a rational way of understanding the situation. "According to my version of Rennie, what happened couldn't have happened. According to her version of herself, it couldn't have happened. And yet it happened." Horner at the end still cannot believe in any version of reality and appears to be entering yet another period of paralysis which may well be, as the last word of the novel suggests, "terminal."

Both these novels are, as I have said, quite realistic examinations of the dilemma created by the failure of logical systems to provide a tenable basis for existence and of the resulting entrapment of the will in a bottomless quagmire of relativism. One derives the strong impression that in writing them, Barth had himself arrived at a point of imaginative development or depletion at which, like his protagonists, he could no longer find real or meaningful any of the conventional methods of cohering experience that are so essential not only to the rational maintenance of life but to the production of realistic fiction. In fact, both books are finally *about* the impossibility of arriving at any secure perspective from which to judge human affairs; their realism is always on the verge of being nullified by their epistemological resistance to the premises of realism. Obviously, this is a clear declaration of impasse for the novelist unless he is able to discover some means of converting the very elements of the impasse *into* his subject matter, while at the same time turning away as completely as possible from materials drawn from the contemporary social scene that require specific realistic treatment.

It was perhaps logical, therefore, that Barth in his well-known essay, "The Literature of Exhaustion," should announce the obsolescence of all the conventions of the realistic novel—"cause and effect, linear anecdote, characterization, authorial selection, arrangement, and interpretation"—(conventions that have formed the basis of our conception of the novel from the beginnings of its history) and insist that the only worthwhile function for the novelist at the present time is to parody those conventions, to produce "imitations-of-novels, which attempt to represent not life directly but a representation of life" or, ultimately, "something like *The Sot-Weed Factor* or *Giles Goat-Boy:* novels which imitate the form of the Novel, by an author who imitates the role of Author."

Barth's implication here is that whether through the exhaustion of the realistic genre, his own imaginative exhaustion and boredom with the overly familiar effects of a worked-out tradition, or the impossibility of giving adequate expression to current social actualities within the formalized modes of that tradition, the novelist today has no choice but to focus his attention on the fiction-making process itself. He must create complication and mystery not through the exploration of human character but through an ironic or parodic manipulation of his fictive resources within the closed precincts of any given novel—the relation between his imagined reality and public social reality being no longer mimetic but at most metaphorical or surrealistic or even finally altogether indefinable and, for that matter, altogether irrelevant.

What Barth in fact does in both *The Sot-Weed Factor* and *Giles Goat-Boy* is transfer his paralysing idea of "versions" from the situation of characters like Andrews and Horner to the interior of his fiction, where "versions" become not the differing and conflicting perspectives that the characters bring to the depicted actions but rather the conflicting ways in which Barth the novelist *does* the depicting. Where for Andrews and Horner "versions" were a prime cause of psychological impasse, they now become dramatic expressions of the author's imaginative impasse. After Barth has put before us a bewildering variety of possible approaches to, and interpretations of, the many events of his narrative and then requires them to undercut and neutralize one another, nothing solid is finally left. All the "versions" have been rendered suspect, leaving the reader to conclude that there is no way at all that reality can be engaged, that, in fact, there is no reality other than the self-canceling efforts of the author to discover that there is none. In this sense *The Sot-Weed Factor* and *Giles Goat-Boy,* ingenious though they may be in conception, are novels made to self-destruct—the one being an imitation and parody of an eighteenth-century picaresque novel in which Barth endlessly invokes the authority of history only to nullify that authority by exposing it as merely another version of an unfathomable truth, the other being a mock epic and comic burlesque of the stereotypical heroic quest in which such figures as Jesus Christ, Oedipus, and John F. Kennedy are deflated and trivialized into farce by a vigorously enforced reductive angle of vision that allows no character or occurrence within the novel to possess more than a momentary and provisional validity.

In *Lost in the Funhouse,* his collection of more or less thematically related short stories, Barth emerges as the author so obsessively conscious of the possible ways of presenting his narrative that finally all possibilities are sabotaged and the very idea of narrative becomes unthinkable. In the title story, which is preceded by a few quite excellent stories done, surprisingly enough, in a fairly conventional realistic manner, a family spends the Fourth of July at an amusement park, and a thirteen-year-old boy either does or does not get lost in the funhouse while Barth interrupts the action regularly to discuss alternative ways of carrying it forward. The funhouse is of course an objectification of his vision of life in its baffling relation to the artist, but the bafflement is in fact the story. The protagonist is not the boy but John Barth demonstrating why the boy can never enter the funhouse or find his way out of it, become either lost or found, be brought to life as a character or made to enter life as a human being. The funhouse with its infinitely magnifying hall of mirrors and labyrinthine passageways leading to illusory deadends is the culminating image of Barth's own imaginative deadend, the exhaustion of his sense of creative possibility, his ultimate capitulation before the challenge of utterance, and in the story called "Anonymiad" he confesses his defeat: "I yearned to be relieved of myself.... I'd relapse into numbness, as if, having abandoned song for speech, I meant now to give up language altogether and float voiceless in the wash of time like an amphora in the sea, my vision bottled."

The only alternative for the writer who has thought himself beyond the limits of narrative possibility is silence, and an insistent yearning to become silent, in effect to kill himself off as an articulating artist, can be felt throughout Barth's more recent work. But in the epistolary novel called *Letters,* he seems to have tried for a brief postponement of suicide by retreating completely into the bottled vision of his previous novels and carrying on an imaginary correspondence with the many characters he created in those novels—or he will have them correspond with one another. Jacob Horner is brought forward to tell—in a letter addressed fittingly to himself in his earlier incarnation in *End of the Road*—what happened to him after the conclusion of that novel. Barth as the author of *Letters* writes to Todd Andrews to ask him if he would be willing to appear as a character in a new work of fiction that will become *Letters,* and even to serve as Barth's attorney in the event that any libel suits should result from the novel's publication. Todd Andrews writes an annual death-day letter to his deceased father, telling him of the resumption of his affair with Jane Mack—that relationship having been terminated by Jane at the end of *The Floating Opera.*

By establishing in this way a series of incestuous relationships with his own fictional progeny, Barth relieves himself of having to create new characters. He is not required to invent alternative ways of presenting his narrative because "reality" has already been established as fixed by the manner in which it was presented in the earlier novels. And that fictional reality has become a substitute for the world of extra-fictional reality, which now need not be consulted at all, since the fiction is all there is. All that is important has occurred in the novels and not in life, while life has been totally fictionalized by the novels. Barth, in his turn, has disappeared as author into his creation and become, like his characters, a fictional version of a hypothetical human being. His vision has indeed become bottled and he voiceless in the wash of his previous vision, an amphora whose only function is to be a surviving artifact of a function that he himself has rendered obsolete.

Barth once remarked that "reality is a nice place to visit but you wouldn't want to live there.... Reality is a drag." The fictional method that he began elaborating after he published *End of the Road* enabled him not only to avoid living in reality but to escape having even to pay it a visit. The extreme internalization of all those technical effects, which in the work of a realistic novelist would serve as mimetic or at most metaphorical points of exit to the external world, resulted in a fiction that sustains itself almost entirely through the consumption of its own entrails. The complex, cross-indexed system of allusions to events and characters that exist solely within the novel that is in process of being written or the novels that have previously been written, the introduction of mythical figures as well as actual historical personages into a context in which they are taken apart and reassembled so as to serve the purposes of a Barthian antimyth—all make it possible for Barth to avoid the immensely difficult problem of having to confront the complexities of the external world. One can remain lost in the funhouse forever and endlessly contemplate the myriad distortions of one's reflection in the hall of mirrors and endlessly speculate on the meaning of those distortions—or on whether they have meaning. And all the while one can be safe from the intrusion of any reality that is not itself one of the distortions, a product of the mirrored scene.

Yet for better or worse, the world outside the funhouse is where the novelist must begin, even if he ends in a world that represents only a fictive version of the outside world. But when the connection between the world and its version is broken or was never made in the first place, then the version is no longer a version but has become its own subject, while the author has appointed himself the observer of the process by which the subject has become the subject and he the observer of the process. The ultimate result, as Barth's early work makes clear, is that the author becomes trapped in the act of creation with a steadily diminishing awareness of just what the materials are that the act was meant to create. Clearly, they should be something more than the materials of creation themselves. The pot of paint and the canvas are not, after all, the painting. But then if Barth believes that the reality that might be painted is a bore, he has no choice other than to make what he can of the emptiness of his canvas.

In view of all this, it comes as a distinct surprise to find Barth in *Sabbatical: A Romance* very nearly reversing his former advance into creative impasse and turning back to something like old-fashioned narrative realism. "Very nearly" and "something like" are necessary because Barth would not be Barth if he submitted easily to the heresy of verisimilitude or avoided showing concern for some of the compositional problems that so vexed him in the past. He therefore devotes the opening sections of the novel to a certain amount of nervous fiddling with camera angles and observational perspectives, as if to contest and qualify the disgrace of his descent into realism by erecting around it a refracting screen of authorial equivocation about how his story should be told and which of its manifold potential meanings should become dominant. In his effort to do this, Barth again erases himself completely as author and appoints his two main characters, a couple named Fenwick and Susan Turner, as co-narrators. The Turners are participants in the experience that, at the same time, they are struggling to translate into coherent narrative form, and so they alternate between living in the action and observing themselves as performers in a fictive account of the action—as both real persons and dramatis personae.

Fortunately, Barth's old concern with the "versions" approach to experience now appears to have become mostly ceremonial and does little to impede the development of his narrative, perhaps because in losing interest in the Turners as fictional constructs, he falls in love with them as people and so makes them loveable as characters. In fact, the Turners are the most thoroughly charming characters to appear in fiction in some years, and their story is—as Barth's subtitle indicates—indeed a romance not only in the sense that it is an account of their deep love for each other but because the realism of the account is periodically stretched beyond its conventional limits in order to accommodate elements that are extraordinary, mysterious, and quite inexplicable by the known laws of reason. The form Barth has chosen is the oldest and most appropriate form of the romance—the voyage at sea, for which not only the Greek and Roman sea epics but Poe's *The Narrative of A. Gordon Pym* are often cited in the text as the authoritative precedents.

The Turners make their voyage aboard their sailboat during a sabbatical year when Susan, a bright and beautiful young professor of American literature, takes leave from teaching and Fenwick, a fifty-year-old ex-CIA officer, languishes between careers. They sail for nine months from Chesapeake Bay to the Caribbean and back, and along the way as the details of their past and present lives are revealed, it becomes evident that their journey represents a descent into the maelstrom or underworld in search of some means of understanding their relation to themselves and the often unbelievable realities of contemporary life. One of those realities is the unsolved disappearance at sea of Fenwick's twin brother Manfred, also a CIA official, and of Susan's half-brother Gus in Chile—both men having perhaps been the victims of CIA conspiracy. At one point in the voyage, the Turners come upon a sinister island in the middle of the Chesapeake but not to be found on any navigational chart. At another point Fenwick loses his beloved and talismanic Spanish beret overboard, and many miles farther on, it magically bobs to the surface and is restored to his head. Then there is the fabulous figure of

Susan's mother, a most stylish and foxy lady gifted with the power to communicate occasionally with souls beyond the grave.

The novel is, in short, a wonderful combination of realism and fantasy, psychological analysis and metaphysical exploration. But its virtue lies not in its overlay of the darkly mysterious but in its realistic depiction of the commonplace, which, as Joyce's *Ulysses,* demonstrated, when scrutinized closely enough and with sufficient artistry, shades into the extraordinary and becomes numinous.

Barth's next novel, *The Tidewater Tales,* both does and does not mark his further progress toward the clarity of narrative daylight. In fact, taken in terms of its characters and central situation, it so closely resembles *Sabbatical* that it can be considered, if not quite a sequel to that novel, at least a companion volume. Once again the story is told by twin narrator-protagonists, this time Peter and Katherine Sagamore, who are very much like the Turners and who are also sailing, although their radius is limited to the waterways of the Chesapeake Bay. They too are involved in a marginal way in CIA activities, and they even have a friend, one Frank Talbott, who once wrote a novel about his and his wife's sailing experiences in the Caribbean, a novel that is actually *Sabbatical* with the Talbotts renamed the Secklers. In that novel Mrs. Seckler has an abortion. In *The Tidewater Tales* Mrs. Talbott has had an abortion but by the end has become happily pregnant, even as Katherine Sagamore, who has had a miscarriage, is also throughout the novel happily pregnant with twins. Her husband, Peter, furthermore, will use the experiences they are having in *The Tidewater Tales* as the materials of a novel to be called, of course, *The Tidewater Tales.* Peter is a writer of minimalist short stories and has adhered so religiously to the principle that less is more that he is on the verge of creative self-strangulation. But by making use of the massively abundant materials provided by the voyage, he will presumably enjoy replenished vitality as well as a new belief in the principle that much more is, after all, much, much better.

If the sheer bulk of this novel is any indication, Barth seems now to share this belief and to have undergone a similar liberation—in his case, from his former obsession with self-canceling versions. In his performance here he reminds one of Saul Bellow who, after being strait-jacketed by formal restraints in his first two novels, burst out in *The Adventures of Augie March* into a loose and baggy picaresque saga, an extravagant sprawl of language, and a huge cast of wildly eccentric characters. Barth seems similarly larky and euphoric, gleefully at play in the fields of his own fiction, sporting outrageously with his medium, clearly loving himself as the creator of all this abundance, and adoring his characters as much as they adore one another. And in truth, while this is not Barth's most intellectually complex novel, it is without question the richest, most ebullient, and technically daring of any he has hitherto written. It is crowded with grand virtuosic effects that seem to have nothing to do with the action except to interrupt it, yet are offered simply because they are such fun.

There are odd excursions into dreams, some of which are uncannily prophetic of the future action. There are encounters with strange exotic people like the beautiful Greek couple who may very well be contemporary incarnations of Odysseus and Nausicaa or like Capt. Donald Quicksoat, a contemporary Don Quixote whose adventures, as imagined by Peter Sagamore, occur in the centuries following the end of Cervantes' novel. Scheherazade comes to life to explain why she told her stories for exactly a thousand and one nights and not sixty-two or ninety-four. The Sagamores carry on conversations with their as-yet-unborn twins who, as the novel proceeds, grow into fetal characters known by innumerable cutesy names like Fore and Aft, Spit and Image, Toil and Trouble, Fish and Chips, and Blam and Blooey. It is all a delightful romp through fantasy, myth, fiction, and fact, and it is also a hugely joyous celebration of life.

It would seem on the evidence of this remarkable novel that Barth has finally found his way out of the funhouse and back into the world. Or perhaps he has learned to adjust its mirrors so that they no longer give back endless images or versions of his baffled self but instead reflect the reality he once disdained in all its diversity and richness.
1983/1987

Robert Coover's Party Animals

From the beginning of his literary career, Robert Coover has been driven by the quite commendable ambition to make radical innovations in the forms and styles of contemporary fiction. Like John Barth who once famously proclaimed the conventional novel obsolete, Coover has for years been burdened by a weary sense that the traditional narrative possibilities for fiction—in particular, the possibilities of classic realism—have passed into exhaustion, not only because they have grown overly familiar but because, since they are so familiar, the response of the reader to them has become habitual and, therefore, imaginatively unproductive.

Coover is convinced that the first responsibility of the truly original writer is to discover new narrative arrangements that will have the effect of shocking the reader out of his habitual responses and forcing him to confront, however painfully, fresh and unorthodox ways of envisioning human experience. In his effort to fulfill this responsibility Coover has produced over twenty years eight works of fiction that include novels, plays, and collections of short stories, all of which are eccentric in form, often brutally unpleasant in content, and fueled by a savage determination to subvert the conventions of plausibility, not to say sanity, so completely that the reader is left stupefied and totally at the mercy of the imperious authority of the writer.

It is a process by which the old-fashioned and usually benevolent relationship between writer and reader is altogether destroyed. The writer ceases to be the helpful mentor and tour guide leading the reader through the unfolding significances of his narrative and becomes an adversarial disrupter of those significances, challenging the reader to find and understand them on his own, if he can, and warning him also that if he does find them, they are not to be understood according to the standard of values he may have inherited from the literature of the past. In fact, the very idea that a narrative may have significance, at least in the usual sense of the word, is called into question because Coover's method is to insist that his narratives are their own artistic subjects, that they are autotelic, wholly about themselves, and that as self-reflexive fictions their meanings are arbitrary and provisional, dependent not upon some crass imitative correspondence to empirical reality but rather upon whatever the writer chooses at the moment to make of them.

This approach is metaphysically very similar to Barth's notion, so extensively elaborated and finally attenuated to the point of exhaustion in his earlier work, that since everything is relative, each of us can have only his version or versions of the truth; hence, it is possible to live one's life by improvising and playing a seemingly limitless series of roles that may be external public expressions of the various versions of the truth one perceives. When applied to the fiction-making process this idea translates into a belief, which in Barth's case became paralysing, that there is an infinite number of ways in which a given piece of fiction may be presented and interpreted, so that finally no one way can be considered better or more plausible than any other. The ultimate result, as Barth's *The Sot-Weed Factor* and *Giles Goat-Boy* make clear, is that the various possible approaches to, and interpretations of fictional events undercut and neutralize one another, and both novels self-destruct in a blaze of relativism.

Coover's own version of the versional approach is best displayed in the stories collected in *Pricksongs & Descants,* the best known of which, the story or perhaps more accurately the narrative exercise called "The Babysitter," is an excellent case in point. The action begins conventionally enough: A teenaged girl arrives at the home of the Tuckers to look after their children while they go to a party. The babysitter's boyfriend, Jack, is wandering around town and thinks he may drop in on her later in the evening, perhaps bringing along his friend, Mark, who may or may not join him in trying to seduce the girl. She wrestles with the two older children on the living room floor and may or may not succeed in giving the little boy a bath, then the little girl. The Tuckers arrive at the party. The babysitter wrestles with the children perhaps a second time, perhaps not. Jack and Mark arrive at the Tucker house. They may or may not rape the babysitter. Mr. Tucker, still at the party, imagines that he returns home alone and rapes her himself or he returns home and finds her making love with Jack, whom he then sends home naked. Or Mr. and Mrs. Tucker arrive home, accompanied by Mark's parents, the neighbors, and the police, and find Mark, Jack, and the babysitter huddled half-naked under a blanket. And so on, and so on. The narrative ends with the ultimate apocalyptic scenario. The Tucker baby is drowned by the babysitter in the bathtub. The two older children and perhaps the babysitter are murdered by Jack and Mark. Mr. Tucker has disappeared. When told this appalling news Mrs. Tucker, still at the party, responds by saying, "Let's see what's on the late late show." On the other hand, it may be that nothing of the sort happens.

Coover has explored most of the imaginable versions of his narrative and revealed, in so doing, a certain technical cleverness. But his versions do not constitute a story but appear rather to be a series of virtuosic attempts to conceal the fact that he does not have a story, if only because the materials of a story are not contained in merely alternative ways of describing an action but consist of a revelation of character and motive, elements Coover evidently lacks the capacity to penetrate. But it would seem that through his abdication of all responsibility to the requirement that narrative be reflective, however obliquely, of some recognizable human situation, he has arrived at a point of imaginative nullity where any technical move is possible because none is necessary.

In Coover's widely discussed novel, *The Public Burning*, this abdication of responsibility results in a narrative that is ostensibly constructed on a basis of historical fact but is such a travesty of fact that it is not satirical but pointlessly surreal, not comically critical but vulgarly slapstick. Using as the occasion for his narrative what is obviously for him the most egregious miscarriage of justice in living memory—the execution of Julius and Ethel Rosenberg for passing atomic secrets to the Russians—Coover composes a preposterous epic-catalogue of culprits responsible for it. They range from Cecil B. DeMille, who stages a massive Hollywood-style extravaganza in Times Square where the Rosenbergs are to be electrocuted before a cheering cast of thousands, to Betty Crocker, who presides over the festivities, and Gene Autry, who will provide vocal accompaniment, while Harry James and his Orchestra play overhead on the Astor Roof. In the audience on Electrocution Night are to be found, in spirit or in flesh, such notables as Dale Carnegie, Ty Cobb, Admiral Halsey, Ezio Pinza, Cole Porter, and Shirley Temple. But, ultimately, just about every prominent national figure and political institution from J. Edgar Hoover and the FBI through the presidential cabinet, Supreme Court, and Congress is indicted as an accomplice in the gigantic conspiracy against the sainted Rosenbergs.

The obvious trouble with the novel—if, in fact, it is a novel—is that in it Coover tells us absolutely nothing about the American political situation at the time of the Rosenberg executions. Instead, he makes an indictment, which is just as pathologically sweeping as any of Joseph McCarthy's, of just about everything and everyone popularly associated with the American way of life, and he does so by adopting the kind of shrill sophomoric bombast with which activist leaders used to harangue street crowds during the more violent demonstrations of the sixties. The sickness for him as for them is universal. It infects every fiber of the national character; it is endemic to our national history and our cultural and political life; and it has been intentionally spread through the secret conduits of the conspiracy engineered by the military-industrial complex, which is determined to brainwash an innocent citizenry and conscript it into the service of its nefarious aims. In short, the novel is not an indignant exposé of the injustices behind the Rosenberg case but a mindless evacuation of spleen, as imaginatively impotent as any graffiti scrawl on the tunnel wall of a subway. Nothing in the novel really signifies or connotes because paranoid hallucination and blind fury have wholly disoriented whatever critical perspective Coover may once have had.

This same failure—which must finally be considered a failure of sensibility—gravely weakens Coover's new novel, *Gerald's Party,* a work that in other respects is technically daring and often fascinating as an example of sick brilliance employed in the service of a hostility so malignant that it shocks the reader with the force of an act of terrorism.

The setting of the action is, as the title suggests, a cocktail party at which Coover assembles a gathering of ostensibly civilized, educated, and sensitive people and causes them to behave in spectacularly uncivilized ways, thereby thoroughly frustrating all of the reader's conventional expectations. His purpose in doing this is unclear. Obviously, it is not satirical, although the novel might superficially be read as a kind of demented burlesque of a British drawingroom farce combined with the classic form of the murder mystery. What Coover actually seems to be saying is that if we were honest enough to follow our deepest impulses, we would do incredibly nasty things—on the order, for example, of the vicious act of anal rape perpetrated upon Richard Nixon by the wildly manic caricature-figure of Uncle Sam at the end of *The Public Burning.* But the problem with this is that we long ago received such a message. The early naturalists for one spelled it out with banal clarity in their beast and blood imagery, and Freud educated us to know what our *real* motives are as we sip our tea with delicate decorum and speak politely of the weather. One can only conclude that this is yet another manifestation of Coover's Betty Crocker syndrome, the derangement of taste and perspective that causes him to carry his point so far beyond plausibility (Betty Crocker, after all, cannot by any standard of sanity be associated with the Rosenberg case) that it becomes aberration—symptomatic perhaps of Coover's complete contempt for all laws of justice and proportion.

But then he also seems contemptuous of the very act of novelistic composition. In fact, his book shows evidence on virtually every page of a kind of surly resistance to being written. The narrative continuity is constantly being interrupted by snatches of conversation that are themselves interrupted by physical descriptions and wisps of reverie, random happenings and the chatter of other people, most of whom one finds it impossible to identify without searching back over the text to sort out their names. Everything in the novel is perceived out of recognizable context and focus, is defamiliarized to the point where the reader is forced into the most stressful contest with the withholding author in order to determine, however vaguely, just what is happening and who is saying or doing what to whom.

This technical resistance is paralleled by the resistance set up by the action itself, which proceeds to subvert all one's assumptions about the conceivable limits of human conduct. The novel begins with the party given by Gerald and his unnamed wife well in progress. The guests are drinking heavily and crowding together in various parts of the house. Some are in the TV room watching a talk show. Others are in a downstairs room playing a game of darts. Still others are wandering around in the backyard. Gerald's wife is in the kitchen preparing hors d'oeuvres. Several amatory explorations have been initiated.

The main attraction of the evening is a celebrated actress named Roz, the star of pornographic films and plays and sometime bed partner of most of the male guests. It is a considerable while before Roz is discovered to be missing and is then found murdered on the living room floor. Her husband, Roger, throws himself on his wife's body and goes berserk with grief. While the police, who finally arrive, try to subdue him, he staggers and flails about, colliding with people, knocking them off their feet, and smearing them with the victim's blood. Later on, because Roger continues to be unmanageable, the police beat him to death with croquet mallets.

Following the discovery of the murdered Roz the party quickly disintegrates into orgiastic chaos. The shock of the murder fades almost immediately. The guests resume their drinking, consume great quantities of food, laugh and joke quite as if nothing dreadful had happened, and proceed to involve themselves randomly and with a kind of sadistic lust in the sexual pursuit of one another. Only Gerald's wife remains placid. She goes about her hostessly duties like a household robot or Stepford wife, preparing food, collecting empty glasses, being cheerful and hospitable.

Later in the evening she walks in on Gerald while he is copulating with a sixteen-year-old girl and courteously introduces him to a couple who have just moved into the neighborhood and whom she is showing around the house. On another occasion after one of the guests, her husband's best friend, is shot by a policeman and lies dying on the living room floor, she says, "I do wish people wouldn't use guns in the house," and "Somehow parties don't seem as much fun as they used to." By the end of the evening something like eight people have been killed by various means, and their bodies are left lying about unattended. The house has been torn apart, windows have been broken out, debris is scattered everywhere, and when the last guests finally leave, Gerald and his wife, in the final scene of the novel, make love amid the wreckage, their "pubes crushing together like remote underwater collisions, as ineluctable as punchlines."

The profoundly frightening aspect of this incredible narrative is the total indifference of the guests to the violence and destruction occurring around them and the ease with which they subvert all normal expectations of compassion, horror, and outrage in a madly manic bacchanal. Only Gerald's wife preserves decorum throughout. But hers is a meretricious decorum, a mechanical conformity to social ritual made possible by complete lack of feeling, and not a decorum based upon humane values that the actions of the others can be seen to violate and, in the violation, brought to moral judgment.

If it was Coover's intention to shock the reader into responding in new ways to a fictional rendering of human experience, he undoubtedly has succeeded. But it is not a response that creates an enlargement of consciousness but rather its diminishment. There is quite simply no meaning to be found in the portrayal of human beings who act in accordance with none of the fundamental laws of humanity. If he is saying that this is the way we are or would like to be if we were freed from the authority of those laws, if he is saying that not so very deep down we are all sexually exploitative, murderous, and indifferent to the suffering of others, then he is offering no instruction that can be used because his premise is false. It may be that in our naked selves we are like that, but we are never that naked because, as Freud saw so clearly, we can never escape the moral and emotional conditions of civilization and would be nothing human if we could.

1986

Norman Mailer
Conquering the Bitch Goddess

The appearance of these two volumes, *The Long Patrol*, a retrospective collection of Norman Mailer's writings and a book of critical essays about him, is one of several recent indications that Mailer has at last begun to suffer the fate he has hoped for years would overtake him. There now seems to be widespread agreement—not only among his literary contemporaries but large segments of the reading public—that he is the most exciting and important writer now at work in America. The interesting question is why this presumably self-evident fact of Mailer's genius has taken so long to be acknowledged, why even sophisticated people have had to *learn* to live with it as if it were a loathsome disease, after overcoming extremely powerful feelings of distaste, while legions of the semiliterate, the sort who never read books but know exactly which writers they detest, appear to harbor the most astonishing hostility to Mailer's face, physique, voice, manners, and morals and seem unable to understand why he was not put away long ago.

This seems rather odd when one considers that we have never expected our best writers to be particularly saintly, and there is a fine tradition among them of behavior ranging from the merely perverse through the boorish, sottish, deceitful, spiteful, disloyal, and infantile to the maddest reaches of paranoia and monomania. The examples of Poe, Whitman, Twain, Frost, Hart Crane, Hemingway, Faulkner, and Fitzgerald all testify in varying degrees to the fact that sometimes the only respectable thing about a writer is his writing. Yet these men have been accepted—in some cases, to be sure, only after they were decorously dead—because the quality of their work finally seemed to justify their peculiarities of character.

The trouble with Mailer is that not only has he been very much alive among us—unforgivably alive—but he seemed for too long a dubious quantity as a writer while his character grew steadily more outrageous. There was a period in the fifties when he appeared to imagine that the way to achieve large literary success was to engage in brawls and try to get arrested or to insult his readers by disparaging their intelligence—as he did to such good effect in the columns he wrote at the time for *The Village Voice.* His strategy then may well have been to create such an offensive public image that people would be moved to read him if only out of hate. But the practical result was that too many people decided that nobody who acted that foolish could possibly be worth reading. Significantly, it was not until the appearance in 1959 of *Advertisements for Myself,* a collection offered quite nakedly, even abjectly, as an appeal for serious recognition, that the tide of opinion began to turn in Mailer's favor, and it did so not because that book contained old material hitherto unappreciated or prompted a reconsideration of his novels, but because in writing about his frustrations and mistakes, the wreck of his literary hopes, the corrosions of failure that drove him to behave badly, he produced a prose so remarkably much better than anything he had done before that a large number of readers saw for the first time how very good a writer he was—because then, for the first time, he was that good.

Mailer also discovered in *Advertisements* what has since become his most complex and vital subject—himself as combined victim, adversary, hero, and fool being simultaneously humiliated and aggrandized as he engages the ogres and windmills of contemporary history. He had learned a great deal about the dramatic possibilities inherent in the multifoliate subject of Norman Mailer, and he was destined as time passed to learn a great deal more. But by 1959 his remarkable sensitivity to the intricate telegraphies of status had already taught him this much: that to be taken seriously as a man and writer you do not *demand* the approval of the public, for this puts you in the position of appearing to feel arrogantly superior to them and insisting on what is rightfully your due. The far better way is to make the public feel superior to you by demonstrating how pathetic you have become in trying to win their approval and just how much their approval means to you. Furthermore, you could always count on good Americans to believe that recognition should come to those who have worked for it hard enough, and Mailer in *Advertise-*

ments had explained with fine eloquence how terribly hard he had worked for it. If, as Leslie Fiedler once remarked, nothing succeeds for Americans like failure, it is equally true that confession of failure is not only cleansing to the soul but absolutely wonderful for one's public image.

Having apparently learned all this by 1959, Mailer went on to learn something even more essential to his future prosperity: how to make himself into the kind of writer who would finally neutralize through his work some of the mistrust and hostility he had generated through his public behavior. He achieved this in two ways. First, he began making much more direct use in his fiction of his own well-publicized obsessions and aberrations—his interest in the mystical properties of the orgasm in *The Time of Her Time*, the spiritually regenerative effects of wife-murder in *An American Dream*, the cathartic possibilities of the scatological in *Why Are We in Vietnam?* This had the effect of dissociating these ideas from his public self and the essays and interviews in which he had first presented them as shockingly offensive personal interests, and giving them the safely general and objective quality of fictional themes. As such, they might still seem offensive, but at least they would be identified with his imaginary characters and no longer be taken as quite such literal evidence of his own moral corruption.

At the same time he was also discovering how to project in his work—primarily in the metajournalism he began to write in the late sixties—a self-image that became steadily more attractive, not so much because the things he described himself as saying and doing had suddenly ceased to seem outrageous, but because a new note of humor had come to characterize the description and to give it an air of ironic detachment and ambiguity that was both appealing and enormously effective as a tranquilizer of enemies. He was no longer the victim of his bludgeoning first-person delivery. Instead, he became his own most derisive critic as he observed his various personae—an aging, hungover activist in Washington, "the reporter" in Miami and Chicago, Aquarius in Cape Kennedy and Houston—pass through the postures of acute embarrassment, ineptitude, braggadocio, affectation, and occasional wisdom, hamming it up for the gallery or putting down a rival, but always finally being put down hardest by himself. The traits displayed by these personae had long been fixtures of Mailer's public character, but when he had displayed them in that character, they had earned him little more than hostility. Now the writer in him had found a way of using them as material, and in the process he turned his worst vices into almost lovable virtues. The early Mailer committed the one sin Americans can never forgive: he took himself seriously. As a journalist, he began to laugh at himself—an action we prize even more highly than failure.

In achieving these realignments Mailer can hardly be accused of cynicism. There is nothing to indicate that he was employing his skills as a politician, although they are recognized to be considerable. He seems rather to have passed into a new phase of personal and creative development in which he was able to engage himself and his material in fresh terms. By the late sixties he had gained in wisdom as well as age, and he had also gained sufficient success to appease at least the larger hungers of his ego and give him a certain benevolent detachment. But the fact that these things occurred at this particular time was immensely fortuitous, and so was the fact that he began just then to offer in his journalism a kind of material singularly appropriate to the historical moment and guaranteed to have a major impact particularly on the younger audience of the moment. It had been obvious for years to others, if not to Mailer, that if he expected, as he claimed, to have a revolutionary influence on the consciousness of the age, he would be unlikely to do so through the novel. The problem was not simply that his best talents were only erratically displayed in the novel, but that the form itself seemed inadequate to satisfy the needs of a generation who had grown to believe that the social realities of this world are far more important than imaginative fictions, and who were trying to relate to issues as the generation before them had tried to relate to ideas. Mailer's interests as a writer and those of his largest potential public thus nicely coincided, for it had been evident—perhaps even as far back as *The Naked and the Dead*—that his particular powers found their most intense stimulus in moments of social and political crisis, in apocalyptic confrontations between individuals and the massive forces of historical and institutional change. The march on the Pentagon, the riots in Chicago, the presidential campaigns of 1968 were all charged with apocalyptic portent. They were as beautifully suited to Mailer's temperament and style as if he had invented them himself—which, in fact, he might have done—and it so happened that all the seismic instruments agreed that these occasions demanded expression in precisely the form he and he alone could give them.

If he had come to envision himself as a symptomatic consciousness, mediating between his personal micro-hells and the major disasters of his age, he now had an audience desperately in need of someone on whom they could project their own more incoherent sense of being both agents and dupes of history, at once personally implicated in and collectively victimized by events. What they found in Mailer was a writer who could bring into focus the contradictory elements of this feeling, a spokesman able to express it in language and action more forcefully than they could or would have dared, and, above all, a human being whom they could accept—as they had accepted no one since John Kennedy—for a hero because he epitomized in his humanness the ambiguities necessary to an acceptable heroism at that time. He was tough, brash, defiantly irreverent, a taker of unbelievable risks. Yet he was also—and openly admitted to being—vulnerable, uncertain, fearful of the impression he was making (on Robert Lowell, Dwight Macdonald, Eugene McCarthy, Sonny Liston), never completely convinced of the possibility that mere quaking guts might stand up to their monolithic self-possession.

Yet that exactly was the secret of Mailer's appeal, the very essence of his heroism, for he was guts at war with all his unmastered contradictions and fears, and he monitored them in battle with that deadly obsessiveness of the general who has never quite grown up to the courage of his command, brooding over the corpses of real men when he should have been figuring the cold statistics of killed and wounded. Such men as Lowell, Liston, and McCarthy might be great poets, fighters, and politicians, but they could not be heroes, at least not in this time and generation, because they were too complete as personages, at once too intact in their fortitude and too remote from their mortality. Mailer was like the early characters of Hemingway, and he would like to have thought that he was more than a little like Hemingway himself. He was all blustering defense mechanism, the hairy fist clutching the fragile rose, bravery earned at the expense of panic, a mass of insecurities constantly in need of the challenge that would force him into at least the appearance of strength. He thus dramatized the antithetical impulses that underlay the protest movement and the psychology of the young. He expressed their strong mistrust of the pieties of the establishment at the same time that he forced them to confront their own even more pompous pieties. He embodied their sense of self-importance and of insignificance, their faith and their cynicism, their desire to make the grand gesture and their intuition that the grand gesture would probably have slight effect on anyone, least of all the blind course of history. Mailer, in short, was the perfect absurd white knight of their mighty absurd crusade, the quixotic figure of fun, nobility, pride, self-derisiveness, and absolute honesty for a generation that had nothing to offer but its indignation, its idealism, and its preposterous nerve.

But one saw that these same qualities that made Mailer so attractive to the younger readers of his journalism also helped to ingratiate him with older readers and even former enemies. That developing note of self-derisiveness which came to characterize his treatment of his various personae was accompanied by an increasing tendency to equivocate about issues and people he at one time most probably would have demolished. Practically every portrait he drew of public events and personalities could be seen to have a dimension of meliorating ambiguity. If he put down liberals, one also noticed that he put down conservatives. He might show irritation over the fact that Ralph Abernathy had kept the press waiting forty minutes in Miami. He might even use the occasion to deliver one of his most agonized and eloquent perorations on the whole oppressive phenomenon of Negro rights: "He [Mailer] was so heartily sick of listening to the tyranny of soul music, so bored with Negroes triumphantly late for appointments, so depressed with Black inhumanity to Black in Biafra, so weary of being sounded in the subway by Black eyes, so despairing of the smell of booze and pot and used-up hope in the blood-shot eyes of Negroes bombed at noon."

He might even acknowledge the presence in "some secret part of his flesh [of] . . . a closet Republican," yet the confession clearly costs him something in "dread and woe." Its impact is softened if not canceled by his so evident guilt, and that, it turns out, is not his loss but his gain, for he has registered his heresy in the very breath of denouncing it, and so may be said to have had it both ways, put into words our most vicious buried hatreds but purged himself and us with the detergents of self-disgust.

In the same manner one also saw him in *Armies of the Night* open an attack on his peers, but with a sure instinct for the right one to destroy—Paul Goodman, lost to him anyway, but not Lowell or Macdonald, who at that moment was known to be at work on a review of *Why Are We in Vietnam?* for *The New Yorker*. Again, it would be unfair to suggest that what has really happened to Mailer is that he has become a politician. Without doubt his vision has simply grown more dialectical, and he has found a way of dramatizing more completely his own intellectual and psychological contradictions. Yet one cannot deny that this often *appears* to be circumspection or that, deliberate or not, it has worked powerfully to his advantage. He now knows how little real profit there is in the self-indulgence of the direct attack, and how much potential risk. To allow oneself the exhilaration of trying with a single blow to kill off all one's literary competitors—as he very nearly succeeded in doing in "The Talent in the Room" and "Some Children of the Goddess"—is to take the chance of undermining one's whole campaign for the championship. He did not dare to afford such luxuries now that he saw he had become the caretaker of a possibly major reputation and a talent for winning the large-scale approval he had fought for throughout his literary life.

The dangers for the public writer in achieving approval of this kind were all rehearsed for us in the sad example of Hemingway. Mailer began by envying Hemingway his reputation, and now that he has won something approaching its equivalent, he may be forced to suffer very similar consequences. If Hemingway finally found it more enjoyable to play at being the celebrity than to persist in the more arduous course of developing himself as a writer, Mailer may not be wholly exempt from the same temptation. Widespread attention is most easily won these days through performing in the mass media, and such performance is far less tiring than creativity. If in order to gain an audience for your important work you make yourself into a media performer, you must also know when to stop performing and get on with your important work. Otherwise, you may end by becoming nothing but a performer, and, worse, you will begin to live for it as an end in itself. Mailer knows this better than most because he knows his own weaknesses better than anybody else. But it would appear to be time now for him to get back to work and begin to live out his fantasies through the creations of his mind and talent and not through such humiliating and disastrous exhibitions as his recent boxing match with Jose Torres on the "Dick Cavett Show" or his nasty debate with Gore Vidal.

The two volumes devoted to representative selections from Mailer's work and to the views of his critics may serve as a reminder to him that he is indeed the caretaker, however careless, of a major talent and reputation, and they may also draw public attention away from his activities as a television pugilist and back to the real matter at hand. *The Long Patrol* contains an excellent sampling of his writings—both excerpted and complete—from *The Naked and the Dead* through *Of a Fire on the Moon,* and is intended, as the editor, Robert F. Lucid, says, to attract readers who may be discovering Mailer for the first time. The critical collection, also edited by Mr. Lucid, should surely win for Mailer both new and more respectful readers, for here are critics writing, whether in praise or condemnation, about a man whom they clearly consider a literary phenomenon of very great importance. The book contains an extremely discerning and appreciative introduction by Mr. Lucid, Richard Foster's fine long study, which first appeared as one of the *University of Minnesota Pamphlets on American Writers,* the early and classic essays by Diana Trilling and Norman Podhorets, Elizabeth Hardwick's delightfully indignant and mostly uncomprehending review of *An American Dream,* as well as other pieces of varying quality and temper by such critics as Alfred Kazin, Richard Poirier, Tom Wolfe, Midge Decter, Leo Bersani, Jack Richardson, and Dwight Macdonald.

The two collections together testify to the size of Mailer's achievement and the solidity of his present reputation. That is what matters to us, and it should be all that matters to him. For now that he has proven that he can survive and triumph over failure, he has still to prove that he can survive his large success. To do this it would seem that he must learn again the lesson every successful writer has had to learn not once but many times: that it is necessary for him to become private once more because his real demons can never be confronted in the public limelight but only in the haunted personal dark. Yeats's lines addressed "To a Friend Whose Work Has Come To Nothing" may be even more appropriate to one whose work has come to a very great deal:

> Bred to a harder thing
> Than Triumph, turn away
> And like a laughing string
> Whereon mad fingers play
> Amid a place of stone,
> Be secret and exult,
> Because of all things known
> That is most difficult.

1971

A Mailer Masterpiece

Mailer's powers of self-rejuvenation are evidently limitless because since 1971, when I published the preceding essay, he has indeed passed beyond that long, tempestuous public phase of his career and, while still and always in public view, has become private once again. In that haunted personal dark to which I admonished him to return, he has addressed himself to the creation of works that are unquestionably more original and important than any he produced before—*The Executioner's Song* in 1979, *Ancient Evenings* in 1983, and now, in 1991, *Harlot's Ghost*.

One might, in fact, argue that in this massive novel he has undertaken the most challenging task of his creative career, the writing of a fictionalized history of the multifoliate operations since World War II of the CIA, an organization that lives at least in our imaginations, if not in fact, as the supreme embodiment of mystery and covert power in the present age. It is not surprising and surely it is no accident that Mailer has chosen for the book a form as labyrinthine and finally as ambiguous in its implications as the conspiratorial system he sets out to explore. For if it is true that the best form in fiction is that which makes the most of its subject, then Mailer has found one which not only makes the most of his subject but almost exactly emulates it.

The novel is composed of two distinct but closely interwoven narratives, each concerning events that take place during different periods of the action and both written by the protagonist, a veteran CIA officer named Harry Hubbard. The long opening section, which Hubbard calls the Omega manuscript, is mainly an account of certain horrendous happenings that occur in the late winter of 1983, ten years after Watergate. Hugh Montague, a brilliant CIA agent (code name: Harlot), Hubbard's godfather, professional mentor, and former husband of his wife, Kittredge, has suddenly disappeared, and a dead man who may be Harlot has been found floating in Chesapeake Bay. The problem is that no identity papers are found on the body; the face has been mutilated by a shotgun blast; the ends of the fingers have been eaten away, perhaps by fish, so that print identification is impossible; and Harlot's x-rays are mysteriously missing from the Agency files.

This dire information is brought by Reed Rosen, a CIA colleague, to Hubbard and Kittredge at their house in Maine. It turns out that Rosen suspects the dead man may actually not be Harlot but someone meticulously prepared to resemble him, right down to his partially intact dental work. But the heavy question is: if the corpse really is Harlot, has the KGB contrived to have him killed in order to eliminate a top CIA agent, or have the members of some secret cabal inside the Agency itself done the deed out of an apparently justified fear that Harlot had amassed evidence incriminating them in a Watergate-related plot to steal billions of dollars from the Federal Reserve? Or could it be that Harlot himself has managed to make it appear that he committed suicide, while he has actually defected to the Soviet Union?

In any case, after Hubbard and Rosen discuss these sobering possibilities, Kittredge, who has been devastated by the news of her former husband's possible death, abruptly announces that she has fallen in love with Dix Butler, another CIA colleague, and that she and Rosen expect him to arrive at the house later that evening. She insists that Hubbard leave so that she can be with Butler, and he most reluctantly does so. He flies to New York and learns the next day that the house has burned down, Rosen's body has been found at the site, but there is no word of Kittredge. At the end of the unfinished Omega manuscript, Hubbard, under a false identity, has gone to Moscow determined to find out whether or not Harlot has defected. Such high gothic melodrama would surely be more than sufficient to sustain any novel of modest length. But in this massive context, it is nothing more than a brief preamble.

The vast center of the book is composed of Hubbard's second narrative, the so-called Alpha manuscript, a heavily detailed and convoluted account of his CIA career beginning in 1955. It extends through his service in postwar Berlin before the building of the Wall, a period of choreographing dirty tricks in Uruguay, his bungled participation in the Bay of Pigs fiasco and an attempt to assassinate Fidel Castro, more dirty tricks in Paris, and ends with the assassination of John F. Kennedy in 1963.

These hundreds of pages are crammed with almost as much arcane but fascinating marginal information as can be found in *Moby Dick,* Balzac's *The Human Comedy,* or in a novel by Charles Dickens. We learn from them about the intricate methods by which information of a secret nature is processed and transmitted between overseas stations and CIA headquarters, about Kim Philby and Guy Burgess, the British intelligence agents who defected to the Soviet Union, how the secret and double agent networks operated in East and West Germany as well as in Cuba and South America, the fundamental principles behind espionage and counterespionage operations, exactly how and where young CIA recruits are trained, and the personalities and domestic habits of Bobby Kennedy, Howard Hunt, then a CIA chief of station and later a key figure in the Watergate scandal, and Allen Dulles, a former CIA director.

The presence of these and many other real-life personages gives the book a close resemblance to the kind of nonfiction novel that Mailer helped to perfect in such a work as *The Executioner's Song,* a strongly factual account of the life of the convicted murderer, Gary Gilmore, who was executed by firing squad in Utah in 1977. But *Harlot's Ghost* escapes that classification because the purely fictional characters and those drawn from life are both imagined with equal vividness and originality. In fact, one might hazard the guess that Bobby Kennedy, Howard Hunt, and Allen Dulles are made more human and attractive in Mailer's treatment of them than any documentary account might indicate that they actually were.

There will probably be readers, particularly among the sound-bite generation, who will want to bring this book up on a charge of criminal excess. And it is true that, in terms of bulk alone, it might be seen as belonging to that category of overstuffed novels that Henry James, with his own bloated productions clearly in mind, once described as "loose and baggy monsters." It may also be generally true, as the late Isaac Bashevis Singer has said, that "no novel should be longer than *War and Peace,* and even that novel is too long." Maybe so. But Tolstoy, after all, managed to get away with it, and so does Mailer.

To be sure, there are moments when the accumulated weight of all those hundreds of events and characters becomes almost more than one can bear, and one yearns to be less thoroughly informed about every last intricate detail of every last intelligence operation that is going forward at the pace of a paraplegic snail. *Harlot's Ghost* is, indeed, a monster of a book. But what a wonderful monster it is, and it would be less wonderful if it were less loose and baggy. For what finally the book becomes is no less than a gigantically discursive, remarkably benign meditation on the subterfuges and perversions, the deceits and betrayals, the compromises and, yes, the honest victories that constitute the dark politics of covert power. No smaller novel could begin to do justice to such a mighty subject. If "form follows function" is a first principle of architecture, it is also a first principle of fiction, and *Harlot's Ghost* conforms to it absolutely.

It is perhaps fitting that, like so many of the espionage operations it describes, the novel does not end with the resolution of its central mystery. It simply stops, and the last words of the text are "To be continued." So a second volume will be necessary to carry the story forward to the present and clarify, or perhaps further complicate the question of exactly what happened to Harlot. But this first volume contains more than sufficient evidence of the great scope and brilliance of Mailer's conception and of his continuing power to achieve the extraordinary. Unlike just about every American writer since Henry James, Mailer has managed to grow and become richer in wisdom with each new book, and he has been able to gain steadily increasing control over the often unruly energies that drive his talent. There can no longer be any doubt that he possesses the largest mind and imagination at work in American literature today.
1991

William Styron's Holocaust Chic

Abstract ideas about the nature of life or death have almost always been poorly served in the American novel. We have had, to be sure, many works of high rhetorical pretentiousness, crowded with the vividly rendered life of raw experience, promising significance on every page but seldom delivering anything very much weightier than the accrued poundage of their pages. We have had other works of great lyrical intensity and still others of the most corrosive social criticism and satire, in which we may learn all about the distresses and stupidities of American life, but almost nothing about what it means.

Our novels have usually lacked what the best of European fiction has traditionally possessed in abundance: the power to deal directly with abstract concepts of being and to depict ideas as concrete modes of dramatic action to be experienced with all the force of physical sensations. For reasons that may derive from the peculiarities of our national history and psychology, American novelists have rarely been able to extrapolate from the immediate and local predicaments of their characters to the general human truths that they may typify—in the way, for example, that Flaubert could create out of the tragedy of one bored provincial housewife a universal portrait of the bourgeois mind, or Dostoevsky out of the sufferings of a poor student a classic study of the psychology of guilt, or Tolstoy out of the disparate lives of some Russian aristocrats the history of an entire epoch. We have had *The Scarlet Letter* but no *Madame Bovary* or *Crime and Punishment, Moby Dick* but no *War and Peace*—we have had novels, that is, possessing a certain kind of greatness, but their significance so often seems confined, even when they strain for allegorical generalization, within the limits of the particular situations they dramatize. The result is that they finally seem to be about merely personal guilt rather than the force of evil, merely individual failure rather than the tragedy of human existence. It is possible that American novelists are by nature limited to the specific and particular, that they have sensations or at best perceptions instead of ideas, and that they write most convincingly when they are absolved of the obligation of having to think.

Part of our problem may be that the Puritan settlers arrived in this country with such a bleak and negative attitude toward experience that, while it may have equipped them admirably to endure hardship, it also helped to impoverish both the realistic and the intellectual content of American fiction throughout the formative years of its development. In the Puritan view, experience of this world represented temptation to sinful indulgence and wherever possible was to be resisted so that the soul might be properly prepared for its sojourn in the City of God. Eternal life in the hereafter was the reward for renunciation of the enticements of this life. As a result of this doctrine, our fiction writers for many years were beset by such a fear of secular reality that most of them very nearly managed to eliminate it from their work altogether and devoted themselves to dramatizing, on the transcendental plane of allegory and theological romance safely removed from corruptive actuality, what were essentially versions of the Puritan struggle for salvation.

This may help to explain why Hawthorne and Melville seem so deficient in a sense of social fact. Their imaginative eye seems always to be fixed on the cosmos, and their novels give the effect of taking place in a sanctified vacuum virtually uncontaminated by the presence of people. The thinness of the human and social scene in Hawthorne is so obtrusive that it is itself almost a presence, and perhaps fortunately for Melville *Moby Dick* had logically to take place at sea, so that there would be minimal worldly intrusions on Ahab's solipsistic battle with the brute force of evil nature.

It is of course true—and it has often been said—that in comparison with Europe the social scene in the America of their time *was* thin. That is an important reason for their preoccupation with romance and allegory and, in Hawthorne's case, the Puritan past. But it is also why our early writers had such difficulty creating thematic meanings that would have some generalizing relation to the human condition as a whole. The wonderfully complicated network of family and national history, political intrigue, traditions of place and creed, titled aristocracy, and institutionalized peasantry that created the rich texture of European life and literature simply did not exist for them, and in addition to Hawthorne, at least two other classic American fiction writers—Cooper and James—made regretful public acknowledgment of the fact.

But as the country expanded westward after the Civil War, it became evident that American life was developing a character quite unlike the European but capable of providing vital materials for the many writers who were eager to declare their independence from both Europe and the Puritan past. The defining feature of that character was linear movement in geographic space, the exploration of unknown territory, the effort to discover and absorb vast new areas of raw experience. It is not surprising that the sternly renunciatory Puritan attitude toward experience could not survive in a nation passionately committed to embracing experience. But what did happen was that the force of Puritan spirituality was diverted from the transcendent to the secular, and in the process the secular was spiritualized. Physical experience became sacramental, and our literature came to treat the quest for salvation in experience with the kind of shrill religiosity once reserved for the soul's quest for salvation in heaven.

Whitman and James both saw experience in this way, as spiritually redemptive, as a mystical boon to be sought through embracing multitudes or, as Lambert Strether says in James's *The Ambassadors*, through living all you can—as if immersion in life were the gateway to Godhead. And so evidently it seemed to many of the American writers who came after them. They formed a priestly cult of worshippers at the shrine of experience, and each in his way made his pilgrimage down the road to some earthly New Jerusalem that was located just beyond the next range of mountains or across the Atlantic Ocean or just about anywhere promising escape from the barren, oppressive towns in which they grew up. Some became insatiable consumers of the Eucharist of merely additive living, great chunks of which came out half-digested in their books because they were governed by no conviction that experience in fiction was supposed to *mean:* its justification lay in the miraculous fact of its having happened. An abstract thought or idea was a threat to the integrity of raw sensation, a blasphemy on the sacredness of pure actuality. It is no accident that even T. S. Eliot, the most cerebral of our poets, could observe of even James, the most cerebral of our novelists, that he "had a mind so fine that no idea could violate it," that famous remark that undoubtedly referred to James's vast nondenominational sensibility, but that might also be interpreted, given the choice of words, as a compliment to James on his having successfully protected his intellectual virginity against despoliation by a rapine idea.

Thomas Wolfe was of course the classic case of the American novelist bent on chasing down and eating up the whole of human experience. But Wolfe's subject was finally merely himself in the act of chasing down and eating up, and his effort to give significance to that act found expression in a wild sentimentality of language that sought its vindication in the inflations of its rhetoric but remained unredeemed by a single idea. Hemingway's contribution to the intellectual enrichment of the American novel consisted of his discovery that "morals are what you feel good after." Fitzgerald, who had by far the better mind, had certain subtler perceptions about the meaning of moral conduct. But his villains and villainesses were more emptily careless or simply spoiled than they were evil, while his heroes were too naive or weak to be heroic. Dos Passos had what might be called an idea of American society—that it was dominated and dehumanized by an exploitative capitalist system—but the idea ultimately hardened into an ideology and ossified his vision.

In more recent times, with the Western frontier long closed and the more obvious features of American life having been thoroughly defined in fiction, our writers have sought to appease their hunger for new imaginative frontiers through an exploration of the internal wilderness of their own psyches, out of which some like Roth, Bellow, and Heller have produced, as I have said, a fictional form that has become characteristic of our time: the novel of vociferous *external* monologue in which the voice of the protagonist is the only important character and his paranoia frequently the only substance. Other writers have executed an inward turning not into the psyche but into the technical resources of the fictional form itself, seeking to find in their experiments with myth, fable, self-parody, and the uses of fictions and nonfictions within fictions some means of creating systems of order and significance in a period of our history that seems to possess little or none. They have perhaps been most successful in producing book-length seriocomic metaphors of contemporary experience, in which they are often able to express the idea—as Pynchon does—that all life is dying, mere entropy is loosed upon the world, or that no idea is tenable as a program for living, as John Barth keeps saying in various ways, or that life is so absurd that one's only hope of remaining sane is to resort to cute little incantations of adolescent stoicism—"So it goes" and "hi ho," Kurt Vonnegut's idea so banal that no mind could possibly want to violate it.

William Styron's problem is not so much that he is unable to express his ideas through his fiction as that he seems not to have ideas to express. Like Thomas Wolfe, the literary predecessor he most closely resembles, Styron has a natural storyteller's gift for concocting enormous quantities of narrative material, but he has the greatest difficulty finding ways to make his material meaningful. This has been particularly burdensome for Styron because, while there is little to indicate that he is a writer struggling to express a major vision of life, he has all along given the appearance of being a writer driven by the most intense ambition to be *considered* major, and he knows that to achieve this he must appear to possess major themes. He seems, therefore, to have tried to assimilate into his work elements conventionally associated with the presence of something important to say. He writes in a style that has come to be identified, at least in more conservative literary circles, as the traditional style of our native form of important fiction. It is grandly rhetorical, seemingly always portentous of some large cosmic or apocalyptic significance, rich with atmospheric perfume, swollen with adjectival bloat, and most effective when it is at work on the experience of the South as previously processed by the imagination of William Faulkner.

Styron's dramatic situations are also those indemnified by past usage as serious and important. He is particularly infatuated with situations that lend themselves to the fullest epical or sentimental orchestration, that will resonate most forebodingly with deep tonalities of disaster and doom—murder, suicide, insanity, rape, incest, miscegenation, ancestral bloodguilt, generalized corruption and betrayal, the kinds of materials that served Faulkner so well just because they were inseparable from the cultural and moral derangement of his southern characters. But in Styron's handling of them they seem to exist for their own sake or the sake of mere theatrics without relation to the thematic meaning they are ostensibly designed to express. They constantly generate promises of meaning far larger than the capacity of his characters to fulfill them.

But Styron has recognized that to be considered major, a writer must not only appear to be engaging major themes but also engage them at the right time, when the public for one reason or another will find them topically important or intellectually fashionable. Thus, by strategy or accident, he published his widely praised first novel, *Lie Down in Darkness,* in 1952, at just the moment when it could be read as the final flowering of the southern novel after Faulkner, a brilliant synthesis of all the elements of southern fiction at the culmination of its renaissance following World War II. The fact that most of these elements had by this time hardened into stereotypes actually worked in Styron's favor because it enabled general readers to admire the novel for qualities that they could readily recognize as belonging to an established literary tradition, but one which had ceased long ago to disturb them with original thought.

Something rather different occurred with the appearance in 1960 of Styron's second novel, *Set This House on Fire,* a massive, meandering work that was heavily swathed in the costumery of would-be majorness and that appeared to represent an effort to exploit trendy highbrow interests, perhaps in order to win the favor of the many intellectuals who had disdained *Lie Down in Darkness* because it was so mechanically derivative of Faulkner. In particular, Styron tried to give coherence and meaning to his endlessly attenuated story, which had to do with some troubled people involved in a mysterious murder case, through windy adumbrations of existential *angst,* the Big Questions about "being" and "nothingness" that Sartre and Camus had a good while before made fashionable. But by the time Styron finished the novel—and he writes very slowly—the fashion had passed, and the intellectuals whose good will the book seemed intended to court savaged it for being out-of-date as well as for shamming a significance it did not and could not deliver.

By contrast, the publication of *The Confessions of Nat Turner* in 1967 nicely coincided with the furor then being generated by the civil rights movement. But Styron's error in that novel was political as well as artistic. His portrait of slave-insurrectionist Turner infuriated many black writers because it seemed to them the height of arrogance for a southern white to disregard many important facts about Turner's life and character and produce a fictionalized account that not only distorted the truth but was clearly racist in its point of view. Nevertheless, the book was sensational and titillating enough to survive the controversy, and it became the most commercially successful of Styron's novels up to that time.

When he conceived the plan for his most recent novel, *Sophie's Choice,* Styron could well have had grounds for believing that this time there was absolutely no way he could lose. He had chosen as his central subject the most calamitous event of modern history, the systematic murder of Nazi concentration camp inmates, and he could be reasonably certain that interest in the Holocaust would persist no matter how long it took him to finish the book. He also had some fat chunks of southern experience that, when heated up by his prose, could be counted on to generate the atmosphere of gaseous gloom and fatality on which the flavor of his work depends. And he had in addition the story of his own early years as a writer when he was struggling to write the book that became *Lie Down in Darkness,* was fired from his job with McGraw-Hill for floating plastic bubbles out of a window on the twentieth floor of their building, and was devoting the rest of his time to trying, in the lust of his virginal frustration, to get as many women into bed as he possibly could—an effort that failed repeatedly but that yielded some fairly savory anecdotal material.

Styron also had a somewhat shopworn but nonetheless great potential theme, the question of responsibility for the Nazi atrocities and in particular the guilt of those who survived them, a theme certified to be great by important thinkers like Hannah Arendt, Bruno Bettelheim, George Steiner, and others whom Styron takes care to cite in his narrative, especially when they offer him free insurance against criticism by remarking on just how difficult it would be for a writer to make such a theme dramatically convincing. But putting it all together, Styron had the makings of a rich heavy brew that seemed guaranteed to give off the aroma of grand significance for a good while to come.

As he did in his previous novels, Styron tries in *Sophie's Choice* to create suspense by resorting to the form of the detective story, a form well suited to the writer who wishes to explore a complicated mystery to its ingenious solution, but that can also be adapted to the purposes of a writer seeking to generate a counterfeit effect of complication out of materials which are in themselves so shallow that he can imagine no other way of making them seem significant. Styron's strategy is to gather together great masses of material having to do with people whose behavior seems strange or inexplicable and then scrutinize every last scrap of information about them as if it were a vital clue to a puzzle that he holds himself interminably on the point of being about to solve. This involves him in an activity which he obviously enjoys above all other things and which most vividly demonstrates his quality as a writer: the dogged documentation of absolutely everything, the creation of vast marathon descriptions that go on and on for hundreds of pages and always have behind them the implication that some wondrous profundity will at any moment be divulged to a stunned world.

In the opening sections of the novel we are introduced to Stingo, Styron's narrator-persona, a character seemingly without thematic relevance to the main action but whose presence in the novel may be justified by the fact that Styron appears to have wanted to work his early literary and sexual experiences into the story and at the same time had need of a narrator. The suspenseful questions about Stingo are whether he will manage without regular income to keep going as a writer and whether he will finally find a woman who will relieve him of his virginity. Styron is able to protract an examination of these questions through a large part of the novel, artfully maintaining suspense by pausing from time to time to explore segments of another character's experience, an exercise in nonsequential narrative that helps to enhance the overall effect of spurious complication.

It turns out that Stingo's survival as a writer is for the time being assured by a most remarkable happenstance, one that must be the purest example of southern gothic moonshine to appear in our literature since the fiction of Thomas Nelson Page. Stingo learns that he has come into a small inheritance left him by his grandmother whose father had received the money from the sale of a slave just before the Civil War. The legacy had for all those years been bricked-up in a cubbyhole in the basement of the family house in North Carolina until Stingo's father had discovered its whereabouts. Thus, Stingo is saved for literature by the miraculous intervention of an ancestral *deus ex machina* and is freed to devote his spare time to seeking a solution to his sexual dilemma.

This proves to be exceedingly difficult. He has encounters with two young women, Leslie and Mary Alice, and much later is able to get to bed with the novel's heroine, the beautiful Sophie. But before that happens he is very nearly driven mad by Leslie and Mary Alice. It seems that Leslie is exclusively lingually erotic and will permit only French-kissing, which she and Stingo indulge in hour after tongue-aching hour. Mary Alice will allow him to take no liberties with her person whatsoever but is quite willing to gratify him by hand, which she does in a pleasureless and perfunctory fashion. While there is a certain dismal comedy in all this, just what it has to do with the central story of Sophie is never made clear, evidently because Styron does not know.

Sophie comes into Stingo's life after he moves into a room beneath hers in a Brooklyn boarding house. He is repeatedly awakened by the noise of savage copulation above him, and of course in his condition he becomes each time crazed with lust. Considerable suspense is developed over whether or not the ceiling will fall in on Stingo and just who the frenzied performers may be. Finally, he learns that they are Sophie, a Polish girl who has survived Auschwitz, and Nathan, a New York Jew who has nursed Sophie back to health after her ordeal and who claims to be a scientist. Stingo soon befriends the lovers and from then on becomes more and more deeply preoccupied with trying to penetrate the meaning of their strange contradictory relationship.

He is particularly mystified by the sudden and seemingly unprovoked shifts in Nathan's mood. He and Sophie will be making riotous love, and immediately afterward he will fall into a screaming rage, beat her bloody, and denounce her for having done something reprehensible in order to survive Auschwitz. This kind of behavior or some variation on it is repeated over and over again, to Stingo's steadily accelerating mystification, until at last Nathan's rage has been inflated into a force of seemingly cosmic vengeance, and Sophie's guilty secret is made to seem as blackly criminal as the Holocaust itself. In fact, so much melodramatic voltage is generated not only by Nathan's violence and Stingo's anguish over it but by the soaring grandiloquence of Styron's prose that one might suppose the stage were being set for a performance of Götterdämmerung.

But it is through such pyrotechnics so carefully calculated to arouse expectations of the deepest tragedy and evil (What, in the name of Heaven, did Sophie DO?) that Styron attempts to justify devoting so much space to a detailed documentation of Sophie's life in Poland before the war: the happiness of her childhood; the unhappiness of her marriage; the arrest and execution of her father and her husband by the Nazis; the birth of her two children; the crime for which she was sent to Auschwitz (she had been caught smuggling a ham into Warsaw); her experiences in the camp; her life in the household of the camp commandant; her relations with other inmates; the lesbian attacks made upon her by various women; her separation from her children and the presumed execution of her daughter; the Allied liberation of the camp. And throughout the narrative Styron is careful to drop periodic hints that if the reader will just stay with him a little longer, the unspeakable truth will come out.

But the fact is that Sophie's story is a windy record of Styron's apparent search for some way to legitimize the direful promises of his rhetoric, the extreme intensity of Nathan's wrath, the whole elaborate orchestration of Stingo's anguish and Sophie's ostensible damnation. For the truth about her supposed sin, when finally, *finally* it does emerge, represents not only a terrible anticlimax but an abdication of authorial responsibility, and the reader has every right to feel defrauded. If Sophie has sinned at all, her sin is at most venial and in the circumstances altogether understandable. Upon her arrival at Auschwitz, she was forced by a drunken SS officer to decide whether her son or her daughter would be sent to the gas chamber. Sophie's choice was to save her son, but since she was *forced* to choose, the culpability belonged to the officer and not to her. Later, she had been able, because of her stenographic skills, to do clerical work for the camp commandant and so had escaped execution. She had also, in the hope of saving her son's life, offered herself to her employer, but he refused her. After he was transferred out of the camp, she suffered just as much as any of the other survivors.

Nathan really has no rational grounds for his suspicion of her and no justification for abusing her, particularly since Sophie has told him nothing about either her "choice" or her relations with the commandant. Furthermore, Nathan, after having been blown up by Styron into a kind of vengeful Old Testament Jehovah, is revealed to be nothing of the sort. He is, we discover, quite simply a paranoid schizophrenic and drug addict who has been lying about the important scientific work he is supposed to have been doing and whose goal is to persuade Sophie to join him in a suicide pact. Her second "choice" of death, therefore, seems not an act of atonement for a guilt which, after all, she lacks sufficient reason for having, but an indication that finally she is as insane as he is.

Thus, with Nathan's role and authority as a force of moral retribution invalidated by psychosis and Sophie's sin revealed to be petty, the novel is deprived of all ethical and thematic rationale, and its great length would seem to be a reflection of Styron's hope that if he described his characters and their actions through a sufficient quantity of pages he would sooner or later blunder on his theme.

Perhaps because of his southern gothic heritage Styron has long had a hunger to engage the large seminal issues of good and evil, guilt, betrayal, revenge, and redemption. This is the message of his often quite eloquent prose: it aches for a subject portentous enough to justify its preacherly hellfire-and-brimstone tonalities. Styron needs, in fact, something of what the Puritan fathers, for all their fierce disdain for the secular life, possessed and we have lost: a coherent metaphysical view of the moral nature of existence. But all he has are urgent moral *sentiments* and quantities of raw material that he is unable to make significant within an ideological context. The result is, as both this novel and *Set This House on Fire* make clear, that Styron is driven, in his effort to create the effect or illusion of significance, to resorting to all manner of sham theatrics and specious intimations that there exist large meanings just beneath the surface of his materials, that dark and inscrutable fates, dooms, and curses are hard at work shaping the grim destinies of his characters, even as they themselves repeatedly prove incapable of sustaining the great epic weight he tries to impose upon them.

Hence, instead of a situation of high tragedy, Styron is left in this novel with a kind of sad comedy. Instead of horrendous sin, he has in Sophie a pathetic case of self-preserving and quite justified expediency. Instead of sacred vengeance, he has in Nathan a case of profound mental disturbance, and in Stingo he clearly has a case of infinitely protracted adolescence. Like the characters in *Set This House on Fire*, they are all too weakly human and spiritually impoverished to become principals in the great Sophoclean melodrama that Styron tries so strenuously to hoke up for them. They are, in short, creatures of the contemporary moral void, while to serve Styron's purposes they need to be survivors of the great age of antiquity when the gods and goddesses laid down the laws and vented their terrible wrath on all transgressors.

Because he is deficient in a sense of what his materials are supposed to mean, Styron has a tendency to lapse into bathos and banality or weepy declarations of what Bellow once called "potato love" whenever he is required to express an attitude or to make a generalization about the events that have occurred in his narrative. An excellent illustration is the closing scene of *Sophie's Choice* where we find Stingo, after having attended the funerals of Sophie and Nathan, lying on a beach in the middle of the night, grieving over his dead friends, and pondering the wisdom of the statement, "*Let your love flow out on all living things.*"

> It was then that the tears finally spilled forth ... tears ... I had tried manfully to resist and could resist no longer, having kept them so bottled up that now, almost alarmingly, they drained out in warm rivulets between my fingers. I did not weep for the six million Jews or the two million Poles or the one million Serbs or the five million Russians—I was unprepared to weep for all humanity—but I did weep for those others who in one way or another had become dear to me, and my sobs made an unashamed racket across the abandoned beach. Then I had no more tears to shed, and lowered myself to the sand on legs that suddenly seemed strangely frail and rickety for a man of twenty-two.
>
> When I awoke it was early morning. I lay looking straight up at the blue-green sky with its translucent shawl of mist; like a tiny orb of crystal, solitary and serene, Venus shone through the haze above the quiet ocean. I heard childen chattering nearby.... Blessing my resurrection, I realized that the children had covered me with sand, protectively, and that I lay safe as a mummy beneath this fine, enveloping overcoat. It was then that in my mind I inscribed the words: "*Neath cold sand I dreamed of death / but woke at dawn to see / in glory, the bright, the morning star.*"

Surely, there is a novel of the greatest tragic dimension to be written about the Holocaust. But just as surely, Styron has not written it, for with all its pretensions to literary majorness, *Sophie's Choice* is clearly a phony book, as imaginatively inauthentic as it is intellectually without content.

1979

Saul Bellow's Struggle with the Cosmos

Saul Bellow has all along been a novelist both burdened and blessed with a highly developed sense of the realities—to say nothing of the madness—of the existing social world. He has also struggled to find in those realities meanings that reach beyond the secular, that will support and validate an essentially metaphysical view of human experience. This suggests that Bellow's imagination is dialectical and is always engaged in a debate between the secular and the transcendental, a debate he can carry on because he is almost alone among contemporary American novelists in having the power to tolerate, without collapsing under the stress of, philosophical ambiguity. And he has, in turn, found this possible because he is a man of great intellectual vitality who has consistently been willing, like Mailer but in marked contrast to Styron, to risk his career by venturing, with each new book, beyond the imaginative territories he has previously explored and consolidated. Where most writers take possession of their subjects, along with the technical means to engage them, fairly early in life and then proceed gradually to exhaust them, Bellow from the beginning has maintained a much more flexible and dynamic relation with the materials of his art, and he has brought to their service an intellectual culture far more extensive than that of his American contemporaries. Ideas for him are not only a primary basis of subject-matter, nor are they—as so much of our literature seems to imply—antithetical to the expression of honest feeling and the actualities of "real" life. Rather, they serve to broaden and intensify his perception of those actualities, and they help him to dramatize what he sees as the vital connections, so complexly explored in all his novels, between worldly experience and the abstracting transcendences of history, morality, philosophy, and religion.

Bellow also has the capacity—very nearly as rare among our novelists as the power of abstract thought—to experiment with a variety of novelistic techniques in which to cast his continuously evolving conception of his materials. From time to time and often within the limits of a single book he has made brilliant use of the effects of naturalist realism, the comedy of manners, Black Humor, the mystery novel, the picaresque, psychological, and philosophical novel, and literary satire (in *Henderson the Rain King,* partly a parody of the mythic narrative of descent into the heart of darkness), and his virtuosity has been reinforced by his very considerable knowledge of American and European literature, philosophy, and psychology. Jung, Wilhelm Reich, Rudolf Steiner, Sartre, Dostoevsky, Dickens, Melville, Whitman, and Mark Twain have all been prominent influences on Bellow, but as is the case with most major novelists, he has not so much imitated as transmuted certain of their features to fit the requirements of his imagination. His indebtednesses, however, are often obvious, and sometimes they are flagrant. For example, his first novel, *Dangling Man,* appears to have been strongly influenced by Sartre's *Nausea,* and the protagonist bears a close resemblance— as, for that matter, do so many characters in post-modern fiction—to Dostoevsky's Underground Man. *The Victim* is also derivative, Bellow himself admitted, of Dostoevsky: in terms of sheer plot, it is virtually a retelling of *The Eternal Husband. The Adventures of Augie March,* the third and most ambitious of Bellow's early novels, is a mélange of styles, characters, dramatic episodes, and literary echoes, and as it represents a radical departure from the tight, highly formalized works with which he began his career, so it marks at least a temporary turning away from European in favor of native American influences—Whitman, Twain, Dreiser, and just possibly Melville.

Augie March was and remains Bellow's great transitional work, an expression of manic energy and high comedic talent that he had not previously been able to release, a kind of fiction sufficiently open and flexible to allow him for the first time to do absolutely anything he chose, in which he was freed rather than inhibited by the technical requirements of his medium. Ever since, Bellow has been experimenting with new arrangements and combinations of forms and styles, different angles of approach to materials which were all essentially present in *Augie March* but which, in his subsequent novels, needed to be processed according to the dictates of his maturing perceptions of experience. *Henderson the Rain King* is basically a mock-heroic rendering of Augie's quest for self-knowledge. Henderson's flight into Africa, where he becomes a buffoon fertility god among primitive tribes and finally believes or *decides* to believe he has discovered himself, burlesques Augie's flight from the various "reality instructors" who want to educate him in their distorted visions of the world.

With *Herzog,* in the writer of unmailed letters to prominent people, the Underground Man reappears. The sufferer who seeks after goodness and wisdom is once again the farcical martyr persecuted by malevolent would-be teachers, and in the end he breaks out into freedom and peace or—depending on one's interpretation of the closing scenes—he capitulates to his situation and to himself as he is, saying, "I am pretty well satisfied to be, to be just as it is willed, for as long as I may remain in occupancy"—a note of complacent resignation which, as I once wrote, seems falsely imposed and which calls into question the authenticity of the novel's narrative voice.

Finally in *Mr. Sammler's Planet,* the novel just preceding *Humboldt's Gift,* the sufferer, now an old man bewildered and put upon by the anarchy of life in the contemporary city, searches for some understanding of the ultimate purpose of human existence, some knowledge that will enable him to accept the fact of his nephew's and his own imminent death as well as, conceivably, the eventual extinction of human life on earth. In a fashion that becomes increasingly evident in Bellow's later protagonists, Mr. Sammler moves from self-preoccupation and secular intellectuality closer and closer to mysticism, seeking what one critic has called "the Tolstoyan moment," the instant of apocalyptic perception in which the patterns unifying the cosmos and linking man to the cosmos become visible and comprehensible.

However dissimilar they may be in other respects, Bellow's novels all tell essentially the same story. They are all informed by what can only be called a *desperately* affirmative view of human experience and possibility, a view too complicated to be reducible to a philosophical proposition, too dialectical and contradictory to be taken as dogma, creed, or panacea. Its central feature is, in fact, ambiguity, a recognition of elements which may be forever irreconcilable, of questions which must be pondered and explored, but for which answers will probably never be found, at least not by the merely human creatures who seek them. Bellow on several occasions has expressed his strong disagreement with the idea of cultural nihilism and alienation which pervades so much of modern and contemporary literature and which he believes has its source far more *in* literature than in the actual life it purports to reflect. As he said in his Library of Congress address in 1963:

> Writers have inherited a tone of bitterness from the great poems and novels of this century, many of which lament the passing of a more stable and beautiful age demolished by the barbarous intrusion of an industrial and metropolitan society of masses or proles who will, after many upheavals, be tamed by bureaucracies and oligarchies in brave new worlds, human anthills.... There are modern novelists who take all this for granted as fully proven and implicit in the human condition and who complain as steadily as they write, viewing modern life with a bitterness to which they themselves have not established clear title, and it is this unearned bitterness I speak of.

Herzog, in one of his unmailed letters to his friend Shapiro, angrily denounced "the commonplaces of the Wasteland outlook, the cheap mental stimulants of Alienation, the cant and rant of pipsqueaks about Inauthenticity and forlornness. I can't accept this foolish dreariness. We are talking about the whole life of mankind. The subject is too great, too deep for such weakness, cowardice—too deep, too great, Shapiro."

Clearly, Bellow wishes to offer in his fiction a view of modern life that will be alternative to "the commonplaces of the Wasteland outlook," for he has said elsewhere that "a man should have at least sufficient power to overcome ignominy and to complete his own life. His suffering, feebleness, servitude then have a meaning," and it is the writer's duty to affirm that meaning, to "reveal the greatness of man." This Bellow has steadily tried to achieve. He has celebrated life with remarkable vigor, and he has created some of the most compassionate portraits of the human condition—even in its thoroughly detestable manifestations—to be found anywhere in contemporary literature. Yet the ultimate revelation of the greatness of man has eluded him, partly because it is much easier artistically to represent evil than to find the terms for the convincing display of virtue, but mostly because Bellow has been thwarted by the very complexity and ambiguity of his view of man.

His problem is that as a writer of great perceptiveness and intellectual honesty he cannot help but be aware and reflect his awareness of all those elements in contemporary life to which the only sane response is despair and which have produced the climate of pessimism and generalized forlornness he finds so oppressive. His *moral* impulse is to affirm life in some perhaps transcendental way that will be commensurate with his sincere belief in human possibility. But the observable facts of life as it exists at the present time not only afford little proof of that possibility but seem to work actively to nullify it. Bellow has thus found himself in a position of wishing to believe amid conditions that do not provide adequate objective justifications for belief, and the consequence for his fiction is that it has tended to break apart into two kinds of dramatic statement that may be developed concurrently but cannot be plausibly reconciled. On the one hand, there is material—usually of a speculative, philosophical, or mystical nature—that expresses Bellow's faith that man can attain self-understanding and transformation, that he can overcome the limitations of his individuality and come into some recognition of his place in the social and cosmic order. On the other hand, there is the far more abundant and vital material that portrays man's cruelty, duplicity, venality, his maniacal self-obsessiveness, his hateful determination to exploit others in any way he can in order to prosper in a world where material value is the only value, success is measured by the standards of the con game, and the reigning morality is a cynicism that Bellow aptly calls "deceit without guilt."

It may be because Bellow cannot bring into single dramatic focus his optimism about man and his pessimism about the conditions of contemporary life that his characters so often seem schizophrenic and the endings of his novels disappointingly equivocal. His protagonists are men of good will and high hopes who make their way through a hellish wasteland in which they are forced to suffer every imaginable kind of humiliation and injustice. Yet at the end, in spite of everything, they are still seekers and believers. Martyred and persecuted though they may be, they remain pure and hopeful, still expecting transformation and revelation—perhaps in quiet confidence like Herzog, "well satisfied to be . . . just as it is willed," or like Augie, laughing at nature because "it thinks it can win over us and the power of hope," or like Henderson who, during a stopover in Newfoundland, gets out of the airplane which is bringing him home from Africa and, believing he has at last begun to find his life, runs in ecstasy, an orphaned child in his arms, "over the pure white lining of the gray Arctic silence." These are all endings which represent cessations of narrative action but not conclusions, pauses in flight but not the attainment of thematic destination.

In *Humboldt's Gift,* his eighth novel, Bellow had still not found a way of successfully reconciling these contradictory attitudes and the two kinds of material in which they are expressed. But he did manage to cope with them more effectively than he had been able to do in any of his previous novels. The protagonist, Charles Citrine, confirms one's impression that Bellow's views of the nature of human existence are becoming increasingly mystical and may eventually find a formally religious framework. Citrine is a student of Rudolf

Steiner's anthroposophy, a doctrine which maintains that through self-discipline cognitional experience of the spiritual world can be achieved, and his meditations on such a possibility become a significant yet unobtrusive leitmotif of the novel. But the critical point is that Bellow treats them throughout as meditations only. They are not required to bear a major thematic weight as are the speculative materials in the earlier novels. Therefore, Bellow's inability to reconcile them with his secular materials does not become problematical, since Citrine merely retreats from time to time into his meditations and at best *only holds out hope* that they may eventually lead him to a perception of spiritual truth.

This is to say that for the first time in this novel Bellow has been able to objectify his own wishful optimism and to accept it for just that, wishful, declining now to try to give it more crucial thematic importance than it can justifiably be given. Citrine emerges as, in other respects, a typical Bellow protagonist, but one who has a mystical turn of mind. He may be another seeker after cosmic understanding but that role is deemphasized because he is first and foremost a suffering victim whose journey through the purgatory of humiliation and betrayal is easily separable from his spiritual pilgrimage. He is therefore placed, with a minimum of distracting metaphysical encumbrances, at the center of the kind of action Bellow has always been able to dramatize with the greatest effectiveness, the action of relentlessly secular existence, and that is surely an important reason why Citrine comes to seem the most convincingly drawn of Bellow's major characters.

As the author of several works of popular biography and a successful Broadway play, Citrine is prosperous and well known but has reached an impasse in his life and career. His work has gone stale. He has been through a divorce and is being hounded by his ex-wife who, he is convinced, is determined to ruin him financially. He has lawyers who seem to be trying to assist her in this effort in every way they can, and a few friends who may or may not be any more trustworthy. His beautiful mistress is pressuring him to marry her, but since she seriously doubts that he is a man of responsibility, she takes the precaution of sleeping from time to time with a wealthy undertaker.

Because of these and other problems Citrine has withdrawn more and more into himself, spending days at a time alone in his apartment meditating on such matters as the fate of the soul after death and the possibilities of reincarnation. He is also obsessed with the memory of the dead poet, Von Humboldt Fleischer, the closest friend and literary mentor of his youth, a creative force of immense size but a talent destroyed by neglect, eccentricity, paranoia, and alcohol. Fleischer has died alone in poverty and obscurity, and Citrine ponders his life trying to understand its significance, wishing he had been a better friend to Fleischer, regretting that he cannot carry on his work or in some way redeem his reputation.

Then all sorts of dreadful things begin to happen to Citrine and, in the fashion of contemporary literature of the absurd, they simply happen at the behest of whatever agencies of capricious fatality govern the universe. One of Citrine's friends, troubled by his isolated existence, insists that he take part in a poker game where he will have a chance to meet people who belong to the real world. During the game Citrine drinks too much, babbles about his personal problems, fails to notice that he is being cheated by some of the players, and writes a check to cover his losses. When the next day he stops payment on the check, he is threatened by a small-time Mafia figure named Cantabile, who takes his revenge by arranging to have Citrine's $18,000 Mercedes 280-SL clubbed to ruin in the street. Cantabile then forces Citrine to make an apology before witnesses for defaulting on the debt, and when Citrine offers him cash, he humiliates Citrine further by again forcing him to accompany him, this time to the top story of a skyscraper under construction. There, on a swaying catwalk high above the city, Cantabile takes the fifty-dollar bills Citrine has given him, folds them into paper airplanes, and sails them off into the wind.

These persecutions, as it turns out, are merely initiatory. A short time later a district judge decides that Citrine must pay his ex-wife an amount of money that will virtually wipe him out and then orders him to post a bond of $200,000. Nevertheless, Citrine goes off on a long-planned trip to Europe where he expects to be joined by his mistress. But while waiting for her in Madrid, he learns that she has gone to Italy and married the undertaker—the betrayal having evidently been carefully plotted from the moment it became apparent that Citrine was no longer a good financial prospect. Left alone in Madrid, he resumes his meditations on the occult and experiments with trying to communicate with the spirits of the dead, in particular with Fleischer. The experiments fail, but in a remarkable way. Fleischer finally does communicate with Citrine and passes on to him his gift or legacy. The proceeds from it will not make Citrine rich, but they will help him begin life again, and he supposes it will be a radically different kind of life, a cessation of struggle, extravagance, self-loathing, and boredom, an attempt to "listen in secret to the sound of the truth that God puts into us."

Described in this way the action in its details may seem trivial or

merely ludicrous. It is surely not redeemed by the metaphysical dimension nor is the ending altogether satisfactory. But the power of the novel derives in the Jamesean sense from the quality and intensity of the felt life contained within it, the brilliant evocation of the social world, and the incredible sensitivity of its characterizations. It is here rather than in his philosophical assertions that Bellow expresses most forcefully his belief in life and the greatness of man. If he has so far failed to achieve a synthesis of his metaphysical and his secular materials, the failure may, after all, be fortunate. For we expect a novelist to be a chronicler and not a visionary, an observer and analyst rather than a seer. In searching for and never quite achieving an understanding of the secret cohering principle of human existence, Bellow has given us a portrait of existence that may contain as much understanding as we can tolerate.
1975

Wright Morris Country

Wright Morris may be the last of our novelists to write with a sense of the whole of America in his blood and bones, to possess a vision of the country as both a physical place and a metaphysical condition. The literary tradition from which he seems most directly to descend—and it is a tradition shared with some incongruity by Henry James, Mark Twain, Edith Wharton, and Sherwood Anderson—may well have passed on to him the materials of this vision, and it may be said to have been reconstituted in his work with very little likelihood that it will survive beyond his work. His immediate predecessors did not, on the whole, display much evidence of possessing it, perhaps because they belonged to a generation that, with the sole exception of Faulkner, did not so much learn from history as write from the perilous assumption that history did not exist until they came along to invent it. For what is involved here is a historical imagination, which is not at all the same as a historical understanding or even a historical perspective. The historical imagination functions within a double matrix of fact and illusion, actual happenings and fictive constructs built upon actual happenings, and it does so because it perceives that what the minds of a people make of a national or cultural past, what their powers of mythic transvaluation remake out of the past for the new uses of the present, may have the profoundest influence on the formation of their collective character. It was the mythic idea of its history that shaped the epic in Homer's Greece. It is the idea of its history as epic that has shaped the myth of America, just as it has greatly affected the actuality of America.

Of Morris's immediate predecessors there may be some truth in saying that Hemingway did not possess the historical imagination at all. It was the contemporary moment in its radical divorcement from history that almost pathologically absorbed him, and his personal myth—however closely it may have resembled certain mythic formulations belonging to our national past—was created out of the urgencies of his need to fashion modes of honorable survival against the threat of contemporary fatalities. It was partly because the precedents of the past were of so little use to him that his work had all the tensions of emergency improvisation. Its codes and rituals were contingency measures taken to help insure coherence amid conditions that were fearsome just because they could not be measured by precedent.

Fitzgerald had moments when the past gave his vision of the present a darkly elegiac dimension. But such moments were rare and so often—as in the pontifically beautiful closing passages of *The Great Gatsby*—they had about them the flavor of contrivance, of something not quite earned by the imagination but opted for by sentimentality. The great expectations of those first Dutch voyagers to the New World—expectations, after all, that were finally so mercenary—do not really join with the holy illusions of the priestlike Gatsby. For a transitory enchanted moment they are simply thrown together within the clutching embraces of Fitzgerald's euphoria. And after we have breathed our sighs in rhythm with his majestic prose, we have paid our respects for good and all to the poetic limitations of a rather affected nostalgia.

Several of Morris's contemporaries have written brilliantly about various single aspects of the American experience—as witnessed in the city, the minority ghetto, the suburban East, the rural South—in most cases, materials recalled from a period of our cultural history seemingly almost as remote from us in time as old Scanlon's Middle West and equally as open to attributions of a half actual, half fictitious vitality and romance. It is of interest that many of our novelists younger than Morris have had little directly to say about the life of this country and have sought refuge from conditions perhaps too amorphous, too vapid, or too unbelievable to be engaged imaginatively, through the making of fables and fictions of fictions, their novels becoming more and more narcissistic and self-consuming as the traditional social nourishments of the novel have been depleted.

Morris alone among these writers has had the distinction of preserving a creative connection with a larger and essential America. Yet even for him it is evident that the supply of nourishments has diminished; the social fabric has thinned, and his fiction has had to compensate by mining steadily deeper into its own technical resources. But then one knows, has always known in reading him, that it is just this thinness that is central to his point. He has been from the beginning an extremely conscious recorder of the subtlest symptoms of our entropy, the dying out of some epic and transfiguring vision of ourselves amid conditions leading to such a massive impoverishment of our sense of possibility that we have responded with outrage or sought the revenge of our frustration in atrocity, suicide, and murder.

The America one encounters in Morris's most important novels may or may not still exist. There are those who will say that, yes, it is very much alive and well and living in Omaha. They could easily be right, for hardy strains of past cultures have been known to survive long beyond their appointed time and to take their place with the biological oddities that live on—always in lessened mutated form—to remind us that giants and dragons once walked the earth, that stretching behind us is a larger past from which we derive and incessantly recreate the legends of our heroic origins and stalwart ancestries.

But one thing is certain: The America of Morris's novels no longer exists as a territory of our collective imagination, and that is because the myth that brought it to life in our imagination is dead. We may think that the myth survives in the popular culture of our day, but we will be wrong. It is not even there in lessened mutated form. What we see in popular culture are imitations and prevarications of the myth, media entombments of artifact, cartoon facsimiles which may have the vague contours of the original with one essential element missing: they bring nothing to life; they no longer fire and transform our aspirations. The true artifact is a sacred relic, a thing of magic consecrated by ceremony and sacrament. It embodies the myth as a talisman embodies a moment of life or history when suddenly something eternal happened, when, perhaps only briefly, experience came alive with meaning because it touched and activated new circuits of possibility within us, when magic for a moment overpowered our natural limitations, and we knew, like Gordon Boyd, that we could walk on water and not drown.

This belief that experience might at any moment achieve epiphany and trigger in us the energies needed for transformation and new birth—this undoubtedly had its connections with the dynamism of the frontier and those mystical regions of the second chance spreading endlessly ahead in both space and mind. Americans have always been a practical visionary people, and early on the vision of the extremely practical frontier became a fixture of our imaginations, so that we ceased to be quite real to ourselves except under the stresses of risk and adventure—or in fantasy lighting out from the void of familiar boredom and dead habits to make yet one more assault upon the existential mysteries. For utopia to us is not a perfect condition of life. Rather, it is a vital state of *coming to* life, of incessantly renegotiating the terms of our contract with Fortune.

It will be obvious why it is that we reverence the time of youth in this country, and why for so many adults life stopped with the end of youth. Experience was meaningful only so long as it lay in the future, had not yet been had, and so could be conceived in relation to the sacramental promises of the fantasy. Only the young were innocent enough and brave enough in their innocence to believe this, and it was such belief that made possible the conquest of the frontier. But for adults who had lived to recognize that the fantasy was incapable of being embodied in the hard facts of life on the plains, the problem was very different. If the frontier had to be won, it also had to be secured and maintained, and that, amid all the bleakness and hardship, was no mean assignment.

A reality had to be confronted and dealt with, and without the gloss of the fantasy, the reality represented brutally hard work. In fact, it demanded so much that whole vital areas of the psychic life—any emotion or impulse that might have threatened to subvert the business at hand—had to be repressed, and the need for repression became the basis for a religion of self-sacrifice, endurance, parsimony, and rectitude, a religion trumped up by pioneer expediency in the name of moral virtue. But since in the prairie world it was the men who conquered and the women who secured and maintained, a sexual split was created that became at last a permanent national schizophrenia. Now it would be the men who in guilty secret did the dreaming, who looked back with nostalgia to the time when they could dramatize their lives in accordance with the fantasy of vital becoming, while the women would be the guardians of what had been territorially won by the men as well as emotionally won at the expense of themselves and the men.

In *The Field of Vision* and *Ceremony in Lone Tree* the grotesque extremes of such sexual polarization define the conflict at the center of the novels. There are Boyd and McKee and old Scanlon, and over there on the other side of the great moral divide stands Mrs. McKee, alone and invincible. Boyd and McKee are sleepwalking steadily backward into the past, to those magical moments when Boyd tried and failed to become a hero and McKee witnessed and failed in emulation. Old Scanlon is petrified in the past, has, in fact, seen nothing else for fifty years. A human artifact, old Scanlon, old outlaw, old gun, captured at last and brought back to justice both dead and alive. Mrs. McKee belongs with a large and ferocious company of women who patrol the precincts of the masculine fantasy in Morris's novels—those spiritually grey grandmothers, aunts, wives, and mothers, feet planted stoutly on the earth, arms folded tight across vast granite bosoms, barring the gates to Godhead, making very sure for the good of all that nothing is ever going to happen to anyone ever again. It is all eloquently and diabolically expressed in that well-known passage from *The Deep Sleep* when Paul Webb, the painter son-in-law, experiences his moment of truth, which is also the Judge's and Mrs. Porter's:

> The first Commandment of the House reads—Thou shalt not give a particle of gratification. Thou shalt drive from the Temple the man who smokes, and he shall live in a tent behind the two-car garage, and thou shalt drive from the bed the man who lusts, and he shall lie in tourist camps with interstate whores, and thou shalt drive from the bathroom the man who farts, and he shall sit in a dark cubbyhole in the basement, and thou shalt drive from the parlor the man who feels, and he shall make himself an island in the midst of the waters, for the man who feels undermines the Law of the House!

In the novels that follow *The Deep Sleep* two things that may or may not be one and the same thing begin to happen to Wright Morris. On the one hand, he moves more and more in the direction of Black Humor, as if to fend off a darkening threat to his sanity through the taking of comic evasive action. On the other hand, he evidently comes to see, in the writing of his more serious work, that an insanity is indeed already abroad in the land, an insanity very probably resulting from the frustration of the old dream of existential becoming, the collapse into dead scar tissues of myth of so many of the imaginative forms by which Americans once dramatized themselves and sought transcendence that there seems no alternative now, no other channel for the discharge of all that anger and blasted fantasy life except violence as cold and brutal as the violence of the West would have been without the redeeming and finally ameliorating power of the myth. Violence has erupted in all sectors of our national life, and as the honest and sensitive artist that he is, Morris has seen no choice but to confront it. The events of *One Day* occur against a background of southern civil rights conflict and the assassination of John F. Kennedy. Where McKee might try to emulate Boyd and Boyd Jesus Christ, the adolescent psychopath in *In Orbit* emulates an actor, William Holden, bombing the bridges of Toko-Ri. So far as one can tell, the Indian in *A Life,* by opening the vein in the old man's wrist, emulates nothing—he is simply a force of nature turned murderous, as the incessantly copulating flower children in *Fire Sermon* are a force of nature turned meaningless. But we also remember from *Ceremony in Lone Tree* young Lee Roy Momeyer who drove his hotrod over two of his classmates because "he just got tired of being pushed around," Charlie Munger who murdered ten people because "he wanted to be somebody," and McKee's experience the day he bought his new station wagon and

> drove it home like he had it loaded with eggs ... four or five of these hoodlums in a souped-up Ford swooped out of nowhere right up beside him, guffawed like hyenas, then leaned far out to scratch their matches on the paint of his hood ... the grinning faces of those hoodlums scared him worse than he dared to admit. McKee had recognized the nameless face of evil—he recognized it, that is, as stronger than the nameless face of good. ... What troubled him was not what he saw, but the nameless appetite behind it, the lust for evil in the faces of the beardless boys.

Finally, in the same novel there is Etoile's angry outburst when the radio announcer says that nobody knew why Charlie Munger murdered all those people. "You want to know why?" she yelled. "It's because nobody wants to know why. ... It's because nobody wants to know *any-thing*! Everybody hates everybody, but nobody knows why anybody gets shot. You want to know somethin'? I'd like to shoot a few dozen people myself!"

A contemporary writer who is not usually considered to have very much in common with Wright Morris once made a statement that reveals just how surprisingly much in common he does have. In an essay called "The Existential Hero," Norman Mailer (yes, Norman Mailer) said this about violence and the Western myth and the relation of both to the national psyche:

> It was almost as if there were no peace unless one could fight well, kill well (if always with honor), love well and love many, be cool, be daring, be dashing, be wild, be wily, be resourceful, be a brave gun. And this myth, that each of us was born to be free, to wander, to have adventure and to grow on the waves of the violent, the perfumed, and the unexpected, had a force which could not be tamed no matter how the nation's regulators—politicians, medicos, policemen, professors, priests, rabbis, ministers, *idéologues,* psychoanalysts, builders, executives, and endless communicators—would brick in the modern life with hygiene upon sanity and middle-brow homily over platitude; the myth would not die ... it was as if the message in the labyrinth of the genes would insist that violence was locked with creativity, and adventure was the secret of love.

It may be that violence was *once* locked with creativity in this country, and adventure was *once* the secret of love. But clearly neither is any longer true. And that, in fact, is our problem, just as it is one of the poignant motifs of our contemporary literature. Violence now is the symptom of the frustration of our creativity, and adventure has been lost along with any secret that may once have been associated with love. At the heart of it all, let us say, is challenge and mystery and the challenge *of* mystery, and we have witnessed the failure of that challenge in the dissolution of mystery.

For those of us who are old enough to remember the very different past, there is nostalgia—the romance and sedation of age in Wright Morris country. For those of us who are not old enough, there is an unfocussed and potentially lethal frustration over the fact that they have no past to remember and nothing in the present that will be worth remembering when they do become old enough. The young, therefore, have tried by other means to reconstitute the challenge of mystery. They have sought their frontiers, their possibly memorable instances of magic, in violence, sex, drugs, and transcendental meditation. And they have seen each of these sterilized of magic even as they have known them, because in knowing them they have merely joined in technology's conquest of all mystery, all secrets, have added a little more statistical data to the void we inhabit in which all things have become known and almost nothing is deeply experienced or felt.

There is much humor and a rare and genuine kindness in the novels of Wright Morris, but the dark strain has deepened in them. It is also to be found—in different guises and because of somewhat different provocations—in the works we consider most original and permanently valuable in the modern American literary tradition. It arises perhaps, as Philip Rahv once said, from a recognition of "the discrepancy between the high promise of the American Dream and what history has made of it.... The inner feeling of this [modern American] novel is one of nostalgic love of nativity combined with baffled (and sometimes angry) disenchantment." That has been the troubled preoccupation of some of our finest modern novelists, and inevitably it is also Wright Morris's—although it should be said that he cannot tolerate without some amusement the faintest note of apocalypse.

Nevertheless, his somber awareness of what has happened to us in the past and is continuing to happen to us today cannot be entirely concealed behind the subtle locutions of his irony and wit. It is perhaps that he is holding in escrow the ultimate pessimism he clearly sometimes feels. For he has, after all, lived much, has found much cause for love and wonder, and has too much practical sanity to make final pronouncements of either hope or disaster. Like Warner in *A Life,* he has been "a good hunter, a killer only when necessary, a man who knew his own mind, kept his own counsel, and lived in the manner he believed he had chosen, not knowing that he had been one of those chosen not merely to grow old, but to grow ripe."

If there is comfort in that achievement, there is also a redeeming challenge and mystery in the far greater achievement of his art—and in the magic still to be engendered in his works to come.
1977

Little Magazines and the Great Gray Middle

I have lately been reading through a great quantity of materials either taken from or devoted to American little magazines of the past fifty or sixty years. The experience has been educational if not altogether exhilarating.

Anyone who has followed the fortunes of this or that literary journal or review over a long period of time is bound to have learned something about the hazards involved in the struggle to keep alive a noncommercial outlet for serious writing. Little magazines come and go with a rapidity that may seem saddening but is, in most cases, merciful for all concerned. There have been thousands of them, far more bad ones than good. Yet all but a few have contributed—sometimes very powerfully—to the collective health of literature. Their very existence has been proof that artistic aspirations can still prevail, however briefly, over the profit motive, and they have made it possible for some good writers to develop in freedom from pressures to tailor their work to the requirements of the mass market—the term "little" referring not so much to the size of the magazine as to the limited and highly sophisticated audience it is intended to reach.

Nevertheless, one can have every sympathy for these publications and still find it depressing to study their histories in depth and to read the many anthologies offering the "best" or "most representative" selections from their pages. All those miles and miles of print running on and on, through deserts of dullness, among mountains of vanity, so often to absolutely nowhere; all those brave or impotent attempts to crystallize in language the honest, the quintessential, and the new; all those names familiar, perhaps even famous, for a year or decade and forgotten now except by friends and antiquarians; all that expenditure of time, money, and love to support the tiny possibility that genius might at some moment appear, find encouragement, and be saved; all that sanctimoniousness on the part of editors about truth and integrity, the coterie paranoia that gives so many of them a defensively inflated sense of their service to art but at times appears to blind even the most perceptive to the real size of their accomplishment. For example, there is innocence both laughable and touching in the remarks of Jane Heap, Margaret Anderson's co-editor on *The Little Review,* as she announces the magazine's demise in 1929 after fifteen years of vigorous life:

> The revolution in the arts, begun before the war, heralded a renaissance. *The Little Review* became an organ of this renaissance.... For years we offered [the magazine] as a trial-track for racers. We hoped to find artists who could run with the great artists of the past or men who could make new records. But you can't get race horses from mules. I do not believe that the conditions of our life can produce men who can give us masterpieces. Masterpieces are not made from chaos. If there is confusion of life there will be confusion of art.... We have given space in *The Little Review* to 23 new systems of art (all now dead) representing 19 countries. In all of this we have not brought forward anything approaching a masterpiece except the *Ulysses* of Mr. Joyce.

What a confession of failure! Nothing to show except the discovery and first publication of the greatest novel of the modern age, that service alone being enough to justify the giving of space to a thousand nonentities and dead systems of art. And what a stable of mules! Between 1914 and 1929 *The Little Review* published the work of most of the writers now recognized as the laureates of modern literature. Sherwood Anderson, Hart Crane, Eliot, Ford Madox Ford, Hemingway, Joyce, Wyndham Lewis, Amy Lowell, Marianne Moore, Pound, Gertrude Stein, Wallace Stevens, William Carlos Williams, and Yeats were all represented in its pages, as were the eccentric and merely notorious such as Baroness Else von Freitag-Loringhoven, Tristan Tzara, and Maxwell Bodenheim. Although shockingly deficient in masterpieces and rich in the usual varieties of ambitious trash, *The Little Review,* together with other magazines of greater or lesser distinction like *The Dial, Poetry, Secession,* and *Broom,* quite simply created the modernist literary movement in its American and Continental phases, and they did so by providing a medium through which the principles and insights of a radical new sensibility could be expressed in collective form and thus be recognized as constituting a movement in fact rather than the products of isolated and disparate minds.

In a very real sense, therefore, the history of the modern little magazine is also the history of literary modernism as we know it. To read from *The Little Review Anthology* through such recent collections as *Short Stories from the Literary Magazines, Best Little Magazine Fiction 1970*, and the three volumes of the annually published *American Literary Anthology* is to move chronologically and imaginatively through a period of the greatest literary achievement we are likely to know in this century. It is also to arrive at a clear and often disturbing impression of just what can happen, perhaps must happen, when a major movement runs its course and ends not in honorable death but in suspended animation, a state in which its influence continues to be operative but upon talents no longer energized by its pioneering spirit, in which its best effects retain their authority even as they have ossified into establishment clichés, and in which its principal organs of expression have produced descendants that exist too often solely because the little magazine has become in our day an institutionalized outlet for an institutionalized literature, an empty memorial to a lost vitality.

The process by which all this came about can be traced in the evolution or devolution of modernism in our time. As the central energies of the movement began to fail, two things appear to have happened, and they happened almost simultaneously. The major modernist figures ceased to be looked upon as mortal men and fallible artists and were elevated by the avant-garde to sainthood, a condition in which, for nearly forty years now, they have represented the best that could conceivably be thought and done by writers in this age. Criticism, meanwhile, was engaged in transforming their works into relics of hieratic subtlety, their aesthetic principles into canonical laws that should govern the practice of all art. The result was a short-circuiting of our sense of creative possibility, a deadening of our power to take new imaginative risks, from which we have not yet recovered and may never recover.

Since the twenties at least three distinct generations of writers have come to maturity, all of them thoroughly schooled in the great heritage of modernism and forced, because of their position in history, to work either in emulation of or rebellion against that heritage. The best minds of each generation have recognized that the literary formulations of modernism have become stereotypes. Yet judging by the record of their individual performances, it would appear that most of them have felt powerless to create fresh formulations of comparable originality. One reason for this is that although their world may be different in certain respects from the world of 1920 or 1930, it is not different enough to invalidate completely the views handed down to them by their distinguished predecessors. Those views may now be stereotypes, but they still have their powerful relevance as descriptions of life at the present time.

Another problem confronting these writers is that, largely because of the influence of criticism, they have become vastly oversophisticated about the methodology of literary production. They have learned the critical vocabulary. They know exactly what the standards are and which great works exemplify them most successfully. They have all the knowledge required for effective performance, but their knowledge seems, in far too many cases, to have withered the life of that certain holy innocence required for truly exceptional performance. This may be why we now have such large numbers of competent writers and so very few—if one can think of any at all—of clearly major stature. It may also account for the high incidence of critics, men who might in another time have written imaginatively but who have been so thoroughly intimidated by the enormous authority of the modernist accomplishment that they have chosen to devote themselves wholly to the study of that accomplishment, knowing that nothing they might do could possibly equal it. Competence and criticism are the natural products of a post-renaissance time in the arts, and they have largely determined the character of our present literary situation.

The history of the American little magazine over the past fifty years is alive with examples of not only the proliferation of competence but the steadily increasing influence of criticism. It is significant that the pioneering magazines of the period—*The Little Review, The Dial, Poetry*—were either devoted almost entirely to imaginative writing or, like *The Dial*, also published critical essays and reviews by men of whom a startling number were themselves imaginative writers of the first rank. For a time in those early years criticism was a vital medium of communication between practicing artists as well as a way of testing out in theory the aesthetic principles they subsequently applied in their own creative work. But the first symptom of a movement's decline is the separation of criticism from creativity, and this separation becomes steadily more apparent as one follows the development of the little magazine.

At some point in the late twenties or early thirties the remaining energies of modernism began to divide, and what had previously been a major force of creative innovation became a major force of critical evaluation. *The Little Review* and other magazines devoted to sponsoring the new revolution in the arts were superseded in influence by critical journals like *The Hound and Horn* and *The Symposium* and later on *The Southern, Kenyon,* and *Sewanee* reviews, which sponsored what came to be recognized as a new revolution in criticism. By the end of the fifties, largely as a result of the authoritative work published in these journals, the New Criticism had become solidly established as the official custodian of modernism; the masterpieces of the movement had been thoroughly analyzed and the critical concepts derived from them incorporated into a technology of literary studies headquartered in major universities throughout the country.

The next step was inevitable and predictable. If modernism under the control of criticism could be institutionalized in the classroom, if the methods of genius could be studied as an academic subject matter, it seemed only logical that creative writing itself could be similarly institutionalized and studied, and young writers, fully instructed in the methods of Joyce, Eliot, Lawrence, and Hemingway, could in effect be manufactured. Professional writers were accordingly invited to the campuses to teach criticism to potential critics and conduct workshops for potential novelists and poets. In the next years we produced—and we continue today to produce—a large population of university-educated young people who, if they have not actually become writers, have at least been exposed to the basic literature of modernism and have acquired some degree of sophistication about the creative process in general. Of those who think of themselves as writers, it is to be expected that only a very few do so because they are driven by strong creative ambitions or talents. The majority have simply been infected with a specious literariness through the study of writing, and of course they are bedazzled by the aura of holiness which has been generated around the image of the writer as a result of the canonization of the modern masters. People of this sort constitute what amounts to a new fabricated literary mass culture, and their works fill the pages of the countless little magazines being published at the present time.

One's necessarily generalized impression in reading some of these magazines or selections from them in the anthologies is that almost nobody writes badly or brilliantly and just about everybody writes passably well. As has happened in other areas of our society, the extremes appear to have been cancelled and the great grey middle has expanded enormously. There are of course exceptions. Now and then a writer will stand out above the others, and a particular story or poem will seem remarkable because it gives every appearance of having been produced by a living human brain rather than a computer. But there is such a very great deal of competent mediocrity, so much boredom, so little genuine excitement.

The editors of one of the recent anthologies have complained that a short story writer today has the greatest difficulty establishing a reputation, first, because over the past several years the widely circulated commercial outlets for fiction have sharply decreased in number and, second, because a writer may now publish in so many little magazines read by so many different little audiences that his name can never become widely known. It is perfectly true that the early modernists did have the important advantage of beginning their careers during a period when there were relatively few magazines in which they had more concentrated exposure and when their reputations were formed and kept alive by a small, vociferous avant-garde until such time as they could be absorbed into the commercial market. But a more accurate, though less flattering explanation for the failure of so many writers to become widely known today is simply that so few deserve to be. Their work is so often without individual character and, therefore, contains nothing that would distinguish it from the work of a hundred others.

One knew when one was reading a Joyce or Lawrence or Hemingway story because it bore on its every page the signature of a unique sensibility responding to experience in an absolutely individual way. One also felt that this quality of freshness resulted at least in part from the fact that these writers were engaging the realities of the modern age at a time when those realities were still new both to them and to their audience. Today, in addition to the homogenization of literary talent, we are up against the difficulty that the distance between the knowledge of the writer and the knowledge of the educated reading public has drastically narrowed just because we are all familiar with the central experiences of our time and the standard literary methods for depicting them. Hence, our reaction to a story or poem is more likely to involve recognition of the familiar rather than the excitement of revelation and first discovery. In these circumstances it is extremely hard for a writer to present material which his audience will find dramatically significant. Unless through sheer intelligence and imaginative power a writer can manage to cut through the thick layers of cliché in which so many of our experiences today are embedded, our response to him must be one of boredom and déjà vu, for like Eliot's Prufrock we have known them all already, known them all.

It is also difficult to imagine how a literature of much vitality can be produced by writers of whom so very many seem to have been completely absorbed into middleclass life and are, therefore, obliged to draw their materials from the limited dramatic resources of that life. Yet this is one of the important consequences of the homogenizing process. It has been accompanied by the democratization of the writer, his demotion from the status of radical iconoclast to that of solid citizen. This is not to suggest that the dissolute life is a prerequisite to major creativity or that the battle of the imagination can only be fought at the barricades. But it does seem significant and more than a little ominous that such a large proportion of the contributors to the little magazines—and, for that matter, the big commercial ones—will be described in biographical notes as members of university faculties, writers employed to teach writing to writers, owners of farms outside Little Rock or Iowa City where in their spare time they raise corn and pigs, or they may be Connecticut exurbanites, free-lance editors in New York, storekeepers in Scarsdale—all so evidently respectable, responsible, and ordinary. One can hardly blame writers or anybody else for surviving as best they can, and the alternatives to the middleclass life are clearly not what they once were. Nevertheless, it is one thing to live conventionally and quite another to accept and live by the values of convention, to become as trivialized imaginatively as the life one leads. It has sometimes been true that the conditions of average existence can produce genius, but most often they produce averageness, the kind of averageness that in writers consists not so much of pedestrian experience as of pedestrian vision.

Over and over again in the little magazines one encounters stories about the small housekeeping details of life, the sweaty anxieties of simple, average people, the sexual daydreams of bored housewives, political intrigues in university English departments, the suicidal impulses of adolescents who do not feel loved, the suicidal impulses of old folks who do not feel needed. The stories, in other words, are about the usual situations and distresses of the world we all inhabit. They are familiar. They may seem trivial. They may even be boring. But the problem is not the subject matter, although surely one of the hazards of writing about contemporary American life is that its banality can perhaps be accurately rendered only at the level of soap opera. The problem is rather that in most cases the author's conception is as banal as his subject matter—banal in the sense that he and it seem to be locked into the same system of values. And just as he has been unable to imagine an alternative to those values, so he has also been unable to imagine a way of endowing his subject matter with a significance that would elevate it above the level of soap opera to the level of art. It would obviously be unfair to expect writers to be exceptional men, and it would be un-American to enact legislation prohibiting a man from becoming a writer unless he had talent. But a writer can be average only at his peril, to say nothing of the peril to his readers. It may be, however, that these particular writers are actually, as someone once said, the green grocers of literature and might just as well be selling potatoes.

The idea of the writer as an exceptional man is uncomfortable, perhaps because so seldom demonstrable, at the present time. Yet it is a measure of just how far we have fallen that in the great period of modernism the idea was not simply taken for granted: it was a concept of such liberating force that from it the movement derived much of its creative confidence and authority. Margaret Anderson provides evidence for this in *My Thirty Years' War,* the first of her three autobiographical volumes. In recalling the history of her association with *The Little Review,* which is also the history of her incurable school-girl crush on art and artists, Miss Anderson describes—without explicitly setting out to do so—the various elements that helped to account for the remarkable productivity and high evangelical fervor of those early renaissance years. She makes it plain that in *The Little Review* she saw herself as carrying on a crusade to stimulate a major revolution in the arts, that her function—indeed, her sacred mission—as a little magazine editor was to provide an outlet for work of high quality which could not be published elsewhere because it violated existing taboos or was too radically honest, that an absolute belief in the supreme value of art, in "Life for Art's sake," must be a first article of religious faith, that the artist, to the extent that he is a genuine shaper of consciousness, is indeed an exceptional man, superior to other men by virtue of his talent and intelligence, and would necessarily be antibourgeois in his attitudes and values, if only because bourgeois society is the enemy of artistic freedom, is corrupted by materialism and hypocrisy, and exists in a state of spiritual paralysis which is a form of death. These sentiments may be old-fashioned now and surely they seem romantic in the extreme, especially so in Miss Anderson's phrasing of them, for she appears to have lived in a condition of permanent gushy euphoria about everything connected with the artistic life of her time. Yet although the facts may to some extent deglamorize her claims, they do nothing to invalidate them. Miss Anderson was surrounded by artists, many of whom actually were exceptional people. She took part with them in an extraordinary creative experience. She recognized earlier than most just how extraordinary it was, she made her vital contribution to it, and she saw it reach fruition and come to an end. In 1929 she announced: "Our mission was accomplished; contemporary art had 'arrived'; for a hundred years, perhaps, the literary world would produce only: repetition." To which *The New Yorker* replied: "A little smug but, to date, not very inaccurate."

Not very inaccurate, yet in the perspective of the present time not really accurate enough. The literary world has undoubtedly produced repetition in the sense that we continue to move around and around in the circle of imaginative possibilities marked out by modernism, and even our efforts to break out are so often only self-defeating attempts to escape from our most central interests and experiences and to exchange an inherited but unsurpassable mode of vision for a merely defiant eccentricity. But it would seem truer of our present situation to say that modernism has ended not so much in repetition as in conventionality and professionalism. Many of its governing attitudes now belong in the public domain and have become part of the chic metaphysical decor of mass culture. Others have been discredited because they do not conform to the pieties of mass culture. A belief in the artist as exceptional being is now open to the charge of elitism. The antibourgeois stance is an insult to our militant egalitarianism. We have seen the old individualist avant-garde dissolve into a proletariat composed of great numbers of interchangeable minor and major-minor talents, literary engineers, pitchmen, writers whose profession is not writing but being writers. The universities and women's clubs subsidize a whole vaudeville industry of poets who travel around the country ostensibly bringing culture to the provinces but mostly selling distraction for the bored, doing their best to act the part made scandalous by Dylan Thomas, reminding us through every bellow, wiggle, and twitch of genitals that the vitality so often missing from the poetry is not really missed. The demonic and outrageous have become costumes for the personality rather than qualities of the work.

Some of their more illustrious colleagues may appear on television and become beloved by millions, not because they are writers but because one may talk like a Mississippi carnival freak and another can always be counted on to say something obscene. Still others may be asked to join the staff of writers' conferences where they are likely to be valued not for their knowledge of writing but for their ability to comfort the customers, tell the sweet little old ladies what they are paying their money to hear, and generally behave like Good Old Boys, living examples of the truth that anybody indeed can become a writer.

As the barriers have fallen that formerly separated talent from mediocrity and achievement from publicity, so the old taboos have been erased that once made it daring to write honestly about sex, a criminal offense to publish *Ulysses,* and a service to literature to run

a little magazine. The thirty years' war of modernism has long been won. It is now possible to write about anything in whatever language one chooses, and clearly almost anything can be published almost anywhere. Writers have become not only socially acceptable but positively fashionable. Our benevolent civilization has taken them in, given them security in the middle class and status in the world of show business. A place has even been made for huge quantities of little magazines that are no longer considered the least bit subversive. We have been freed at last to create the major literature we of course knew would be produced as soon as the forces of censorship and repression were overcome.
1972

It is of some comfort to me to realize that during the years that have passed since 1972, the American literary situation may have grown more complicated but seems otherwise not basically to have changed. In one particular only would I revise the foregoing assessment if I were making it today. Where in 1972 the short story was little read and was, therefore, a distinctly unpromising form by which a young writer might make his reputation, today it is a strong competitor of the novel for popularity and has become the usual mode through which young writers begin and often establish their careers. A first book is now as likely to be a collection of stories as it is a novel and perhaps even more likely.

In other respects, the schools of creative writing I discussed when they were more or less in their infancy have since proliferated to an awesome degree, and the numbers of the faintly talented attracted to writing partly through their attendance at such schools have risen into the hundreds and hundreds. Literature now is being produced in great quantity, but it does not flourish.

For a further and more extensive discussion of the influence of these schools on the character of current literary production, I refer the reader to my book, *Talents and Technicians: Literary Chic and the New Assembly-Line Fiction* (Charles Scribner's Sons, 1992), a critical study of some of the more prominent younger American fiction writers.

Index

Aaron, Daniel, 23
Abernathy, Ralph, 191
Adams family, 7
Adams, Henry, 8
Adams, J. Donald, 112
Aichinger, Peter, 130
Aiken, Conrad, 13
Aldington, Richard, 20
Aldridge, John W.: *After the Lost Generation*, x, 130, 131; *Talents and Technicians*, 234
Algren, Nelson, ix, 108–11, 145; *The Devil's Stocking*, 109; *The Man with the Golden Arm*, 109
Alighieri, Dante, 15
American Literary Anthology, 227
Andersen, Henrik, 5, 6
Anderson, Margaret, 226, 232; *My Thirty Years' War*, 232
Anderson, Sherwood, 65, 70, 72, 217, 226
Apocalypse Now, 150
Arendt, Hannah, 204
Auden, W. H., 66, 156

Baker, Carlos, 29, 30, 33, 37, 88
Balzac, Honoré de, 196; *The Human Comedy*, 196
Barth, John, 147, 152, 153, 166, 171–79, 180, 181, 201; *End of the Road*, 172, 175; *The Floating Opera*, 171, 175; *Giles Goat-Boy*, 173, 174, 181; *Letters*, 175; "The Literature of Exhaustion," 173; *Lost in the Funhouse*, 174; *Sabbatical: A Romance*, 176–78; *The Sot-Weed Factor*, 153, 173, 174, 181; *The Tidewater Tales*, 179
Barthelme, Donald, 111, 152, 154–56, 157, 158; *Come Back, Dr., Caligari*, 154; *Unspeakable Practices, Unnatural Acts*, 154, 155
Baudelaire, Charles, 91
Beauvoir, Simone de, 64
Beckett, Samuel, 90, 91, 93, 158
Beebe, Lucius, 115
Bell, Millicent, 100
Bellow, Saul, 120, 178, 201, 209–16; *The Adventures of Augie March*, 178, 210; *Dangling Man*, 210; *Henderson the Rain King*, 210; *Herzog*, 211; *Humboldt's Gift*, 211, 213–16; *Mr. Sammler's Planet*, 211
Bennett, Arnold, 3, 22
Bergonzi, Bernard, 15
Bersani, Leo, 192
Best Little Magazine Fiction, 1970, 227
Bettelheim, Bruno, 204
Bird, William, 73
Birmingham, Stephen, 99, 100; *The Late John Marquand*, 99
Bishop, John Peale, 13, 27
Blackmur, R. P., 83, 86
Blair, Mary, 26
Blotner, Joseph, 49, 50
Bodenheim, Maxwell, 226
Bourjaily, Vance, 130, 131, 132
Bowen, Stella, 19
Brandt, Carl, 102
Brandt, Carol, 100, 102
Brooks, Cleanth, 83
Brooks, Van Wyck, 3, 75, 84; *The Pilgrimage of Henry James*, 3
Broom, 226
Broughton, Rhoda, 8
Brown, Slater, 73
Brown, Ford Madox, 22

235

INDEX

Browning, Robert, 6
Bruccoli, Matthew J., 113, 114, 116; *James Gould Cozzens: A Life Apart* 114; *A James Gould Cozzens Reader* (ed.), 113
Brustein, Robert, 145, 146, 148
Burke, Kenneth, 83
Burns, John Horne, 130, 132, 146
Burroughs, William, 94
Butor, Michel, 93

Camus, Albert, 90, 98, 203; *The Stranger*, 93
Canby, Margaret, 26
Carlyle, Thomas, 6
Carpenter, Meta, 52; *A Loving Gentleman*, 52
Céline, Louis-Ferdinand, ix, 57, 87–94, 136; *Bagatelles for a Massacre*, 91; *Death on the Installment Plan*, 91, 93; *Journey to the End of the Night*, 89, 91, 93; *School for Cadavers*, 91; *Some State of Affairs*, 91
Channing, William Ellery, 101
Chicago Tribune Book World, The, x, 1
Churchill, Randolph, 126
Cohn, Roy, 147
Commentary, xi, 147
Connelly, Cyril, 126
Conrad, Joseph, 6, 17, 19, 20, 21, 98, 99, 123
Cooper, James Fenimore, 200
Coover, Robert, 180–85; "The Babysitter," 181–82; *Gerald's Party*, 183–85; *Pricksongs and Descants*, 181; *The Public Burning*, 182–83
Cosmopolitan, 95
Cowley, Malcolm, ix, x, 30, 31, 69, 70, 79–86, 130; *And I Worked at the Writer's Trade*, 79; *Exile's Return*, 70, 79; *A Second Flowering*, 69, 79; *Think Back on Us*, 84
Cozzens, James Gould, ix, 112–17; *By Love Possessed*, 112, 113; *Confusion*, 115; *Guard of Honor*, ix, 112, 115, 116; *Michael Scarlett*, 115
Cozzens, Sylvia Bernice Baumgarten, 115
Crane, Hart, 77, 78, 80, 186, 226
Crane, Stephen, 7, 20, 22, 136; *The Red Badge of Courage*, 136
Crosby, Harry, 73, 80
Cummings, E. E., 59, 61, 62, 77, 131

Decter, Midge, 192
DeVoto, Bernard, 84, 112
Dial, The, 226, 228
Dickens, Charles, 6, 66, 158, 196, 210

Dos Passos, John, 40, 73, 77, 80, 83, 96, 97, 131, 132, 146; *U.S.A.*, 83
Dostoevsky, Fyodor, 66, 198, 210; *Crime and Punishment*, 198; *The Eternal Husband*, 210
Dr. Strangelove, 150
Dreiser, Theodore, 70, 210
du Maurier family, 7
Durrell, Lawrence, 54, 55; *The Henry Miller Reader*, 54

Edel, Leon, 1, 2, 3, 5, 6, 23, 25, 26; *Henry James: The Master*, 1
Eliot, George, 6
Eliot, T. S., ix, 1, 2, 9–16, 22, 80, 99, 104, 137, 200, 226, 229, 230; "Ash Wednesday," 14; "The Four Quartets," 14, 15, 16; "The Love Song of J. Alfred Prufrock," 11, 16; "Portrait of a Lady," 11; "Preludes," 11; "Rhapsody on a Windy Night," 11; "The Waste Land," 11, 12, 13, 16
Eliot, Valerie, 9, 10
Eliot, Vivienne Haigh-Wood, 11, 12, 13, 14
Ellmann, Richard, 1, 9; *James Joyce*, 1
Emerson, Ralph Waldo, 6, 69, 80, 101
English Review, The, 18, 20
Executive Suite, 97

Farrell, James T., ix, 108–11; *Sam Holman*, 109, 110
Faulkner, Estelle Oldham, 51
Faulkner, William, ix, 40, 49–53, 59, 61, 62, 63–68, 78, 113, 120, 121, 122, 186, 202, 203, 217; *The Bear*, 68; *The Hamlet*, 67; *Light in August*, 67, 68; *Mosquitoes*, 51; *Sanctuary*, 52, 65, 67; *Soldiers Pay*, 51; *The Sound and the Fury*, 52, 68
Fenichel, Otto, 46; *Psychoanalytical Theory of Neurosis*, 46
Fenton, Charles, 130
Fiedler, Leslie, 73, 188
Fiske, Gardiner family, 102
Fitzgerald, F. Scott, 12, 19, 24, 40, 42, 50 72, 73, 74, 76, 77, 80, 81, 83, 96, 113, 121, 128, 186, 201, 218; "Babylon Revisited," 76–77; *The Great Gatsby*, 77, 121, 218
Fitzgerald, Zelda, 12, 72
Flaubert, Gustave, 6, 198; *Madame Bovary*, 91, 198
Ford, Elsie, 21
Ford, Ford Madox, ix, 7, 17–22, 226; *The Good Soldier*, 17, 18, 22; *Parade's End*, 17

INDEX

Ford, Gerald, 163
Foster, Richard, 192
Freitag-Loringhoven, Baroness Else von, 226
Friedman, Bruce Jay, 152, 153; *Stern*, 153
Frost, Robert, 59, 61, 62, 186
Fuller family, 7
Fullerton family, 7
Fussell, Paul, 130

Gaddis, William, 147, 150, 165–70; *JR*, 166–70; *The Recognitions*, 165
Galsworthy, John, 20
Genet, John, 91
Gide, André, 64, 98, 99, 121, 127; *The Immoralist*, 121
Gold, Herbert, 147
Gold, Michael, 84
Goldring, Douglas, 17, 18
Goodman, Paul, 191
Grass, Günter, 94
Graves, Robert, 131
Greene, Graham, 65

Hale, Emily, 10
Hardwick, Elizabeth, 192
Hardy, Thomas, 20
Hargrove, Marion, 146
Harper's, xi
Hassan, Ihab, 130
Hawkes, John, 94, 135, 166; *The Cannibal*, 135; *Second Skin*, 135
Hawthorne, Nathaniel, 7, 65, 127, 199
Hayes, Alfred, 130, 132
Heap, Jane, 226
Heggen, Thomas, 146
Heller, Joseph, x, 94, 133, 134, 144–51, 152, 158–64, 201; *Catch-22*, x, 133, 144–51, 159, 163; *Good as Gold*, 160–64; *Something Happened*, 149, 150, 159
Hemingway, Ernest, ix, 19, 22, 24, 29–38, 39–48, 59, 61, 62, 72, 73, 74, 75, 76, 77, 80, 82, 88, 96, 113, 128, 131, 136, 145, 158, 186, 190, 192, 201, 217, 226, 229, 230; *Across the River and into the Trees*, 31, 32, 33, 36, 39; *The Dangerous Summer*, 29, 37, 38; *Death in the Afternoon* 37, 39; *A Farewell to Arms*, 82, 131; *For Whom the Bell Tolls*, 33, 34, 35; *The Garden of Eden*, 29, 30; *Islands in the Stream*, ix, 33–38; *Men at War* (ed.), 31; *A Moveable Feast*, 29; *The Old Man and the Sea*, 31, 32, 39; *The Sun Also Rises*, 39–48, 77; *To Have and Have Not*, 34
Hicks, Granville, 84
Higginson, Thomas, 101
Higginson family, 7
Hitler, Adolf, 132
Hoffman, Frederick J., 75
Holmes family, 7
Hound and Horn, The, 229
Howarth, Herbert, 11; *Notes on Some Figures Behind T. S. Eliot*, 11
Howe, Irving, 113
Howells, William Dean, 7
Hudson, W. H., 20
Hunt, Violet, 21
Huntley, H. Robert, 17; *The Alien Protagonist of Ford Madox Ford*, 17
Huxley, Aldous, 128, 133; *Brave New World*, 133

James, Henry, ix, 1–8, 4, 16, 17, 20, 22, 24, 25, 26, 61, 65, 76, 113, 127, 196, 197, 200, 217; *The Ambassadors*, 3, 4, 200; *The Bostonians*, 4; *The Golden Bowl*, 3, 6; *The Other House*, 4; *The Portrait of a Lady*, 5; *Watch and Ward*, 4; *The Wings of the Dove*, 3, 6
James, William, 2, 4
Jeffers, Robinson, 59
Jones, James, x, 139–43, 146; *From Here to Eternity*, 139, 140, 141, 142; *Go to the Widow Maker*, 139; *The Merry Month of May*, 139; *Some Came Running*, 139; *The Thin Red Line*, 139, 141, 142; *Whistle*, 139, 141, 142, 143
Joyce, James, 1, 80, 94, 99, 165, 178, 226, 229, 230, 233; *Finnegans Wake*, 165; *Ulysses*, 178, 233
Jung, Carl, 46, 210; *Psychology and Religion*, 46

Kafka, Franz, 15, 63, 133, 136, 137
Karl, Frederick R., 49, 50, 51, 53
Kazin, Alfred, 192
Kennedy, John F., 190
Kenner, Hugh, 46; *A Homemade World*, 46
Kenyon Review, 229
Kierkegaard, Søren, 15
Kiernan, Thomas, 104, 105; *The Intricate Music*, 104
Kipling, Rudyard, 7
Kissinger, Henry, 163
Klein, Marcus, 130
Knapp, Bettina L., 87; *Céline: Man of Hate*, 87

238 INDEX

Kosinski, Jerzy, 135, 136, 137; *Being There*, 136; *Blind Date*, 136; *Cockpit*, 136; *The Devil Tree*, 136; *The Painted Bird*, 136; *Steps*, 136

Ladies' Home Journal, 95
La Farge family, 7
Lawrence, D. H., 19, 20, 22, 229, 230
LeClair, Thomas, 149, 150
Lewis, Sinclair, 70, 75, 97
Lewis, Wyndham, 20, 22, 226
Life, 29, 30, 37
Lincoln, Abraham, 7
Liston, Sonny, 190
Little Review, The, 226, 228, 232
Little Review Anthology, The, 227
Look, 31
Lorre, Peter, 96
Lowell, Amy, 226
Lowell, Robert, 190, 191
Lowell family, 7
Lowry, Robert, 130, 132
Lucid, Robert F., 192
Lyons, Leonard, 31

M*A*S*H, 150
McAlmon, Robert, 73
McCarthy, Eugene, 190
McCarthy, Joseph, 85, 147, 183
McCarthy, Mary, 41
McCarthy, Patrick, 87, 88, 92, 94
MacDonald, Dwight, 113, 190, 191, 192
MacLeish, Archibald, 84
MacShane, Frank, 17, 18
Mailer, Norman, 54–58, 71, 109, 112, 120, 130, 132, 135, 136, 146, 147, 150, 186–93, 194–97, 209, 222; *Advertisements for Myself*, 187–88; *An American Dream*, 136, 188, 192; *Ancient Evenings*, 194; *Armies of the Night*, 191; *The Executioner's Song*, 109, 194, 196; "The Existential Hero," 222; *Harlot's Ghost*, 194–97; *The Long Patrol*, 186, 192; *The Naked and the Dead*, 112, 132, 150, 189, 192; *Of a Fire on the Moon*, 192; "Some Children of the Goddess," 191; "The Talent in the Room," 191; *The Time of Her Time*, 188; *Why Are We in Vietnam?*, 136, 188, 191
Malamud, Bernard, 147
Malory, Sir Thomas, 105; *Morte d'Arthur*, 105
Man in the Grey Flannel Suit, The, 97
Mann, Thomas, 98
Marquand, Adelaide Hooker, 102
Marquand, Christina Sedgwick, 102

Marquand, John P., ix, 95–103; *B. F.'s Daughter*, 96; *H. M. Pulham, Esquire*, 96, 102; *The Late George Apley*, 96, 97; *Melville Goodwin, USA*, 96; *Point of No Return*, 96; *Repent in Haste*, 96; *Sincerely, Willis Wayde*, 96; *So Little Time*, 96; *The Unspeakable Gentleman*, 95; *Wickford Point*, 96, 101; *Women and Thomas Harrow*, 96, 98
Matthews, T. S., 9, 10, 11, 12, 14, 15; *Great Tom*, 9
Melville, Herman, 113, 196, 199, 210; *Moby Dick*, 199
Mencken, H. L., 70, 75, 82
Michelet, Jules, 24
Millay, Edna St. Vincent, 27
Miller, Henry, ix, 54–58, 87, 93; *Black Spring*, 54, 56; *The Colossus of Maroussi*, 54, 56; *Tropic of Cancer*, 54; *Tropic of Capricorn*, 54
Miller, Merle, 130
Mirrlees, Hope, 12
Mizener, Arthur, 17, 18; *The Saddest Story*, 18
Moore, Marianne, 226
Morris, Willie, 139
Morris, Wright, 217–24; *A Life*, 221, 224; *Ceremony at Lone Tree*, 220, 222; *The Field of Vision*, 220; *Fire Sermon*, 221; *In Orbit*, 221; *One Day*, 221
Murphy, Gerald and Sara, 73

Nation, The, x
New Republic, The, x, 84, 145
New York Herald Tribune Book Week, The, xi
New York Review of Books, The, xi
New York Times Book Review, The, xi, 145
New Yorker, The, 84, 191, 233
Nin, Anaïs, 55
Norton family, 7

O'Hara, John, 145, 152
Orwell, George, 104, 133; *1984*, 133
Ostrovsky, Erika, 87; *Voyeur, Voyant*, 87
Owen, Wilfred, 131

Page, Thomas Nelson, 205
Pater, Walter, 71
Perkins, Maxwell, 139
Perry family, 7
Persse, Jocelyn, 5, 6

Podhoretz, Norman, 148, 192; "The Best Catch There Is," 148
Poe, Edgar Allan, 177, 186; *The Narrative of A. Gordon Pym,* 177
Poetry, 226, 228
Poirier, Richard, 192
Pound, Ezra, 7, 12, 22, 72, 75, 80, 99, 226
Prescott, Orville, 112
Pynchon, Thomas, 94, 134, 147, 150, 152, 158, 166, 201; *The Crying of Lot 49,* 134; *Gravity's Rainbow,* 134; *V.,* 134, 147, 166

Rahv, Philip, 223
Ransom, John Crowe, 83
Reich, Wilhelm, 210
Remarque, Erich Maria, 131, 132, 146; *All Quiet on the Western Front,* 131
Richardson, Jack, 192
Ricketts, Edward F., 105, 106
Robbe-Grillet, Alain, 87, 93, 136; *In the Labyrinth,* 136
Rockwell, Norman, 63
Roethke, Theodore, 59
Rossetti family, 22
Roth, Philip, 120, 147, 201; "Writing American Fiction," 147

Salinger, J. D., 41, 147
Sartre, Jean Paul, 87, 93, 203, 210; *Nausea,* 93, 210
Sassoon, Siegfried, 131
Saturday Evening Post, 63, 95
Saturday Review, xi
Schine, David, 147
Secession, 226
Sedgwick, Theodore, 102
Semmelweis, Ignaz Philipp, 89, 90
Sencourt, Robert, 9; *T. S. Eliot: A Memoir,* 9
Sewanee Review, 229
Shakespeare, William, 145
Shaw, Irwin, 130, 132, 146; *The Young Lions,* 132
Short Stories from the Literary Magazines, 227
Sill, Rev. Frederick, 114-15
Singer, Isaac Bashevis, 196
Smith, Henry Ladd, x
Smith, Roger H., 145
Snow, C. P., 116
Southern Review, The, 229
Spender, Stephen, 6
Stallings, Laurence, 84
Stearns, Harold, 80
Stein, Gertrude, 22, 41, 47, 72, 75, 226

Steinbeck, John, ix, 104-7; *Cannery Row,* 105; *Cup of Gold,* 105; *The Grapes of Wrath,* 105, 107; *Sweet Thursday,* 105; *To a God Unknown,* 105; *Tortilla Flat,* 105; *Travels with Charley,* 107
Steiner, George, 204
Steiner, Rudolph, 210, 213-14
Stevens, Leslie: family, 7
Stevens, Wallace, 59, 226
Strachey, Lytton, 9
Styron, William, 66, 147, 201-8, 209; *The Confessions of Nat Turner,* 203; *Lie Down in Darkness,* 202, 203; *Set This House on Fire,* 203, 207; *Sophie's Choice,* 203-8
Swinburne, Charles, 22
Symposium, The, 229

Taine, Hippolyte, 24
Tate, Alan, 22, 78, 83, 86, 123
Tennyson, Alfred Lord, 6
Thackeray, William Makepeace, 6
Thoreau, Henry David, 6, 69, 80, 101
Time Magazine, 115, 116
Tolstoy, Leo, 196, 198; *War and Peace,* 196, 198
Tomlinson, H. M., 20
Torres, José, 192
Transatlantic Review, The, 18
Trilling, Diana, 192
Trilling, Lionel, 83
Trollope, Anthony, 6
Turgenev, Ivan, 6
Twain, Mark, 7, 84, 186, 210, 217
Tzara, Tristan, 80, 226

Vanderbilt family, 7
Verdenal, Jean, 13
Vidal, Gore, 130, 131, 192
Vonnegut, Kurt, 135, 150, 201; *Slaughterhouse Five,* 135

Waldmeir, Joseph J., 130
Walpole, Hugh, 5
Warren, Robert Penn, ix, 83, 118-25; *All the King's Men,* ix, 118, 119, 124; *Band of Angels,* 123; *Flood,* 118; *Meet Me in the Green Glen,* 118, 124; *Wilderness,* 118
Waugh, Evelyn, ix, 126-29; *Brideshead Revisited,* ix; *The Diaries of Evelyn Waugh,* 126-29
Wells, H. G., 3, 7, 19, 20, 22
Whitman, Walt, 186, 200, 210
Whittier, John Greenleaf, 101
Wilder, Thornton, 78, 84

Williams, Tennessee, 4
Williams, William Carlos, 59, 226
Wilson, Earl, 31
Wilson, Edmund, ix, x, 3, 10, 23–28, 81, 83, 84, 85, 86, 107; *The American Earthquake,* 23, 84; *Axel's Castle,* 24, 83; *The Bit Between My Teeth,* 23; *Classics and Commercials,* 23; *I Thought of Daisy,* 23, 27; *Memoirs of Hecate County,* 23, 27; *A Piece of My Mind,* 23; *A Prelude,* 23; *The Shores of Light,* 23, 84; *Upstate,* 23

Winters, Yvor, 83
Wister family, 7
Wolfe, Thomas, 73, 76, 77, 201, 202
Wolfe, Tom, 192
Woolf, Virginia, 7, 155
Woolson, Constance Fenimore, 5

Yeats, William Butler, 66, 193, 226; "To a Friend Whose Work has come to Nothing," 193

Zola, Émile, 106